Norman Allison Calkins, Henry Kiddle, Thomas F. Harrison

How to Teach

A Manual of Methods for a Graded Course of Instruction

Norman Allison Calkins, Henry Kiddle, Thomas F. Harrison

How to Teach
A Manual of Methods for a Graded Course of Instruction

ISBN/EAN: 9783337778255

Printed in Europe, USA, Canada, Australia, Japan

Cover: Foto ©Paul-Georg Meister /pixelio.de

More available books at **www.hansebooks.com**

How to Teach.

A

MANUAL OF METHODS

FOR A

GRADED COURSE OF INSTRUCTION:

EMBRACING THE

SUBJECTS USUALLY PURSUED IN PRIMARY, INTERMEDIATE, GRAMMAR,
AND HIGH SCHOOLS; ALSO, SUGGESTIONS RELATIVE
TO DISCIPLINE AND SCHOOL MANAGEMENT.

FOR THE

USE OF TEACHERS.

BY

HENRY KIDDLE, A.M.,
City Superintendent of Public Instruction, New York.

THOMAS F. HARRISON,
First Assistant Superintendent of Grammar Schools, New York City; and Professor of Methods and Principles of Teaching in Saturday Normal School.

N. A. CALKINS,
First Assistant Superintendent of Primary Schools and Departments, New York City; and Professor of Methods and Principles of Teaching in Saturday Normal School.

NEW YORK:

J. W. Schermerhorn & Co.,
14 BOND STREET.

1875.

PREFACE.

THE system of graded instruction, which has become so general in this country, requires for its successful application, the constant use, on the part of the teacher, of a guide, or chart, to which he may refer in order that his present work may harmonize with that which preceded, and that which is to follow it. The ground to be covered in a complete course of school education, however elementary, is quite extensive, and hence needs to be divided and subdivided according to certain established principles, so that the mind of the instructor may not be diverted from that which should engage his immediate attention, by the necessity of considering and choosing the best means of supplementing it. Such a graded system of teaching can best be prepared by those who have had not only a long experience in the practical business of teaching, but whose field of observation has been sufficiently comprehensive to enable them to give to the scheme an adaptability to a great variety of circumstances.

The system laid down in the work here offered to practical educators, whether teachers, superintendents, or school officers, is designed to afford such a guide as is above indicated. It is essentially the system which has been in use in the city of New York for some years, only differing from it in the number of grades into which the course is divided. This difference is, however, rather nominal than real, since the number of grades into which a course of study is divided is entirely arbitrary, except so far as it may be dictated by special circumstances. Where schools are very large, and the attendance of pupils is fluctuating, as must be the case in so populous a city as New York, the necessity of constantly reorganizing classes, renders frequent promotions, or transfers from class to class, indispensable, and, hence, a large number of grades becomes a convenience. In schools having a smaller and steadier attendance, the number of grades need not exceed what is requisite for a proper classification and division of subjects for simultaneous study. The *order* of studies —the main point in every course of instruction—corresponds, as here arranged, precisely with the New York plan ; the time requisite for its completion is also about the same.

This course, with its division into grades, constitutes, however, only the frame-work for the series of practical suggestions designed to assist teachers in the performance of their professional duties—that is, in some degree, to show them *what to teach*, as well as *how to teach*. All the precepts and directions here given have been dictated by an earnest desire to aid in the effort now universally put forth by the ablest and most intelligent school officers to abolish the pernicious rote method of teaching, by book and formula, formerly so prevalent, and to make universal the system which appeals, from first to last, to the intelligence of the pupil, and adapts itself to its progressive stages of development. In the lower grades, the objective, or perceptive, system is, of course, made prominent, to be succeeded by those subjects and methods which, as they dispense to a considerable extent with the actual objects themselves, and appeal to the acquired ideas of the pupils, may be properly denominated *conceptive.*

The natural and physical sciences, it will be observed, are largely drawn upon for the materials necessary to accomplish this object, the sciences of observation and classification, such as zoology, botany, and mineralogy, properly taking precedence of those which require a more special application of the reflective and reasoning faculties, such as physiology, natural philosophy, and astronomy. By this kind of teaching, it is designed that the pupil shall acquire the ability to gain an experience of his own, instead of depending exclusively upon that of others, and at the same time, shall acquire a taste for the observation and study of nature.

Certainly such a system for the common schools of our country is far preferable to that which, although insuring proficiency in the "three *R's*" left the pupil's mind in a condition of matured stolidity, and while, perhaps, a most ready talking, writing, and parsing machine, sent him forth to go through this beautiful world, blind to its manifold wonders and glories, and fit only to become the easy prey of the demagogue and the bigot.

It is an evidence of the increasing earnestness of teachers, that the demand for practical suggestions and exact information in regard to their work is now so great. More especially is this so in the case of those engaged in primary school instruction. This department of teaching requires very much special knowledge as well as peculiar tact to produce successful results. A complete exposition of the various methods which are applicable to each stage of this work would require a much larger space than could be devoted to it in the book here published. Hence, references to more full and complete works on the subject have been given in connection with several of the grades, in order to aid teachers in finding the additional information which they may need in this direction.

The demand for copies of the "Manual of Instruction and Discipline," recently prepared by the authors of this work, for the use of the primary and grammar schools of the city of New York, has induced them to endeavor to put the work into a shape in which it might be generally useful; and they trust that, as it is now presented to those engaged in practical education, it will prove an acceptable addition to the literature of American pedagogy, now so scanty and insufficient.

CONTENTS.

INTRODUCTION.

No task can be more responsible, or require the exercise of greater care than that which has for its object the proper education of the young. To perform it efficiently, special preparation and study are indispensably necessary, not only in regard to the branches of knowledge which may have been selected as a basis for the instruction, but also in respect to the proper methods and appliances to be employed, in order to render the instruction truly effective. These methods must be determined by a consideration of the faculties to be trained and educated, as well as the nature of the subject taught; hence, the teacher should be familiar with at least the outlines of mental science,—the office of each of the faculties of the mind, the order in which they are naturally developed, and the proper means of aiding in this development. so that the training and instruction given may result in that most valuable of all characteristics, a well-balanced mind. It is the remark of Professor Henry, that "the laws (which govern the growth and operations of the human mind) are as definite, and as general in their application, as those (which apply to the material universe); and it is evident that a true system of education must be based upon a knowledge and application of those laws." How important then that the teacher should make himself familiar with these laws! Certainly no true success can be obtained without this knowledge ; for destitute of it, the teacher is only an empiric, applying rules the reason of which he does not know, and mechanically following methods, the rationale of which he does not understand.

If the teacher have sufficiently mastered these elementary principles of his profession, it will not be difficult for him at all times rightly to understand his pupils' mental condition and grade of advancement—a matter of the greatest importance, especially at the first stage of school instruction. Failing in this respect, many teachers are often found most laboriously occupied in the useless task of attempting to do that for the child which nature, without any assistance, has already accomplished. They do not seem to be aware of the extent to which the pupil's mental faculties, more especially these concerned in observation, have been developed in this way. The acquisitions made by a child of four or five years of age, before being placed under any regular tuition at all, or subjected to any of the manipulations of the school teacher, are indeed wonderful. The senses, actively awake, have brought the young mind into communication with the multifarious objects of external nature ; the faculty of conception, peculiarly active in childhood, has given it a number of ideas corresponding to its perceptions, and the faculty of speech has enabled it to connect with thousands of these ideas, words and combinations of words, so as to designate and express them.

Thus is the foundation of the intellectual character unerringly laid by the unaided operation of nature herself. Here is no senseless cramming of words, for words are only learned after the ideas which they represent have been acquired. Under the guidance of a teacher properly conversant with the laws of the mind and its growth, this natural process would be continued, and would be directed to its proper objects; but, instead of this, a mental treadmill is often used, the effect of which is to counteract the work of nature, and check the mental activity of the young pupil. To learn A, B, C is, of course, necessary as one of the rudimental steps of primary instruction; but this, like everything else, should be so done, that the intelligence of the pupil may be fostered, not deadened, in the acquisition. In every stage of intellectual training, let the teacher always remember, that his pupil's mind is *not* to be treated as a "passive recipient" of the thoughts and experience of others, but as an active agent, to be enabled to acquire an experience of its own, and apply it to useful purposes. Let him constantly apply the principle, so tersely expressed by Sir William Hamilton : " *The primary principle of education is the determination of the pupil to self-activity—the doing nothing for him which he is able to do for himself.*" This principle is equally applicable to every stage of the mind's development, as well as to the different processes of instruction adapted to these stages; but it will be impossible accurately and effectively to apply it, without a complete knowledge of the order of mental development, and of the relation of that development to the study of each of the branches prescribed for the instruction and the cultivation of the mind.

Knowledge is to be considered as the *food of the mind;* since by the proper reception, digestion, and assimilation of it, the mind is to attain a maturity of strength and efficiency; and upon its quality and quantity it must depend whether that mind is to be healthy and vigorous, or puny, sickly, and imbecile. It is, therefore, of the greatest importance to ascertain the

effect produced upon the mind of the pupil by the
study of each separate branch of knowledge—what
faculties it exercises and develops, and what it keeps in
a state of abeyance or passiveness. The future wants of
the pupils as to information, must, indeed, be a prominent consideration in selecting the subjects to be taught;
but the teacher should, in the classification, as well as
the instruction, of his pupils constantly keep in view the
present status of their minds—what they especially need
in order to acquire vigor, promptitude, and efficiency of
action. In the first stages of education, the latter
should be the almost exclusive consideration; but as
education advances, the practical usefulness of the
knowledge imparted should have paramount weight and
importance.

The adaptation of the *processes of teaching* to the
various subjects taught, as well as to the faculties which
they call into exercise, should be a prominent object in
the teacher's mind. Young, untrained, inexperienced
teachers commit the error of bringing into play, with
regard to all subjects, association or memory. This,
with imitation, enables the pupil to present a show of
knowledge, very gratifying to the unintelligent obser-
ver, but exceedingly pernicious as a substitute for real
acquisitions. When a teacher conceives that the sole
end of his efforts is to enable the pupil to recite *verbatim* the contents of a particular text-book, or to repeat
with verbal accuracy and fluency certain rules, definitions, and formulæ, whether their true meaning is
grasped or not, it is natural that he should resort to the
shortest and most direct means of accomplishing it, that
is, constant rote drill—an appeal to the law of arbitrary association. The injury, however, done to the
mind by this continued process, is incalculable; since,

finally, ideas and facts suggest each other according to no intrinsic or philosophical relation, but only from their accidental connections, or such as this constant repetition may have established; and thus all logical flow of thought is necessarily precluded.

A determination of what are the best methods of presenting the subjects to be taught must depend upon the relations here referred to. Rules and methods may, indeed, be arbitrarily learned and mechanically applied to practice, without any investigation of principles, but no such hap-hazard process can, in any case, be sure of success; while in very many it must result in failure. This important part of the theory of teaching should be carefully studied, not only as preliminary to entering upon the duties of an instructor, but through every stage of their performance. It involves not only a knowledge of the laws of mind, but a thorough familiarity with the subjects taught. "A teacher," says Edward Everett, "ought to know of everything much more than the learner can be expected to acquire. The teacher must know things in a masterly way, curiously, nicely, and in their reasons. He must see the truth under all its aspects, with its antecedents and consequents, or he cannot present it in just that shape in which the young mind can apprehend it. He must, as he holds the diamond up to the sun, turn its facets round and round, till the pupil catches its luster."

A very important inquiry in connection with the right manner of presenting the subjects to the pupils' minds, is in what manner the subjects should be divided into topics, and how these topics should be arranged, and in what order they should be taken up. The following work, embodying, as it does, a graded course of instruction, is designed to deal with this inquiry quite exhaustively, and it is in furnishing a guide to the teacher in this important part of his duties that its usefulness will be found to consist.

The teacher should study, too, the phenomena of morbid as well as of healthy growth; for teaching, in the complete discharge of its functions, has much to do in reforming, as well as forming, the mind. While very much, in this regard, can be learned only by experience, there are many facts and principles already established, which the teacher should, as an essential part of his professional preparation, acquire. In this connection, the *automatic tendencies* of the mind are to be studied— the tendencies, that is, to fall into habits, these when depraved constituting what may be called the morbid growth of the mind. No part of the teacher's duty is more important than the exercise of a constant vigilance, in order to arrest the formation of deleterious habits, or to aid in forming such as are calculated to confirm the healthy progress and development of the pupil's mind. It is on this account that teachers are constantly to be reminded that habits are always more valuable than facts—that it is not the quantity of knowledge acquired that constitutes a criterion of mental advancement, but the mode of employing the mental faculties—the *habits of thought* into which the mind has settled in making its acquisitions or in applying them. In such useful arts as require a mixed exercise of the muscular system and the mental faculties, such as penmanship, drawing, elocution, etc., this automatic tendency has a most important application. Elegant hand-writing, distinctness of articulation, correctness of intonation, ease and grace of deportment, may all be made to rest so firmly on thoroughly fixed habits as to become a kind of "second nature."

How to use text-books, as well as when and for what purposes to employ them, is at the present time particularly, a most important subject of study to the teacher. Though in some branches, and for the attainment of certain objects of mental discipline, it is best to dispense with them altogether and bring the mind of the teacher in direct contact with that of the pupil, yet good text-books must always be among the most important instrumentalities of school instruction, both as regards the effect which their judicious use has upon the mind of the pupil, and the economy of time and labor of which it is the source to the teacher. The latter must have learned how to use them aright in order to be successful in his work, and the pupil must learn how to make effective use of books to be truly educated.

Most children enter school for the first time with minds athirst for knowledge. They have received this craving at the hands of Nature, and their whole existence has been passed in the effort to satisfy it. By their own unaided intelligence they are able to proceed to a certain limited extent; observation is on the alert, and reflection begins to be active; but without the guidance of a mature and trained intellect, there can be no method in their acquisitions, and the limit of their researches is soon reached. The teacher and the book are the instruments for affording this necessary aid and direction; but in doing this, the tendency should always be to stimulate, not repress, intellectual activity—to bring into play the higher faculties of the mind, not to render its energies dormant by offering only the dry forms, the mouldy skeletons of knowledge, instead of the vital germs of intelligence and thought. If, after the various grades of school study have been passed, the pupil is left with a torpid, vacant mind, the loss which he has sustained is too great to be compensated by even the ability to read, write, and cipher. On the other hand, a pupil that has not only mastered the elementary principles of science, but has learned how to use books so as to supplement the result of his own observations by the experience of others, has been more effectually educated than he could possibly be by an exclusive dependence upon oral instruction.

One of the most serious abuses to which the employment of elementary text-books is liable, is the practice of requiring the pupil to commit to memory, *verbatim*, all the definitions of a subject before teaching the subject itself, so as to enable the pupils to understand the nature of the things defined. It is, of course, most logical in the scientific treatment of a subject to place the definitions first, and the reasoning based upon them afterward, but this is not the order of investigation. The definitions are the results of an induction based upon the facts obtained by observation; they are generalizations of those facts, and are unintelligible to those entirely unacquainted with the facts themselves. Thus the order of investigation is *inductive;* the treatment is *deductive,* and in elementary teaching the method should conform rather to the former than the latter. Give the pupil accurate and vivid conceptions of the facts, encourage him to observe the phenomena—to collect an experience of his own; tell him, or let him learn from the book what has been discovered by the experience of others; and when the facts thus obtained form a sufficient ground-work, lead his mind to the proper induction, after which the definition, principle, or rule, based upon it, comes naturally, and will be thoroughly understood. The definitions thus taught should be brief and accurate in language, and, as a general thing, should be committed to memory *verbatim;* for great skill is required to construct a good definition, and it is of the greatest value to the scholar and thinker to have his mind well stored with these landmarks and guide-posts of knowledge.

There is a numerous class of subjects in which text-books, in the hands of the pupil, are apt to be a bane rather than a benefit. The general recognition of this fact is quite an interesting feature in the educational history of our times. *Object Teaching* and *Oral Instruction* have assumed a prominent place in every rational course of study. Both these terms necessarily exclude the use of text-books. Teaching from objects is merely training the young child to acquire knowledge, in a systematic way, from his own experience; that is, by the regular exercise of his observing faculties. It presupposes the presentation of the actual object during the early stages of the work, so that perceptions may pass from it to the mind, and thus ideas be obtained. In teaching natural science, at an advanced stage of the course, the same method is needed; for it is of very little use to attempt to teach facts in relation to the phenomena of nature when those phenomena have never been observed. It is of no use to talk of the laws of light, heat, and electricity—of the movements and appearances of the heavenly bodies—or of the chemical composition of ordinary substances, as if they were mere abstractions. The teacher should never forget that the study of the book is the instrument, not the end of instruction; its lifeless representatives of ideas cannot dispense with those vivid expressions of thought which come fresh from the lips of the teacher. Besides, there is a language other than words—a language to which the eye, the tones of the voice, the movements of the body, all give force and expressiveness, and added to these there is the influence of sympathy, which, though a kind of " unconscious tuition," is perhaps the greatest element of the teacher's power; and this not alone, or chiefly, in intellectual training, but in that which is far more important—moral education.   The government of his pupils—the training of their sensibilities, their emotional nature, and their impulses—the instilling of right principles of conduct—all these constitute a greater part of what may be called a good education, than the teaching of the rudiments of knowledge. " Give me the child," says Everett, " whose heart has embraced without violence the gentle lore of obedience, in whom the sprightliness of youth has not encroached on deference for authority, and I would rather have him for my son, though at the age of twelve he should have his alphabet to learn, than be compelled to struggle with the caprice of a self-willed, obstinate youth, whose bosom has become a viper's nest of unamiable passions, although in early attainments he may be the wonder of the day."

GRADED COURSE OF INSTRUCTION.

TENTH GRADE.

(LOWEST PRIMARY.)

Time allowed, about five months.

LANGUAGE.

Reading.—Words, and what they represent; their sounds, and letters; also short sentences composed of familiar words. The alphabet, by review.

Phonetics.—Simple sounds of letters for training the organs of hearing and of speech.

Spelling.—Words of regular formation—to be taught from the blackboard, charts, etc.

ARITHMETIC.

Counting and Adding.—Objects—as balls on the Numeral Frame, pebbles, etc.

Figures.—From 0 to 100, as symbols of the numbers, taught by counting objects.

OBJECT LESSONS.

Form.—Common shapes, as square, oblong, ball, cylinder, cube; different kinds of corners, and of lines.

Color.—Common colors, as red, yellow, blue, green, orange, purple, to be distinguished.

Objects.—Names of common objects, their uses, and principal parts.

Human Body.—Principal parts of the body.

DRAWING AND WRITING.

On Slates.—Making dots and small crosses in rows; drawing short lines, corners, etc.   Printing or writing simple letters.

MANAGEMENT.

Length of Exercises.—Fifteen minutes at one time.

Discipline.—Constant, but varied employment the best means.

How to Teach

LANGUAGE.

Reading.—Children learn words as *audible* signs or names of objects, actions, and qualities, when they begin to talk. These words are learned as wholes, at once, by hearing them spoken; not by first learning their elementary sounds. In this manner young children gradually become familiar with new words until they possess a vocabulary which enables them to make known their wants, and to express their thoughts. The words which the children thus learn make but little impression upon their minds, as *words*, but they are so intimately associated with the objects, actions, and qualities which they represent that they convey to the mind the same ideas as the objects or the actions themselves convey.

When a child first goes to school it has already learned many words, by hearing, as symbols of objects, etc. The first duty of the teacher is, to ascertain what words the child thus knows, then to teach the young pupil to recognize them by their *forms*. The spoken words are first learned as wholes; the printed words should be learned first as wholes and associated with both the spoken words and the objects which they represent.

Therefore, teach first *short* words, which the children have learned by hearing; beginning with the names of familiar objects which can be shown to the pupils, or the pictures of which may be presented. Also, during the first lesson in reading, print the words on the black-board several times, and point them out on charts, etc. Let the pupils point out the words on the blackboard, and on charts; also let them print the words on their slates.

Special pains should be taken to lead the children to associate the printed words with the objects which they represent, either by the use of the objects themselves, or by pictures.

In teaching words that are not *names*, care should be taken to illustrate their meaning by simple phrases, conversations, etc. During the earlier lessons, omit words of irregular formation, having *several silent letters*, such as *tongue, knife, know, though, thought*, etc. This class of words may be presented when the pupils have learned the alphabet, and its regular combinations, and the sounds represented by the letters have been taught.

Let each word be taught first at sight, as a whole, and the sounds and names of the letters which compose the word be taught afterward. After the children have learned a few words at sight, they may be taught the *sounds*, and the *letters* which form those words. For the purpose of teaching the *sound-elements* of words, select those in which the sounds and letters are similar, as *cat, rat, hat, mat, ox, fox, box*, etc. The teacher should sound the elements or letters of the words first, then require the pupils to imitate the sounds thus made. But before this can be done successfully the pupils must be trained *to distinguish*, and *to produce* these sounds, as directed under the head of *Phonetics* for this grade, which see. As additional words are learned, the children may be required to name such of the letters as they know, in the new words, and then taught the remaining ones in those words. In this way let the twenty-six letters of the alphabet be taught, progressively. Subsequently these should be reviewed, and their usual order learned by repetition. The *small* letters are, of course, to be taught first.

After the pupils have learned several single words, simple sentences may be presented, as " The dog can bark." " The horse can draw a cart." The other words that make up these sentences can then be learned easily, as parts of the sentence.

The rapidity with which a child may be taught to read by learning to recognize the simple *forms* of words, at first, is surprising. And no less astonishing is the readiness with which spelling is afterward learned.

Let the order of teaching reading be, *first, the idea ; then, its sound-symbol,* or spoken word ; *next, the form-symbol,* or printed word ; and *subsequently, its representation by writing ;* and the order of learning to read the language will correspond with the order of using it. Words, then, will become as mirrors, reflecting objects and ideas to the minds of the pupils. *Sense,* and *sound,* and *form,* and *use* will become so intimately blended together that pupils may easily be led to use conversational tones in reading, and a natural style of expression will follow as the necessary result.

But it may be asked, How can the pupils acquire the means of learning the new words which they will find in reading ? By observing their resemblances to words already learned. The child, while learning to read, is constantly comparing the forms of new words with the forms and sounds of those previously mastered. The teacher may and should aid the young pupils

2

in acquiring the ability to learn new words by arranging in groups, on the blackboard, those already learned, and showing them how to compare the *forms* and *sounds* of these words with others.

For the purpose of leading the children to observe readily the *analogy of words*, in their sounds and in the arrangement of their letters, after they have learned, objectively and singly, to recognize several words at sight, place on the blackboard, in columns, such of these words as are similar in spelling and in sound, as in the following groups:

cat,	*pin,*	*pen,*	*ox,*	*cup,*
rat,	*tin,*	*hen,*	*fox,*	*gun,*
hat,	*fin,*	*ten,*	*box,*	*run,*
mat.	*in.*	*men.*	*top.*	*fun.*

When the children have learned to pronounce the words in a column, at sight, let them learn to give the sounds of each, as—*k ă t*, cat; *r ă t*, rat; *h ă t*, hat; etc., *not* as a *spelling* exercise, but to impress upon their minds the relation of sounds, and of letters as their representatives.

As other words are learned, let new groups be arranged, and comparisons made with words of similar form, as:

old,	rake,	me,	line,	mule,
cold,	make,	we,	fine,	rule,
told,	cake,	see,	nine,	cube,
scold.	bake.	bee.	pine.	tube.

If further descriptions of methods for teaching children to read during their first term in school be desired, see Suggestions for the Teacher, pages 329–332 of *New Primary Object Lessons.*

Jeffers's Panoramic Reading Chart will be found exceedingly useful during the early lessons in reading, for presenting the words objectively.

Phonetics.—The object of teaching this subject should be, *first—to train the organs of hearing,* so that the children may readily distinguish the sounds heard in speaking our language ; *second—to train the organs of speech,* so that the pupils may learn to produce those sounds correctly in using the language. In presenting this subject—and this should be done as soon as the children begin to learn words by sight—the teacher should herself make the sounds, and then require the pupils to imitate them, as: $\bar{a}, \bar{a}$; $\hat{a}, \hat{a}$; $\bar{o}, \bar{o}$; $\breve{o}, \breve{o}$; $\bar{e}, \bar{e}$; $\breve{e}, \breve{e}$; $\bar{i}, \bar{i}$; $\breve{i}, \breve{i}$; $\bar{u}, \bar{u}$; $\breve{u}, \breve{u}$; $\ddot{a}, \ddot{a}$; $\underline{a}, \underline{a}$; afterward, thus: $\bar{a}, \breve{a}, \ddot{a}, \underline{a}$; $\bar{e}, \breve{e}$; $\bar{i}, \breve{i}$; $\bar{o}, \breve{o}, \varrho$; $\bar{u}, \breve{u}, \underline{u}.$

When their organs of hearing and of speech have thus been trained, both to *distinguish* and *to imitate* sounds, proceed to teach what sounds are represented by the letters of simple words, as—*m e, m a t, c a t, m a n, n o, n o t, p i n, c u p, m e t, c a k e, m a k e, l a t e, s l a t e.*

Should more definite directions relative to methods for giving the first lessons in Phonetics be desired for this and the following grades, see pages 297–308 in *New Primary Object Lessons.*

Spelling.—After the words have been learned by sight and sound, let them be learned by spelling, and the children requested to observe that similar spelling and similar sounds usually accompany each other. Of course many words must be taught simply as signs of things, or actions, or qualities, etc., but the plan of grouping words by similarity of sounds, as indicated on a preceding page, under the head of *Reading,* will greatly facilitate learning to read, and to spell, also.

Various modes may be used in teaching the reading and the spelling of words singly—for instance: Let the pupil point out given words on the blackboard, and on the charts, as they are named by the teacher. A word may be erased from the blackboard, and the pupils requested to pronounce the word, and name the letters composing it. Parts of words may also be erased, and the pupils required to name the missing letters. Let the pupils, also, print the words on slates, copying them from charts, or the blackboard.

The list of familiar words taught during the first term in school should include those commonly used, as, names of articles of dress, food, furniture, and utensils used in the house, different things used in the school-room, common animals, plants, names of familiar qualities, actions, etc.

It is not the small number of letters of which a word is formed that renders it easy to be learned objectively, but its familiarity by use in conversation. Do not, therefore, confine the pupils to words which are composed of only three or four letters. Long, difficult, or anomalous words should, however, be omitted in this grade.

N. B.—In all these exercises of reading and spelling, the teacher should—

Train the pupils to pronounce words readily at sight.

Never allow them to use unnatural tones in speaking or reading.

Correct their faults in the use of language as they occur.

ARITHMETIC.

Counting and Adding.—The child's knowledge of *number* commences with counting objects. He cannot learn the value of *figures* from 1 to 10 until he can count *ten* objects. Therefore *counting* should be attended to first. The *Numeral Frame* is the most convenient apparatus to aid in teaching counting, and in giving children first ideas of simple numbers. The following illustration is intended to represent one mode of using the Numeral Frame for teaching counting. This mode of using it consists simply in holding the Frame before the pupils, and moving the balls on the first wire, one at a time, while the children count "one, two, three, four, five, six, seven, eight, nine, ten." The same counting may be repeated on the second, third, and on each succeeding wire. At first the counting should not extend beyond *ten.* When all the

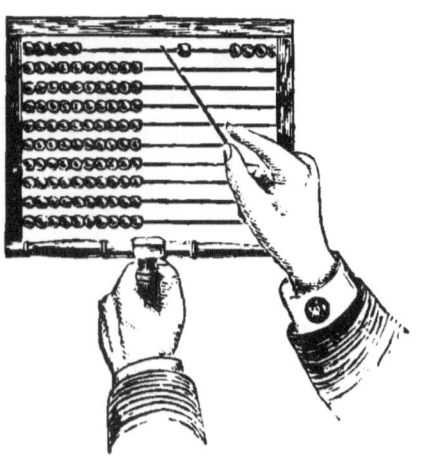

COUNTING.

balls on each wire have been counted in this manner, proceed to move *one ball on each wire,* and let the children count to *ten,* as before. Let this exercise be continued, from day to day, until each child can count from one to ten, alone. Afterward, the counting may be extended to *twenty,* by moving the balls on *two* wires; then to *thirty,* by moving the balls on three wires, and so on to one hundred. When the pupils are allowed to count in concert, care should be taken to have them use the falling inflection at each number, to prevent them from acquiring a sing-song tone.

Adding.—When the pupils can count to one hundred by *ones*, the teacher may move *two balls* at a time,. and thus train them to add by *twos*. As the teacher moves two balls on one wire, and two more on the next, and so on, the pupils say, " two, four, six, eight, ten, twelve, fourteen," etc.

After the pupils can count, or add thus by *twos*, as far as fifty, and have also learned to read and write figures as far as 20, the teacher may write a column of 2's on the blackboard, and train the pupils to add the *figures* in the same manner as the balls were added.

Next, the pupils may copy the column of 2's from the blackboard, on their slates, and each one add it as it was added on the blackboard, and write the sum under the column.

When the pupils have had sufficient practice on a column of 2's, both on the blackboard and on their slates, to be able to add it readily, the teacher may again take the Numeral Frame, move *one* ball on the first wire, and *two* balls on each succeeding wire, while the pupils say, " one, three, five, seven, nine, eleven," etc., to fifty-one. When the pupils have learned to add the *balls*, thus, the teacher may write a column of 2's with a 1 under it, on the blackboard, so as to make the combinations produce the odd numbers. After sufficient training upon these combinations, both with the Numeral Frame, and the blackboard, require the pupils to write similar columns of 2's with a 1 underneath, and add as before, writing the sum below the column.

Let the same process be pursued in teaching the addition of *threes;* first, by balls on the Numeral Frame, as three, six, nine, twelve, etc., then by figure 3's on the blackboard, and lastly by each pupil's writing the figures in columns on the slate, adding them, and writing the sum below. Then the *threes* should be combined with *one*, next with *two*, so as to produce different combinations of numbers, as with the *twos*.

During a still later stage, the pupils may be taught to add by alternating *twos* and *ones;* then *threes* and *ones;* then *threes* and *twos;* then *threes, twos,* and *ones.* Each of these steps should be taken first with *objects*, then with *figures* on the blackboard, and finally by the pupils' writing the columns on their slates and adding them. The same method may be pursued for teaching the addition of *fours, fives*, and *sixes*, and their combinations with *ones, twos, threes*, etc., in the next or Ninth Grade. The order of the steps is indicated by the objects employed in teaching, viz.: Numeral Frame, Blackboard, Slates.

Of course, these exercises with columns of *figures* should not be introduced before the pupils have been taught to know figures as symbols, and to make them on their slates.

Value of Numbers.—It is exceedingly important that the first ideas of the value of numbers, and of figures, be associated with numbers of objects counted. Both the *value of numbers* and the *value of figures* should be taught in connection with counting objects. Here, again, the *Numeral Frame* is the most useful apparatus. When the pupils can readily count *ten*, the teacher may hold the Numeral Frame before the class, move *one ball* on the second wire from the top, and request the pupils to say "*one* ball." Then the teacher may move *two* balls, one at a time, on the third wire, the pupils counting them as moved, thus: "one, two; two balls." Then move *three* balls, one at a time, on the fourth wire, the pupils counting thus: "one, two, three ; three balls." Then move *four* balls in the same manner; then *five* balls, and so on. The position of the balls on the wire while the pupils are counting, may be seen on the sixth wire in the accompanying

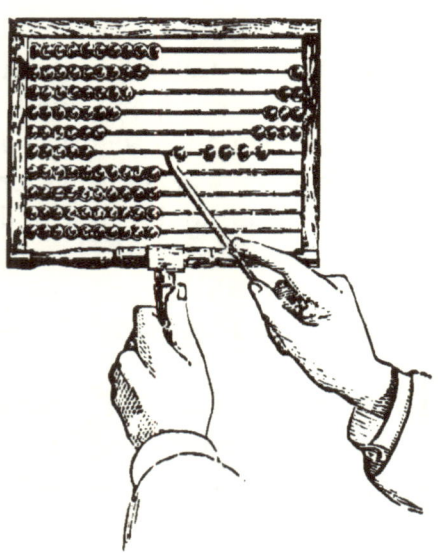

VALUE OF NUMBERS.

illustration of the *Value of Numbers*. While the pupils are counting "one, two, three, four, five," the teacher does not move the balls to the side of the frame, but leaves a space between each two balls, as may be seen in the illustration on this page.

The illustration on the next page —*Simple Value of Figures*—represents the teacher in the act of moving the *five balls* to the side of the frame; and, as he does this, the pupils tell the number of balls, thus, "five balls." Let the same mode be pursued with each number, from *one* to *nine*. First, the children count the separated balls, as each is moved part way; and as all are moved to the side of the frame, the pupils tell the whole number of balls moved.

Next let the pupils tell the number of balls. on each wire, thus: one ball, two balls, three balls, four balls, five balls, six balls, etc., to nine balls; nine balls, eight balls, seven balls, etc., to one ball, no ball. By these means the *Value of Numbers* will be learned thoroughly.

Figures.—Figures should be introduced as symbols of the number of objects counted, and presented first consecutively, in groups, or steps, as follows: from 0 to 9; from 10 to 19; from 20 to 29; from 30 to 39, etc. No succeeding group should be presented until the preceding one has been thoroughly learned, so that the pupils can read them at sight, in order, and out of order. While teaching the Simple Value of Figures, the Numeral Frame will be found a most valuable aid. During this stage of instruction the teacher should make frequent use of the blackboard, and the pupils of slates.

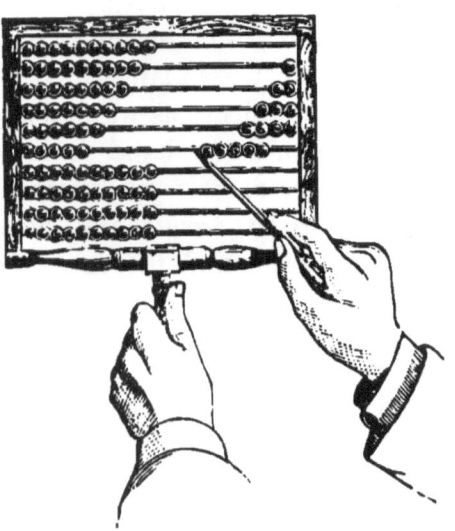

SIMPLE VALUE OF FIGURES.

Additional suggestions relative to methods for teaching the First Ideas of Numbers and of Figures, may be found on pages 194–209 of *New Primary Object Lessons.*

2*

OBJECT LESSONS.

N. B.—Each exercise in object lessons should be conducted with a view to forming habits of attention and careful observation through the use of the senses.

Form.—In Nature's school, children first learn to know things as wholes; they learn to know their parts afterward. The teacher who would be successful must follow Nature's plan of instruction. Present, therefore, common objects, as wholes, and lead the pupils to notice resemblances in shape, first; afterward direct their attention to prominent differences.

A Box of Forms and Solids, containing forty-eight plane Forms and fifteen Solids, has been prepared for the special purpose of *Object Teaching.* This is the most important aid in illustrating the various forms and solids.

Select the Form to be taught from the Box of Forms, and lead the pupils to observe it, then tell them its name; next require them to mention other objects having the same shape. Proceed in this manner with each Form and Solid mentioned for this grade, and continue these exercises until the pupils can recognize and name each.

Color.—The pupils should be led to distinguish resemblances and differences in color from "colored cubes," or cards, and to group together objects of like colors. They should also learn the names of the six principal colors.

Objects.—The lessons on *Common Objects* in this grade should be simple and conversational, treating only of their most obvious parts and uses. Such common objects as a bell, chair, slate, pencil, hat, cup, knife, etc., are appropriate for this purpose. The pupils should be led to notice and point out the principal parts, and encouraged to tell what they see and what they know of each object shown them.

Human Body.—In this Grade the lessons on the Human Body should lead the pupils to notice and name the parts, as head, neck, trunk, arms, hands, legs, feet; also parts of the head, as crown, face, forehead, cheeks, chin, mouth, nose, eyes, ears, etc.

N. B.—If more explicit information be desired relative to methods for giving lessons on *shapes of lines, corners, square, oblong, ball, cylinder, cube,* and *common objects;* also on *colors,* and on the *human body,* it may be found in *New Primary Object Lessons.*

DRAWING AND WRITING.

Drawing on Slates, etc.—The exercises of *Drawing* and *Printing on slates* should be introduced in such a manner as to give an interesting variety to the class-work; also, so as to aid in the discipline of the class, by giving the children something *to do* that will interest them after they have become tired with their other lessons. The children might be allowed to use slates for drawing, as a reward for good order and attention. Short daily exercises may be made very useful.

MANAGEMENT.

Length of Exercises.—The exercises of this Grade should not be continued upon the same subject longer than fifteen minutes at one time, without materially changing the manner of the exercise.

Discipline.—Young children cannot attend to the same thing for a long time without change in the form of attention. Their natural activity demands frequent changes in the position of the body; also constant but varied employment. If the teacher does not furnish the needed employment and changes of position by variety in her methods of instruction, the children will seek to gratify their needs by play. Therefore children *should never be compelled to sit without employment, either for the mind, the hands, or the body.*

Children should be led to do right by encouragement rather than driven by fear. Judicious praise is more efficient than scolding. Teach them to be cleanly, mannerly, truthful, and obedient. Let good examples of these traits be commended frequently.

NINTH GRADE.

(PRIMARY.)

Time allowed, about five months.

LANGUAGE.

Reading.—In the *First Reader.*

Phonetics.—Pupils to be taught to recognize and to make the sounds of the letters in words of one syllable.

Definitions.—Pupils to be practiced in illustrating the meaning of words by their use in short sentences; also in telling what the words mean.

Spelling.—Words from the reading lessons; also familiar words in common use.

ARITHMETIC.

Adding.—With objects, and with figures; twos, threes, fours, and fives.

Figures.—Numbers of two and of three figures to be read at sight, without numeration; also, to be written on slates from dictation.

Roman Numbers.—I, V, X, L, with their combinations to *sixty*, inclusive; also their use on the face of the clock.

OBJECT LESSONS.

Form.—Common shapes, continued; adding those of rhomb, rhomboid, circle, semicircle, crescent, sphere, hemisphere, cone; also position of lines.

Color.—Shades of common colors, as light and dark red, light and dark blue, etc.

Human Body.—Names and uses of the limbs, and of their parts; also the names and shapes of the principal bones.

Objects.—The principal parts and chief uses of common objects.

DRAWING AND WRITING.

On Slates.—Connect dots by lines; draw squares, oblongs, rhombs; divide lines into equal parts. Write simple words with small letters.

MANAGEMENT.

Doing.—*Train* children *to see, to do,* and *to tell.*

Manners and Morals.—Use the appropriate daily incidents of school as occasions for giving instruction in Manners and Morals.

HOW TO TEACH

SUBJECTS OF THE NINTH GRADE.

LANGUAGE.

Reading.—The manner of teaching *Reading* during the first term in which books are used by the pupils, has a very important influence on the future progress of those pupils. In the processes of instruction, only one difficulty should be presented to the pupils at a time. Among the difficulties which children have to encounter during their first lessons in reading from books, are, learning *to know the words at sight,* so as to pronounce them readily; learning *to know what the words and sentences mean;* learning *to read in such a manner as to imitate good conversation.*

First Step.—With each new reading lesson the first step should be to make the pupils familiar with the words of the lesson, by printing them on the blackboard in columns, and teaching the children to pronounce them at sight; next teach them to pronounce at sight the same words in the book, but out of their order in the sentences of the lesson, lest they learn them by rote, instead of by sight.

Second Step.—Train the pupils to find out what each sentence means, and to tell the meaning in *their own* language.

Third Step.—Train the pupils to read each sentence so that the reading may resemble good conversation.

Finally, when the lesson has been read in a proper manner, the teacher should talk with the children about it, and encourage them to tell, in their own language, what they have read.

N. B.—*Let the standard for good reading be its near resemblance in manner to good conversation.*

Further suggestions relative to first lessons in reading from books may be found on pages 333–337, of *New Primary Object Lessons.*

₊*₊ The work of teaching children to read may be facilitated by using, for the First and Second Reading Books, those printed with the modified types invented by Dr. Edwin Leigh.

Phonetics.—The object of exercises in Phonetics should be the same in this grade as in the preceding— to secure a ready recognition of the several sounds of our language, and the ability to utter them distinctly in conversation and reading. Time should not be wasted in the endeavor to teach children definitions or descriptions of the various sounds of letters.

Let the chief aims of the teacher be, to train the organs of hearing to acuteness in the perception of sounds, and the organs of speech to flexibility and accuracy in producing sounds.

Definitions.—During the lessons of this grade, it is appropriate to teach the children to use the principal words of the lesson in brief sentences, to enable them to show readily that they understand what the words mean, as: "A horse can draw a *cart.*"—"I must be *good.*"—"I can *hold* a book."—"*Snow* is white."—"I will try to *learn* to read."—"I must *obey* my mother," etc., etc. Such exercises will be found to be much more useful to young children than teaching them formal definitions to be recited. The meaning of difficult or unusual words must, of course, be *explained* and *illustrated* by the teacher.

Spelling.—In oral spelling, the words should be distinctly pronounced by the pupil before they are spelled, then each letter clearly uttered, *a pause made between the syllables,* and the word again pronounced after all the letters have been given. The familiar words taught, in addition to those in the reading lessons, should include such appropriate words as the children most commonly hear and use. These should be printed or written on the blackboard by the teacher, and copied by the pupils, on their slates. The same words may also be spelled orally.

The chief use of spelling consists in writing words; therefore, as early as possible, it should be taught by writing. As the first step in this direction, let pupils commence in this grade to *study spelling lessons by copying the words on slates.*

ARITHMETIC.

Adding.—It would be well for the teacher, before commencing the lessons of this Grade, in Arithmetic, to read the directions for teaching "Adding" in the preceding Grade.

During the exercises of counting and adding with the Numeral Frame, do not allow the children to count and add by *rote.* See that due attention is given to the objects counted. When the pupils can add readily

single columns, each composed of like numbers, as all
2's, all 3's, 4's, 5's, etc., teach them to add single columns
composed of different small numbers, as 2's and 3's;
2's, 3's, and 4's; also 2's, 3's, 4's, and 5's.

2	4	5	These combinations should be illustrated
3	3	4	on the Numeral Frame at first, then
2	2	3	taught with figures on the blackboard;
3	4	2	and subsequently copied by the pupils on
2	3	5	their slates, and added by them silently.
3	2	4	In adding, let the pupils be trained from
2	4	3	the first to name only the sums, thus:
3	3	2	3, 5, 8, 10, 13, 15, 18, 20, 23, 25;—4, 6,
2	2	5	9, 13, 15, 18, 22, 24, 27, 31;—4, 9, 11,
3	4	4	14, 18, 23, 25, 28, 32, 37.
—	—	—	To make the pupils familiar with the
25	31	37	sums produced by adding the separate
			numbers, 1, 2, 3, 4, 5, 6, 7, 8, 9, to

each number below 20, arrange the figures on the blackboard thus:

0	1	2	3	4	5	6	7	8	9	10	11	12	13	14	15	etc.
1	1	1	1	1	1	1	1	1	1	1	1	1	1	1	1	
1	2	3	4	5	6	7	8	9	10	11	12	13	14	15	16	

0	1	2	3	4	5	6	7	8	9	10	11	12	13	14	15
2	2	2	2	2	2	2	2	2	2	2	2	2	2	2	2
2	3	4	5	6	7	8	9	10	11	12	13	14	15	16	17

Continue this arrangement until the pupils can add,
both on the blackboard and on slates, each number
from 1 to 9 to each number below 20, both in the order
given, and out of this order.

Reading and Writing Figures.—Both the reading and writing of numbers in figures can be taught most thoroughly in steps, or groups. The figures should be presented first in their order, in connection with counting ; then out of their order. In this Grade the figures should be taught *without numeration.* The following groups will indicate appropriate steps :

First Step.	Second Step.	Third Step.	Fourth Step.	Fifth Step.
10	100	100	200	300
11	200	101	201	301
12	300	102	202	302
13	400	103	203	303
14	500	104	204	304
15	600	105	205	305
16	700	106	206	306
17	800	107	207	307
18	900.	108	208	308
19		109	209	309
20		110	210	310
21		111	211	311
etc.,		etc.,	etc.,	etc.,
to		to	to	to
99.		199.	299.	399.

These steps may be continued in this manner through 999. As much time will be required to teach the *first* and *third* steps as for any *four* other steps. Let the children be trained to *read* and *write* the numbers contained in each step, readily, before taking up the next one in order.

If properly conducted, these lessons will train the pupils to read and write numbers through 199 in one month, and any number expressed by three figures in two months.

Roman Numbers.—Besides teaching what numbers are represented by I, V, X, and L, and their combinations to *sixty*, the pupils should be trained to tell the time of day as indicated on the face of a clock.

OBJECT LESSONS.

Form.—When the pupils have learned to recognize a given shape by means of its representative form in the set of "Object Teaching Forms and Solids," they should be led to discover the same shape in several other objects. See remarks on page 34, relative to Form and Methods for teaching it.

During the first lessons on lines, the attention of the pupils was properly directed to their *shapes* only, as straight, crooked, curved, waved, spiral. When they are taught to recognize and name the *positions* of lines, as vertical, slanting or oblique, and horizontal, they should be trained to apply these names of positions to *objects* as well as to lines.

Color.—In lessons on color, the name should first be associated with the *color* which it represents, by showing that color and requiring the pupils to point it out on the chart, and among colored objects. To recite names and descriptions of colors, without also knowing the color when seen, is of no use. The teacher should use "Color-Cubes," "Colored-Cards," "Color-Charts," and other colored objects for illustrating these lessons, and require the pupils to show, by placing in groups colors that nearly resemble each other, with what degree of accuracy they *distinguish colors;* and at the same time they should be taught to know common shades and tints by their names.

Human Body.—In giving the lessons on the *human body*, let the pupils point out and give the names and uses of parts, as parts and uses of the arm, hand, leg, foot, etc.

Objects.—Let the pupils point out parts of objects, and the teacher give their names and uses; then let the children give the names and uses of the parts as the teacher points to them.

N. B.—Should the teacher desire more explicit information relative to methods for giving lessons on *plane forms, solids, position of lines, shades of colors,* the *human body,* and on *common objects,* for this and the succeeding Grades, than the space will allow in this book, it may be found in the treatment of these topics in *New Primary Object Lessons.*

DRAWING AND WRITING.

On Slates.—In this Grade, the instruction should be continued in a manner similar to that for the Tenth Grade, which see. The teacher should give full illustrations on the blackboard, relative to each point and step of the lessons.

MANAGEMENT.

Doing.—*Children learn much faster by doing* than by merely repeating what they have been told. Therefore, whenever possible, arrange the exercises of each subject so that the pupils may be called upon *to do* something which relates to that subject, *with their hands;* also so as to require them *to tell* what they *see* and *do.*

***Regular Occupation for all the Pupils.*—**
A teacher who furnishes that regular and constant occupation which commands the attention of all the pupils during the several exercises of the .day, thereby
gives the best assurance of ability to manage a school
successfully. Indeed, the secret of maintaining good
discipline chiefly lies in this. Hence the *manner of
teaching* becomes an important element of good management as well as of good instruction, for it is this
which chiefly determines the order of the class. Fur-
thermore, habits of learning are acquired from the prevailing methods of teaching.

To learn how to manage a class or school, so that all
the pupils may have constant occupation, and may give an
interested attention to all the exercises, should be the
aim of every teacher. Proper changes in the manner
of presenting the different lessons upon the same subject,
and even changes in the manner of conducting the exercise of a single lesson will be useful to the teacher
toward the attainment of this aim.

In a class composed of young children, frequent alter-
nations from answers by individual pupils to responses
by the entire class will aid in maintaining the attention
of all the pupils. Great care, however, will be necessary,
on the part of the teacher, to prevent the pupils, while
speaking in concert, from using sing-song tones. This
may be prevented by requiring them always to use the
falling inflection in answers by the entire class, and by
never allowing them to repeat the answer, or statement,
without a request from the teacher, *made after each response* by the class.

EIGHTH GRADE.

Time allowed,—about five months.

LANGUAGE.

Reading.—*First Reader* completed, and an easy *Second Reader* commenced; pupils to be able to read fluently in good conversational tones, with proper attention to the *pauses*.

Phonetics.—Sounds occurring in words of one syllable, and silent letters to be distinguished.

Definitions.—Meaning of the words read to be shown by using them in short sentences.

Spelling.—From reading lessons; and lists of other familiar words.

ARITHMETIC.

Adding.—Single columns of ten figures; adding by decades, through 9s'.

Numeration and *Notation.*—Reading and writing figures through nine places (987, 654, 321).

Mental.—Simple, practical questions which require the adding of numbers from 5 to 9 to numbers below 30; also, subtracting similar numbers.

Multiplication table commenced.

Roman Numbers.—Their combinations through two hundreds. The Key to Roman Numbers to be taught.

OBJECT LESSONS.

Form.— Parallel and perpendicular lines, angles, prisms, pyramids, surfaces, circumference, diameter, etc.

Color.—Primary and secondary colors.

Human Body.—Principal bones and their uses.

Animals.—Names and uses of familiar animals ; also where they live.

Plants.—Names of trees, plants, flowers, fruits, etc. ; also where they grow.

Objects.—Principal qualities, parts, and uses.

DRAWING AND WRITING.

On Slates.—Drawing plane figures ; writing simple words ; formation of capitals taught.

MANAGEMENT.

Physical Training.—Daily physical exercise and pure air are indispensable to the health of children. Provide them with both during the hours of school duties.

How to Teach

SUBJECTS OF THE EIGHTH GRADE.

LANGUAGE.

Reading.—The exercises for teaching *Reading* in the Eighth Grade may be divided into *three steps*, as in the Ninth Grade.

First Step.—Training the pupils to know the words at sight; also what the words mean.

Second Step.—Attention to the thoughts expressed.

Third Step.—Reading in easy, conversational tones.

1. The pupils may be trained to know the words at sight by writing them in columns on the blackboard—by pronouncing them from their books, commencing with the last word of the paragraph and proceeding in an order the reverse of that pursued in reading.

2. As soon as the words are known readily at sight, *chief attention should be given to the thoughts expressed.* The pupils may be led to attend to the thoughts expressed by requiring them to find out what the sentences tell, without reading them aloud. The teacher may aid them in this matter by proceeding in a manner similar to the following: Request the class to look at the first sentence, and each member to raise a hand when able to tell what the sentence is about. When several hands are held up, call upon different pupils to state, in their own language, what the sentence tells. Proceed in a similar manner with other sentences of the lesson, and

3

require the pupils to tell what those sentences say. The teacher may ask: What does the first line tell us? What do the words in the next sentence say? Who can tell what the next paragraph is about?

3. When the pupils have accomplished the first two steps in a given reading lesson, they will be prepared to take the *third step*, and will readily learn to read with easy, conversational tones. Special care should be taken in this grade to train the pupils in habits of clearness and distinctness of enunciation, also to read in an easy, speaking voice.

Faults in reading are most readily overcome when the efforts to correct them are chiefly directed to one kind at a time, and the training continued until the pupils clearly perceive the fault and take the proper means to correct it.

Punctuation.—The time commonly spent in teaching children to recite definitions of punctuation-marks is wasted. Instead of this, lead the pupils to observe that *a short pause is made at a comma, a little longer pause at a semicolon,* and still *longer pauses at the question-mark* and *period.* Lead the pupils to see that the question-mark points out a question, and a period the end of a sentence. The uses of all the marks of pauses, as well as the hyphen, apostrophe, and quotation-marks, should first be explained from the blackboard, then examples of their use should be pointed out by the pupils in their reading books.

Phonetics.—In this grade the pupils should be taught to distinguish the sounds of given letters in words of one syllable, and to make these sounds, as, the sound of *a* in *slate, a* in *ball, o* in *not, o* in *do, u* in *full, f* in *far*, *f* in *of*, *k* in *kite*, *m* in *man*, *c* in *cow*, etc. When the pupils can distinguish and make the sounds in words of one syllable, they may be required to tell which letters have no sound in given words; also, to name the vowel sound by its number; as in the word *make*, *m-a-k*, make, *a* has its first sound, the *e* is silent; *bought*, *b-*$\overset{4}{a}$*-t*, bought; *ou* represents the fourth sound of *a*, *g* and *h* are silent.

As a method for training pupils to distinguish the *silent* letters, let them first *sound* a word, giving each sound as heard when the word is properly pronounced —then *spell* it, naming each letter in order—next tell which letters have no sound.

Care needs to be taken, in each grade, to prevent the pupils from making the short sounds of *a*, *e*, *i*, *o*, and *u*, too long, when sounded alone. Let each of these sounds be made *very* short, as heard in *at*, *net*, *it*, *not*, *nut*.

Definitions.—In giving the meaning of separate words, in some instances a description of the object, or of its use, if the word be a name, or a simple statement about that which is meant by it, will illustrate the pupil's understanding of it better than the use of the word in a sentence. Let this exercise be so conducted as to avoid mechanical forms of definition, and with a sufficient variety and simplicity to secure a clear knowledge of the *meaning of the words*. The practice of using the given words in sentences, so as to illustrate their meaning, should be continued in this grade.

Spelling.—Care should be taken in oral spelling to have each pupil pronounce the word before spelling it, to name each letter distinctly, *to make a pause between* *the syllables,* and to pronounce the word again when all the letters have been named.

As soon as the pupils can write words on their slates they should have much practice in spelling by writing words from dictation.

In selecting familiar words it would be well to request the pupils to name words for the teacher to write on the blackboard, and all the class, afterward, to copy these on their slates. But teachers should not depend entirely upon the pupils for such words; they should add to the list other appropriate common words.

ARITHMETIC.

Adding.—Continue the exercise of adding single columns, in the same manner as in the Ninth Grade, making them more

6	6	7	7	8	8	9	9
6	5	7	6	8	7	9	8
6	4	7	5	8	6	9	7
6	3	7	4	8	5	9	6
6	6	7	3	8	4	9	9
6	5	7	7	8	8	9	8
6	4	7	6	8	7	9	7
6	3	7	5	8	6	9	6
6	6	7	4	8	5	9	9
6	5	7	3	8	4	9	8
6	4	7	7	8	8	9	7
6	3	7	6	8	7	9	6

difficult, gradually, until the pupils can add readily, without counting, columns of ten or twelve figures each, which are composed of 7s, 8s, and 9s. The progressive arrangement of these columns is illustrated here. When the pupils have learned to add a column on the blackboard, they should copy it on their slates, and then each add it singly, writing the sum underneath it.

Adding by Decades will greatly facilitate learning to add accurately and rapidly.

Appropriate steps toward teaching pupils to *add by decades* may be taken by writing various combinations of numbers on the blackboard, in the following form and order, and requiring the pupils to add the numbers orally, and afterward to copy them on their slates and add them again:

5	15	25	35	45	55	65	75	85	95
4	4	4	4	4	4	4	4	4	4
9	19	29	39	49	59	etc.			
7	17	27	37	47	57	67	77	87	97
7	7	7	7	7	7	7	7	7	7
14	24	34	44	54	64	etc.			
9	19	29	39	49	59	69	79	89	99
7	7	7	7	7	7	7	7	7	7
16	26	36	46	etc.					

When the various combinations with each of the nine digits have been made thus in the form of decades, the pupils may be required to review them by writing on their slates, in groups, combinations of two numbers each, that, when added, will produce in the unit figures the following: 0, 1, 2, 3, 4, 5, 6, 7, 8, 9.

By means of these and similar exercises, children can be led to observe that the same numbers always produce.a like figure when added, as that 9 and 7 always give the unit 6, whether the numbers be 19 and 7, or 29 and 7, or 37 and 9, or 87 and 9; and thus, by attending to this fact, while adding single columns, they can readily acquire the habit of *adding without counting*. One of the most effectual means toward securing this habit, in addition to the adding by decades,

is to teach the pupils to give special attention to the
figure representing the *units* as each successive number
is added, i. e., attention to *adding the units.*

To explain this process, the teacher may write a column of figures on the blackboard, as represented here

a.	b.
7	— 0
8	— 3
9	— 5
6	—
8	— 0
7	— 2
5	—
9	— 0
9	— 1
5	— 2
9	— 7
8	—
—	
90	

by the one marked *a.* Then the pupils may be
led to notice the *unit* figure in each case by
the teacher's pointing to the successive numbers to be added, and saying: "8 and 9
will give 7 for the *unit* figure; 7 and 5 will
give 2 ; 2 and 9 will give 1; 1 and 9 a 0; 5
and 7 will give 2; 2 and 8 a 0; 6 and 9 a 5;
5 and 8 a 3; 3 and 7 a 0."

During this explanatory process, the
teacher may write the *unit* figure opposite
the number added which produces it, as represented in the column marked *b.* So soon
as the pupils understand this process of
adding and naming the *unit* figures only, the
teacher should erase the column, *b,* representing these units, and require the pupils to add by
naming the *units,* as follows: 8, 7, 2, 1, 0, 5, 2, 0, 6, 5,
3, 0. When they can do this readily from the blackboard, the pupils may copy the same column on their
slates, and add by naming the *units* in the same manner.

Then columns made up of other figures may be given
for similar practice. Afterward the pupils may be
trained to add by naming the sum. as each number is
added, as follows: 8, 17, 22. 31, 40, 45, 52. 60, 66, 75, 83,
90. This last form should be followed in the usual
practice of addition. The preceding ones are intended
to be used in teaching pupils *how to add*, that they may
acquire correct habits.

Teachers may observe that the *number* of figures in
the column marked *b,* corresponds with the number of

tens in the sum of column *a—nine*—and that 9 *tens*, with the last *unit* figure, 0, gives the sum of column *a*. But this fact is not of sufficient practical importance to render it desirable that much prominence should be given to it.

After pupils have been thoroughly trained in adding single columns, and understand Numeration and Notation, they can be taught the process of "carrying" in examples of two or more columns, by a few lessons. For teaching the pupils "to carry," at first the examples should be very short, consisting of two columns, only. Afterward the examples may be made longer, gradually, more difficult ones being given by extending both the length of the lines and of the columns. Give many more examples with a few long columns than with long lines. Care should be taken not to embarrass children by giving them *long and large* examples in addition before they can readily add short ones. Let the training be thorough in each step, and the progress gradual. The work of each succeeding week ought to embrace larger examples than were given during the previous one, and to furnish sufficient practice to enable the pupils to master all the difficulties.

Numeration.—On commencing Numeration, the three places in the unit's period should be taught by the order of their places, and by their names; as, *unit's* place, the *first* place on the right-hand side; *ten's* place, the *second* place from the right-hand side; *hundred's* place, the *third* place from the right-hand side. When the pupils can name each place at sight, both in order and out of order, from the blackboard, and can write any number in this period from dictation, proceed to teach the thousand's period in a similar manner. The places in this period should be taught first as the fourth, fifth, and sixth places; then the pupils should be led to observe the similarity of *names* between the first, second, and third places of the *unit's* period, and the first, second, and third places of the *thousand's* period; as units, tens, hundreds of *units*; units, tens, hundreds of *thousands*. When the pupils can both read and write any number readily, from units to hundreds of thousands, proceed in the same manner to teach the *million's* period. Train the pupils so that they can name any place at sight, in order and out of order, and give the order of any place when its name is mentioned; also write readily any number through hundreds of millions, from dictation. Care should be taken to teach the pupils to write the figures neatly, and in straight columns. Two or three weeks may be spent on the unit's period, before proceeding to the thousand's period.

Mental Arithmetic.—In the Eighth Grade the answers to the questions in Mental Arithmetic should be simple and concise. The language used should be sufficient to render the solution of the example, and the answer to it, clearly intelligible to a listener, yet so brief as not to retard, unnecessarily, the process of mental calculation. Appropriate forms for answering questions in Mental Arithmetic, in the Eighth Grade, may be seen in the following examples:

How many are six apples and three apples? *Ans.*—Six apples and three apples are nine apples.

If a coat cost $15, and a hat $5, how much will both cost? *Ans.*—Both will cost the sum of $15 and $5, which is $20.

Henry had 8 marbles and bought 4 more; how many marbles had he then? *Ans.*—Henry then had the sum of 8 marbles and 4 marbles, which is 12 marbles.

A boy had 9 apples and gave away 5 of them; how many apples had he left? *Ans.*—He had 4 apples left; because, when 5 apples are taken from 9 apples, 4 apples will remain.

Multiplication Table.—In presenting the Multiplication Table, it is very desirable that each step be thoroughly mastered before taking the succeeding one. This table may be illustrated first by means of balls on the numeral frame, by arranging the balls in groups of *twos,* then of *threes.* When the groups of *twos* have been illustrated by the balls, the teacher may write the table of twos on the blackboard, thus:

First Form.	Second Form.	First Form.
2 times 2 are 4	$3 \times 2 = 6$	$2 \times 3 = 6$
3 " 2 " 6	$6 \times 2 = 12$	$3 \times 3 = 9$
4 " 2 " 8	$9 \times 2 = 18$	$4 \times 3 = 12$
5 " 2 " 10	$4 \times 2 = 8$	$5 \times 3 = 15$
6 " 2 " 12	$7 \times 2 = 14$	$6 \times 3 = 18$
7 " 2 " 14, etc.	$5 \times 2 = 10$, etc.	$7 \times 3 = 21$, etc.

On placing the *Second Form* before the class for the first time, the teacher should explain the use of the *signs* × and =. The pupils may be told to read the sign of multiplication the same as the word " times," and the *sign* of *equality* the same as " are."

Let the pupils copy and learn the *First Form,* so as to repeat it, both forward and backward. Afterward place the *Second Form* on the blackboard, and let the pupils give each answer orally; also copy the table and write the answers. When the table of *twos* has been learned in both forms, teach the table of *threes* in the *First Form,* then in the *Second Form,* and afterward *review* both of them, in combination, in a *Third Form,* somewhat as follows:

Third Form.

$4 \times 2 =$	$8 \times 3 =$	$9 \times 3 =$	$4 \times 3 =$
$5 \times 3 =$	$5 \times 2 =$	$8 \times 2 =$	$6 \times 3 =$
$9 \times 2 =$	$7 \times 3 =$	$2 \times 6 =$	$7 \times 2 =$
$2 \times 3 =$	$6 \times 2 =$	$3 \times 4 =$	$3 \times 9 =$

All the tables may be taught on the same plan—first in order, then out of order, then by combination with the tables previously learned. New tables should not be presented before the pupils have learned thoroughly each preceding one through the *three forms*.

Roman Numbers.—In the Eighth Grade, the Key to Roman Numbers should be explained to the pupils, and numerous applications of it made to a variety of combinations, viz.: When letters representing equal values stand side by side, and when a letter representing a smaller number stands on the *right*-hand side of one representing a larger number, the values of each are to be added, as II *two*, XX *twenty*, VI *six*, XV *fifteen*, LX *sixty*, XXX *thirty*. When the letter representing a smaller number stands on the *left*-hand side of one representing a larger number, the value of the *left*-hand letter is to be taken from the value of the *right*-hand letter, as, the value of I is to be taken from the value of V in the combination IV, which gives *four*, the number represented by IV; the value of X taken from the value of L in XL gives *forty* as the number represented by XL, etc. Training the pupils in numerous applications of this Key will save much of the time usually spent in memorizing the Roman Numbers. It will be well to give unusual combinations, occasionally, as—VL; VC; VX; VV; XXXX; LC; XLLV; etc., and request the pupils to apply the Key and tell what number each stands for.

OBJECT LESSONS.

Form.—Special care should be taken, in teaching various Forms and Solids, to cause the pupils to discover the given shape in other objects than those shown by the teacher from the set of " Object-Teaching Forms." For the accomplishment of this purpose frequent reviews should be had, without presenting the forms which represent the shapes that have already been learned, when the pupils may be requested to mention several objects of the given shapes.

Lead the pupils to observe that all *prisms* have oblong sides, and all *pyramids* triangular sides; that prisms differ in the number of their sides, and in the shape of their ends; that pyramids differ in the number of their sides, and in the shape of their bases.

Lines and Angles.—In teaching pupils what constitutes parallel lines, lead them to notice the fact that the lines are *side-by-side ;* that they are the *same distance apart at all opposite points ;* afterward, in a subsequent grade, they can easily be led to observe that both lines extend in the same direction ; also that they can never meet.

In previous grades, the pupils have become familiar with the terms sharp, square, and blunt, as applied to corners ; use this knowledge to illustrate the different kinds of angles, and give the terms *acute, right, obtuse,* to be applied to angles, instead of sharp, square, and blunt. In explaining the terms relative to lines, angles, diameters, etc., each of them should be illustrated on the blackboard, and the pupils also required to represent them on their slates.

Color.—All the lessons on Color should be illustrated with "Color-Charts," "Color-Cubes," "Colored Cards," pieces of ribbon, silk, worsted, or other colored objects; also with good water-colors. Care should be taken to make the pupils understand that by mixing two Primary colors, a Secondary color will be produced; also that no Primary color can be formed by mixing two Secondary colors. They should also be taught which Primary colors will produce each of the Secondary colors; and what two Primary colors each Secondary color contains.

If desired, more definite directions relative to this matter may be found in *New Primary Object Lessons.*

Human Body.—It is important that the pupils should learn to point out the location of those bones and other parts of the body for which they are taught names and uses.

Animals.—The lessons on animals should at first be conversational, and of such a character as to lead the children to notice, when away from school, the various kinds of movements of different animals, as, walking, running, jumping, hopping, flying, swimming, etc.; so that they may be able to tell what animals move in a given manner.

After the teacher has led the children to observe the different classes of animals, as beasts, birds, fishes, etc., by showing them pictures of each, let them be requested to give the names of some animals of each class which they have seen. The names thus given might be written on the blackboard in groups corresponding to their several classes.

During these lessons on animals, let the names of those used for food, and of their flesh, be written on the blackboard as the children mention them, and the spelling of each be taught.

Plants.—After talking with the children about different kinds of flowers, plants, grains, fruits, trees, etc., which they have seen, and after they are able to name several of those most common, their attention may be directed to different parts of trees, as, roots, trunk, branches, limbs, leaves, etc. The teacher will find efficient aid in presenting this subject, by the use of " PRANG's *Natural History Series,* for Plants."

Objects.—Pupils should be led to point out and name the parts of common objects, to tell the shape of the parts, and the uses, color, etc., of the objects. This exercise should be so conducted as to give the children the ability to describe readily objects which they see.

Objects having special *qualities* in a prominent degree should be shown, and the pupils led to observe a given quality in several objects, as a means of teaching them to recognize the same quality whenever it may come within their observation. The spelling of the words representing the objects, their parts, uses, color, and qualities, may be taught.

DRAWING AND WRITING.

On Slates.—All necessary explanations and illustrations as to the manner of drawing figures, the formation of small letters and capitals, should be made by the teacher from the blackboard, first to the whole class; afterward, attention may be directed more to the work of individuals of the class, for the purpose of giving special instruction.

Let the teacher of the class select, each day, six slates from those pupils who have made the most commendable improvement in drawing and writing, and place them on her desk for inspection by the class. If properly managed, this plan will prove a good incentive to improvement in neatness in the drawing and writing.

Use of Pencils.—The pupils should not be allowed to write with short pencils. Particular care must be taken as to methods of holding both pencil and pen, also to the position of the body while writing and drawing, to avoid permanent curvature of the spine from bending sideways; and serious injury to the eyesight from inclining the head too far forward, and holding it too near the desk.

MANAGEMENT.

Physical Training.—The pupils in all the grades should be exercised daily in such a manner as to expand the lungs, develop the muscles, and impart an easy and graceful carriage to the body. Calisthenic exercises may be employed for the attainment of these objects.

Five minutes spent once an hour, or even more frequently, in simple changes of the position of the body, by requiring the school or class to stand and to sit together three or four times in succession, also to exercise the arms briskly, will do much for the physical comfort of pupils, and even increase the progress in their studies.

The necessity of pure air in a school-room is a matter too serious to be neglected by any teacher for a single hour. Yet quite too commonly, even where the means for securing it have been provided, teachers carelessly neglect ventilation.

SEVENTH GRADE.

(PRIMARY.)

Time allowed, about five months.

LANGUAGE.

Reading.—In a *Second Reader;* with conversational tones—the use of *Italic* letters to be explained.

Phonetics.—Sounds of short words in common use to be given by the pupils—exercises to be had for correcting indistinct enunciation.

Definitions.—The meaning of words to be given, chiefly by their use in short sentences.

Spelling.—Oral and written—words from the reading lessons; also, other common words.

ARITHMETIC.

Addition.—With practical examples.

Subtraction.—The processes taught and practical examples given.

Multiplication.—Multipliers from 1 to 12 inclusive.

Mental Arithmetic.—Practical questions in *Addition, Subtraction,* and *Multiplication.* Also *Oral Drills* for rapid combinations of numbers.

Multiplication Table.—Continued through 12 times 12.

Roman Numbers.—Reviewed.

Tables of Measure.—United States money; time; liquid and dry measures.

OBJECT LESSONS.

Form.—The polygons, arc, radius, and other forms.

Size.—Comparative, and measured.

Color.—Harmony of colors.

Human Body.—Organs of the senses.

Animals.—Comparison and simple classification by groups, *families,* etc.

Plants.—Shapes of roots, leaves, flowers, etc. Plants used for food, etc.

Objects and Qualities.—Continued.

Occupations.—Trades, tools, productions, commodities, etc.

GEOGRAPHY—PREPARATORY STEPS.

Place and Direction.—*First.* Position of objects on a table. *Second.* Position of objects in the class-room. *Third.* Location and direction of streets and other objects near the school.

DRAWING AND WRITING.

On Slates.—Words and short sentences to be written from dictation ; Capitals to be used. Drawing simple figures.

On Paper.—Simple words of small letters. The pupils to be taught to write their names, with their ages, and the date.

How to Teach

SUBJECTS OF THE SEVENTH GRADE.

LANGUAGE.

Reading.—The methods given for teaching *Reading* in the Eighth Grade should be continued in the Seventh Grade. It is exceedingly important that children be early trained to give attention to the subject-matter of what they read.

Should the teacher find her class using monotonous or unnatural tones, several selections should be made of reading lessons that are composed chiefly of conversations. These may be used for training the pupils to read in easy, speaking tones. Afterwards, other selections may follow, and special care be taken to teach the pupils to read in a pleasant, colloquial style. Call upon different pupils to imitate the style of the best readers in the class.

Two extremes, as to the amount of reading which the class is taken over, should be avoided—that of keeping the pupils too long on the same lesson, and that of reading over many lessons without sufficient attention to the *matter* and *manner* of reading. The first extreme destroys the pupils' interest in this exercise, and prevents them from acquiring the habit of reading to gain information; the second leads to carelessness in manner, and the habit of reading without sufficient attention to the subject of the lesson, and to what is related concerning it.

The use of *Italics* should be illustrated from the blackboard first, and afterward the pupils should be required to find examples in reading lessons, and to tell why the given Italic words are used.

Phonetics.—Care should be taken, in conducting the exercises in sounds, to train the pupils in habits of distinctness of enunciation, and in the use of smooth tones of voice;—uttering the separated sounds of words will aid in accomplishing the first; and making the sounds with varying pitches and different volumes of voice will aid in producing the second. Silent letters should be pointed out by the pupils. They should also be required to tell what sound each letter has in given words, and to make the sound. These sounds may be described somewhat as follows:—*Call*, c has the sound of *k*, a has its fourth sound, the first *l* has its own sound, the second *l* is silent. *Bought*, b has its own sound, *ou* represent the fourth sound of a, *gh* are silent, t has its own sound. *Think*, *th* are sounded together, i has its second sound, n has the sound of *ng*, k has its own sound.

Definitions.—All modes of teaching that will allow pupils to give mere memorized definitions, without the ability to illustrate the meaning of the given words by their use in complete sentences should be avoided. During the exercises in definitions, the pupils' faults of language should be corrected.

Spelling.—The exercises for teaching spelling in the Seventh Grade may be continued as in the Eighth Grade.

ARITHMETIC.

Addition.—The exercises in this grade should be extended to examples with from four to six columns of twelve or fifteen figures each; and with occasional examples of six or eight lines, embracing millions. Practical examples, relating to matters of daily occurrence in business, should be given.

Exercises for training the pupils to add without counting should be continued in this grade in a manner similar to those described for the Eighth Grade, on pages 52, 53 and 54.

Subtraction.—The processes of *Subtraction* may be arranged in three steps, and taught in their order, as follows, viz.:

First Step.—With short examples in which each figure in the subtrahend represents a number that is smaller than the one above in the minuend.

Second Step.—With examples in which it is necessary to take or "to borrow" from the column of a higher denomination.

Third Step.—With examples having naughts in the minuend, making it necessary to take from the third or fourth column on the left.

The *Second* and *Third Steps* may be illustrated first by the use of bundles of sticks; also by the use of cents, dimes, and dollars, somewhat as follows: From 5 dollars, 4 dimes, and 2 cents take 2 dollars 8 dimes and 5 cents. Since I have only 2 cents, I must take one of the dimes and get it changed into cents. This will leave 3 dimes, and give me 12 cents in all. From the 12 cents I can take 5 cents, and 7 cents will remain. I wish to take away 8 dimes, but find that I have only 3 dimes remaining; therefore I must take one of the dollars and get it changed into dimes, which will leave 4 dollars, and give me 13 dimes in all. Now I can take away 8 dimes and have 5 dimes left. Then I can take 2 dollars from 4 dollars, and have 2 dollars left. This explanation may be followed by another in which the same figures (542—285), are used as *units, tens,* and *hundreds.*

The process of representing these illustrations may be shown on the blackboard, thus:

	10				10		
4	3	10		4	3	10	
8$	4d	2c		5h.	4t.	2	units
2	8d	5c		2	8	5	
$2	5d	7c		2	5	7	

Afterward the process of the *Second* and *Third Steps* may be further represented on the blackboard, with common examples in subtraction, by cancelling the figures *from which one has been taken,* and writing the remainder above it thus:

								9	9	10	
3	10	5	10		5	10	1	10		3	10	10	4	10
4	2	6	3		1	6	3	2	0		2	4	0	0	5	0
1	4	4	5		1	5	4	1	5		1	3	5	4	5	3
2	8	1	8		9	0	5				1	0	4	5	9	7

After this process, commonly called "borrowing" (but which is really a change in a part of the higher denomination without altering the value of the entire number), has been illustrated on the blackboard by the teacher, the pupils should be required to copy on their slates the same examples, also the process of *taking from* a figure representing a number of a higher denomination, by cancelling; then similar examples should be given them to write out in full, that they may become familiar with the process of *taking from,* by cancelling.

Forms of illustration for explaining a subject should be continued no longer than may be necessary to enable the pupils·to understand the subject. The process of cancelling in illustrating subtraction should be used for a few days only. When it is first dropped. another plan may be adopted to represent the changes in the figures. A *dot* may be placed over the figure in the minuend to indicate that *it* must be considered *one less* in the subtraction, thus:

	..		..		....
	4263		16320		240050
	1445		15415		135453
	2818		905		104597

In subtracting these examples, the pupil might say: 3 from 10 leave 7 ; 5 from 14 leave 9 : 4 from 9 leave 5; 5 from 9 leave 4 ; 3 from 3 leave 0 ; 1 from 2 leaves 1— remainder 104,597.

This process is shorter and less liable to mistakes in practice than the common way of " borrowing one " from a figure in the minuend, and " carrying one " to the next figure in the subtrahend ; besides, it prepares the way for readily understanding the operations in " Compound Numbers."

Multiplication.—Instruction in regard to the processes of *multiplication* may be presented in four steps, as follows:

First Step.—Give examples in which no single product will exceed *nine*, as

243	3,142	3,231	231,232
2	2	3	3
486	6,284	9,693	693,696

Second Step.—Give examples in which it will be necessary " to carry " to the next column, including multipliers of a single figure only, from 2 to 5, as:

345	4,583	2,435	32,563
2	3	4	5
690	13,749	9,740	162,815

Third Step.—Give examples, including naughts in the multiplicand, and use as multipliers 6, 7, 8 and 9.

2,034	3,102	14,020	10,050
6	7	8	9
12,204	21,714	112,160	90,450

Fourth Step.—Give examples with multiplicands, as in the third step, and use for multipliers 10, 11 and 12. Teach the pupils where to write the *first figure* in each partial product.

24,065	3,108	40,207
10	11	12
240,650	3108	80414
	3108	40207
	34,188	482,484

First, illustrate the step on the blackboard, then give the pupils similar examples for practice on their slates. When they have become familiar with one step, proceed with the next in order.

Mental Arithmetic.—The forms of the answers, in this grade, may very properly employ more language than in the preceding grade. The following examples and solutions of them will represent suitable forms:

Examples :—A man paid $12 for a barrel of flour, $8 for a ton of coal, and $5 for a load of wood; how much did he pay for all ? *Ans.* He paid for all the sum of $12, $8, and $5, which is $25.

A farmer paid $40 for a cow, and sold her for $36; how much did he lose ? *Ans.* He lost the difference between $36 and $40, which is $4.

What will 5 oranges cost, at 4 cents each ? *Ans.* If one orange costs 4 cents, 5 oranges will cost 5 times 4 cents, or 20 cents.

Oral Drills.—Exercises for the rapid combination of numbers should be introduced during this grade, in addition to a continuation of drills by the "decades."

The class may be trained to add several numbers, and each pupil to write the result on a slate, or give it orally. The teacher may give $7 + 3 + 4 + 5 + 6 + 4 + 2 + 4 + 5$, are how many ? In giving these examples for addition, the teacher may say, at first, 7 and 3 and 4 and 5, etc. Subsequently the pupils should be taught the meaning of the word *plus*, and then these examples may be given thus: 7 plus 3 plus 4 plus 5, etc.

Each pupil, having added these numbers mentally, should write the sum obtained on the slate, and the teacher should then ascertain which pupils have performed the addition correctly.

Multiplication Tables.—When all of these tables, through 12 times 12 have been taught by the

three forms as described in the Eighth Grade, they may
be reviewed from the blackboard in the following form,
the pupils reading thus: 5 times 6 are 30 ; 6 times 5
are 30 ; 9 times 5 are 45 ; 5 times 9 are 45, etc.

5 × 6 are 30 ;	6 × 5 are 30 ;	4 × 8 are 32 ;	8 × 4 are 32.
9 × 5 " 45 ;	5 × 9 " 45 ;	6 × 8 "	8 × 6 "
7 × 6 " 42 ;	6 × 7 " 42 ;	5 × 8 "	8 × 5 "
4 × 9 "	9 × 4 "	7 × 9 "	9 × 7 "

In writing these tables on the blackboard for this
review, the several products may be omitted, and the
pupils required to give them from memory. At this
stage the teacher should explain the use of the sign (×)
of multiplication.

Roman Numbers.— Review and give further
applications of the key, as indicated in the directions
relative to this subject for the Eighth Grade.

Tables of Measure.—The tables of weights and
measures should be introduced first, by talking with
the pupils about their experience in the use of them,
and by familiar illustrations given by this means.
Thus the table of United States money may be illustrated by cents, dimes, and dollars ; that of liquid
measure, by what the children know about buying milk,
molasses, kerosene, etc., by the pint and quart ; that of
dry measure, by purchases at the grocery, by quarts,
small measures, pecks, etc. ; that of time, by observing
the hours marked on the clock, and by attention to the
days, weeks, months, etc.

After talking with the pupils about the uses of a
given table, write it on the blackboard, and let them
repeat it ; then they may copy the items on slates, both

in the order of the table and in a different order. Continue the repetition and copying until the table is thoroughly learned. Each of the tables may be presented and learned in a similar manner.

TABLES FOR THE SEVENTH GRADE.

UNITED STATES MONEY.

10 mills make 1 cent.	100 cents make one dollar.
10 cents " 1 dime.	50 " " one-half dollar.
10 dimes " 1 dollar.	25 " " one quarter of a dollar.
10 dollars " 1 eagle.	75 cents make three quarters of a dollar.

LIQUID MEASURE.

DRY MEASURE.

4 gills make 1 pint.	2 pints make 1 quart.
2 pints " 1 quart.	2 quarts " 1 small measure.
4 quarts " 1 gallon.	8 quarts " 1 peck.
31½ galls. " 1 barrel.	4 pecks " 1 bushel.

TIME MEASURE.

60 seconds make 1 minute.
60 minutes " 1 hour.
24 hours " 1 day.
7 days " 1 week.
30 or 31 days " 1 month.
12 months " 1 year.
52 weeks " 1 year
365 days " 1 year.
100 years " 1 century

Days of the Week.

Sunday,
Monday,
Tuesday,
Wednesday,
Thursday,
Friday,
Saturday.

Seasons of the Year.

Spring,
Summer,
Autumn, or Fall,
Winter.

March,
April, } Are the Spring mos.
May,

June,
July, } Are the Summer months.
August,

September,
October, } Are the Autumn, or Fall months.
November,

December,
January, } Are the Winter months.
February,

Review.—In reviewing these tables, the teacher may question the pupils somewhat as follows: How many hours make a day? How many days make a year? How many days make a week? How many weeks make a year? How many minutes make an hour? How many months make a year? What is the shortest measure of time? What does it take to make the longest measure of time? How many quarts make a gallon? How many quarts in three gallons? How many quarts make a peck? How many pints in two quarts? How many quarts in two pecks? Which is more, one bushel or three pecks?

A variety of similar questions may be asked after the tables have been learned in their order.

OBJECT LESSONS.

It is not intended that each topic under this heading shall be made the subject of a lesson each day; but it is expected that a lesson will be given each day upon some one of these topics, and that these shall be varied so as to embrace all the topics of the grade during each month. Much more time and a greater number of lessons will be required for some of these topics than for others.

Form.—It is very desirable to have the manner of presenting the lessons on this subject varied in each succeeding grade, so as to avoid the possibility of memorizing and reciting any formula. To secure this end, let the reviews of the matter taught in preceding grades be so conducted as to compel attention to the shape of the various objects.

By requiring the pupils to describe the shape of objects placed before the class, the teacher will be enabled to test their knowledge of *form*.

Size.—This subject may be illustrated by various objects, as strings of different sizes and lengths, slips of paper of different lengths and widths, and small pieces of wood. The pupils will obtain clear perceptions of size and of length, by being required to judge of the size and length of objects before them, and of lines on the blackboard, then to measure these and ascertain the approximate correctness of their estimates. Drawing lines of given lengths on the slate, followed by a careful measurement of them, is a valuable means for training pupils to accuracy in determining size and length by the eye.

Color.—The lessons on color, for this grade, should lead the pupils to perceive that some colors appear well when placed side by side, while others do not. For this purpose lead them to compare *red* and *green* with *blue* and *green ; blue* and *orange* with *yellow* and *orange; yellow* and *purple* with *blue* and *purple*, or *red* and *purple*.

All lessons on color should be illustrated with colored objects. Pieces of ribbon, silk, worsted, colored paper, water colors, etc., may be used for this purpose.

Human Body.—In teaching children the names and uses of the organs of sense, and their parts, special effort should be made to lead them to understand the subject by means of observations made with their own organs of sense. The actual seeing, hearing, feeling, tasting, and smelling of objects teach children facts which it is impossible to convey to their minds by means of the memorizing of language, however thorough and precise.

Animals.—The lessons on this subject should lead the children to notice the most distinguishing points in the structure of animals, and to see how their structure is adapted to their habits of life; for instance, how the webbed feet of some birds fit them for swimming, and how the long legs of others fit them for wading; how the strong claws and strong beaks of some birds enable them to feed on flesh; how the cushion-like feet of the cat enable it to walk noiselessly about in search of its prey; how the teeth of the cat and dog are fitted for tearing flesh, while those of the rat and squirrel are formed for cracking nuts and gnawing hard substances.

The chief aim of these lessons being to train the pupils in habits of observing nature, so that they may be enabled to gain therefrom the most useful knowledge, the exercises should be conducted in such a manner as to lead them to notice accurately the structure and habits of the various animals that come within their own observation. The facts thus learned should be, by the aid of the teacher, properly classified, as a foundation for subsequent study of the same subject.

Prang's Natural History Series, with the "Manual" which accompanies it, will be found a valuable aid in giving instruction on *Animals* and *Plants*.

Plants.—The lessons on plants, in this grade, may appropriately lead the pupils to learn the most common *shapes of roots*, as turnip-shaped, branching, fibrous, conical, tuberous, etc.; also the *shapes of leaves,* as needle-shaped, arrow-shaped, egg-shaped, heart-shaped, hand-shaped, etc.; also the common *shapes of flowers,* as funnel-shaped, bell-shaped, pink-shaped, butterfly-shaped, helmet shaped, cross-shaped, etc. By suitable exercises the teacher should also direct the attention of the pupils to plants which are used for food, and lead them to observe their mode of growth, form, uses, etc.

Objects and Qualities.—Two distinct classes of exercises may be given under this heading. One consists in training the pupils to distinguish given qualities, by using several objects having the same quality, for illustration; the other, which is more appropriate for review exercises, requires the pupils to ascertain what qualities a given object possesses. Instruction on this subject cannot be considered complete without the use of both of these classes of exercises, in their proper order.

Observation and Comparison.—Habits of observing various objects, and noticing their several *shapes, colors, qualities* and *materials* of which they are made, are exceedingly useful as a means of gaining knowledge; yet habits of *comparing* two or more objects, and observing what qualities, shapes, colors and materials they possess in common, constitutes an advanced stage of development which not only adds additional power of gaining knowledge, but gives to the possessor practical ability in whatever sphere of life that person may be placed.

In the preceding grades the pupils have been taught to distinguish, and to name the common *forms, colors,* and most obvious *qualities*. It is therefore appropriate that they now should be trained to discover *which* of these forms, colors, and qualities may be found in given objects to which their special attention may be directed.

This kind of training should be so conducted as to develop the individual powers of the pupils. To accomplish this, the teacher must avoid asking such questions as might suggest to the pupil what to say, rather than leave him to discover the shape, color, quality, or material without aid. The teacher should aim to train the pupils to discover the principal characteristics of an object, instead of telling them what those characteristics are, and then asking them questions to see if they remember them.

Steps somewhat like the following are appropriate to be taken by the teacher :—

First. Write on the blackboard the words, *Materials, Shapes, Colors, Qualities,* leaving room to write other words under each. Then place some object before the pupils, as a common slate, and request them to tell what materials, shapes, colors, and qualities they observe in it. As these are mentioned by the pupils, singly, the teacher may write the word on the blackboard under its appropriate heading. When the lesson is finished, the blackboard will contain something like the following :

Materials.	*Shapes.*	*Colors.*	*Qualities.*
slate,	oblong,	black.	opaque,
wood,	right angles.		brittle,
iron.			combustible.

Occupations.—The exercises on this topic should cause the children to ascertain the names of tools used in different occupations, and what is done with these tools; also what articles are made or produced. For instance, the teacher might write on the blackboard the word carpenter, shoemaker, or painter, and request the pupils to ascertain what tools are used by those who pursue the given trade, and report on the next day after the subject is thus assigned—the teacher writing the names of tools mentioned by the pupils on the blackboard, and the pupils copying them subsequently on their slates. These exercises will furnish an excellent opportunity for practice in observation, and in describing what has been seen. They may be made useful, also, for first lessons in composition.

The form in which these lessons may be placed on the blackboard is represented by the following:—

Name of Occupation.   *Tools used.*

Carpenter. { Saw, Plane, Chisel, Auger, Awl, Hammer, Mallet, Rule, Square.

Shoemaker. { Last, Knife, Awl, Pincers, Hammer.

Painter. { Pots, Brushes, Knife, Ladder.

CABINET-MAKER.

Tools Used.	Materials.	Articles Made.
Saws,	Black-walnut,	Tables,
Planes,	Mahogany,	Stands,
Chisels,	White Oak,	Bureaus,
Bits,	Cherry,	Sofas,
Hand-screws,	Pine,	Bedsteads,
Squares,	Glue,	Desks,
Scrapers,	Varnish, etc.	Book-cases,
Mallet.		Sideboards.

GEOGRAPHY-- PREPARATORY STEPS.

Place and Direction.—The exercises in this subject must be objective in their character; and they should be conducted with a view to prepare the pupils for understanding the elementary steps of Geography. The manner of giving the lessons in steps will prove most useful to the pupils.

First Step.—Train the pupils to observe and describe the position of objects on the table in front of them, using the terms right, left, front, back, front left-hand corner, back right-hand corner, etc. Then let the teacher represent the positions of these objects on the blackboard. Afterwards request the pupils to copy the representation from the blackboard, on their slates.

Second Step.—Train the pupils to notice and describe the *positions* of the parts of the class-room, and of the principal articles in it, as: door, windows, blackboard, seats, table, chair, closet, etc.

The teacher should draw the outlines of the class-room, and represent the positions of the articles in it, on the blackboard, at the same time requiring the pupils to tell where to place the representation of each object, before drawing it. Subsequently the pupils should copy the same on their slates.

Third Step.—Teach the pupils the location of the streets near the school, and require them to observe and tell in what streets they go while on their way to and from school. The terms of direction, as east, west, north, south, may be introduced in this step, and the

Points of Compass taught. Represent the locations of streets, buildings near the school, etc., on the black-board, and let the pupils copy them, as before.

DRAWING AND WRITING.

On Slates.—The lessons in Drawing and Writing, for this grade, must necessarily be simple, yet they should be progressive, and so arranged as to lead to a proper training of the eye and hand ; indeed this train-ing should be made a prominent object. The black-board should be used much in illustrating the exercises of both drawing and writing. Enlarged copies of good drawing cards, also simple drawings from objects may be made on the blackboard, and the pupils required to copy them on their slates.

Care should be taken to teach the pupils proper posi-tions for sitting, for holding their slates, also for the hand and fingers in holding the pen or pencil.

On Paper.—When writing is commenced with ink, do not confine the pupils too long to making the simple *elements* of letters ; let them learn to write simple words as soon as practicable. It is not necessary that the pupils should write all the lines under each copy of a common writing-book. Whenever the pupils have made sufficient progress to be able to proceed with the next copy in order, let them go on with it. But there should be system in the progress ; all the pupils in the grade should receive instruction relative to the same points, and write the same words simultaneously ; thus all will attend to the same thing, at the same time, and proceed to a new lesson together. Faults in writ-

ing should be pointed out and illustrated on the blackboard, and such directions given as will enable the
pupils to correct those faults.

Before leaving this grade, the pupils ought to be able
to write simple words neatly with the pen; and to
write their own names, and their age; also the day of
the month, and the year, in a proper form for dating a
letter. They should also be able to write familiar
words, and short sentences from dictation, readily and
plainly.

SIXTH GRADE.

Time allowed, about five months.

LANGUAGE.

Reading.—*Second Reader* completed, or an easy *Third Reader* commenced.

Phonetics.—Words to be analyzed by sounds; names of the sounds to be stated; faults of enunciation to be corrected.

Definitions.—The meaning of words to be given orally, and in writing.

Spelling.—Words from the reading lessons, also familiar words, and short sentences from dictation, both orally, and by writing on slates.

ARITHMETIC.

Addition and Subtraction reviewed.

Multiplication continued through multipliers of five figures.

Division.—Both the long and the short forms. Simple practical examples to be given in each of these rules.

Mental Arithmetic.—Practical examples in each of the four simple rules.

Division Table.—Taught in connection with a review of the Multiplication Table.

Tables of Weight and Measure.—The tables of Common or Avoirdupois Weight, of Long, Cloth, and Surface measure, also a miscellaneous table to be taught, and those of the Seventh Grade to be reviewed.

OBJECT LESSONS.

Form.— The shapes of objects to be compared and described, and their resemblances and differences stated.

Human Body.—Lessons to be continued as in previous grades, and extended.

Animals.—Comparison and classification continued; also size, and where found.

Plants.—Parts of leaves; shapes of margins; shapes of flowers; and comparison of members of the same, and of different families of flowers.

Objects.—Various objects to be examined and their shape, color, most obvious qualities, and properties to be stated. The distinctions between miner vegetable, and animal substances to be taught.

Occupations.—Exercises to give the pupils habits of observing and describing common productions, commodities, etc.; also to give them ideas of the exchange and sale of these.

GEOGRAPHY.

First Step.—The location and direction from the school of the most prominent objects near the school, and of the places in its vicinity.

Second Step.—Definitions relating to the forms of land and water, from cards, blackboard, and outline maps.

Third Step.—Teach the name of the city or town, the county, and state in which the pupils live, and also of the places in the vicinity, showing their location on an outline map.

Fourth Step.—Teach the shape of the Earth by means of a globe and hemisphere maps.

Fifth Step.—Teach the location of the principal countries by associations with their most familiar animals, inhabitants, and productions ; also the location of the warm and the cold countries.

DRAWING AND WRITING.

On Slates.—Writing to be continued as in the Seventh Grade.

On Paper.—Writing in books, from copies, with necessary instructions in regard to the position of the body, hand, and paper.

How to Teach

SUBJECTS OF THE SIXTH GRADE.

LANGUAGE.

Reading.—Before a new lesson is read, the unfamiliar and difficult words in it should be selected, written on the blackboard, carefully pronounced by the teacher, and repeated by the pupils; also both the meaning and the spelling of these words should be taught;—afterwards the teacher should request the pupils to find the same words in their reading lessons, and to pronounce them again.

Occasionally call upon a pupil to read while the other members of the class close their books and listen; then, at the close of the reading request those who listened to state the substance of what was read. This exercise will train pupils to habits of attentive listening, and to a proper regard to the subject-matter.

In efforts to correct the faults of a class in reading, select first the most common fault, and direct almost exclusive attention to that until it is understood and easily overcome by the pupils. Then select another common fault and proceed in the same manner, giving attention to the first one also. Afterward select another fault, and proceed in a similar manner, giving attention to the three. By this means a class may be trained to *perceive* and *overcome* faults in reading, much more effectively than by trying to point out half a dozen different kinds of faults at once.

Phonetics.—The phonic analysis of words should train the pupils readily to distinguish and make all the sounds in given words, also to determine which letters are silent. It should also lead the pupils to such habits of distinctness in articulation as will remove the fault of neglecting to sound the final consonants, as *d* in an*d*, sen*d*; *r* in fa*r*, ca*r*; *ing* in sing*ing*, eat*ing*, etc.; also the errors of sounding improperly both consonants and vowels in the pronunciation of common words.

No other means is so efficient for training the organs of speech in clearness and correctness of articulation as that of elementary sounds. By suitable exercises with these, the ear and the vocal organs may be successfully cultivated, and the means furnished to the pupils for determining what are the correct sounds of the language, how to produce them, and the ability to cultivate their own organs of speech and tones of voice.

Definitions.—Exercises in which the definitions are to be written on slates, in short sentences, should be introduced in alternation with oral exercises of a similar character. It is desirable that an oral exercise of this kind, given as a lesson on one day, should be followed on the next day with the same words to be defined in a written exercise, thus training the pupils to write as well as to talk.

In the oral definitions, let the pupils be required to tell what given words mean, in their own language, as well as to use them in short sentences. One pupil may be requested to give a brief definition of a word, another pupil to use it in a sentence, and another one to illustrate its meaning by describing its use. Habits

of reciting formal, memorized definitions would be
avoided by using thus several modes of giving the meaning of the same word, and the pupils would learn to
define, and use words intelligently.

Spelling.—More attention should be given to written than to oral spelling, in this grade. Words may
be dictated for the pupils to write on their slates; short
sentences may be given for the same purpose; the pupils may be requested to write the names of classes of
objects, as names of kinds of food, articles of clothing,
of furniture, kinds of tools, names of occupations, of
animals, of trees, of fruits, of articles that may be purchased at a grocery etc., etc. These exercises will enable
pupils to learn the spelling of a large class of words
in common use.

ARITHMETIC.

Addition and Subtraction.—It is intended that
the *processes* of adding and subtracting shall have been
taught so thoroughly, before the pupils are placed in
the Sixth Grade, that each one will be able to add and
subtract with facility, and with a good degree of accuracy. Now, special pains should be taken to teach the
uses of Addition and Subtraction by means of practical examples. A brief review of these rules should
be had at least once each week, during the entire term
of the Sixth Grade.

Multiplication.—Instruction may be arranged
and presented in three steps, as follows:

First Step.—Give examples with multipliers of two figures only—12 to 99.

Second Step.—Give examples with multipliers of three figures—100 to 999—including some with naughts in the multiplicand.

Third Step.—Give examples with multipliers of four or five figures, containing one or more naughts. Both the multiplicand and multiplier should be so varied as to include all the difficulties arising from the different positions of naughts.

Pupils should be carefully trained to write the first figure of each partial product in its proper place—*under the figure used as a multiplier.*

Review each step with practical examples, embracing transactions that come within the observation of the pupils.

Division.—This rule can be taught most thoroughly by commencing the instruction with the " Long Division " form, and using a small number for a divisor. *Four Steps* will indicate the methods and order for teaching *Division.*

First Step.—Give examples in which each figure of the dividend will contain the divisor without a remainder, thus:

```
2) 486 (243        3) 963 (321
   4                  9
   ──                 ──
   08                 06
    8                  6
   ──                 ──
   06                 03
    6                  3
   ──                 ──
    0                  0
```

Second Step.—Give examples with the divisor less than *ten*, in which remainders will occur during the partial divisions, thus:

```
4) 976 (244        8) 9856 (1232
    8                  8
   ──                 ──
   17                 18
   16                 16
   ──                 ──
   16                 25
   16                 24
   ──                 ──
    0                 16
                      16
                      ──
                       0
```

Third Step.—Give examples with divisors from 10 to 15, then teach the "*Short Division*" form; and subsequently require the pupils to use the *Short* form for all examples where the divisor does not exceed 12.

```
10) 2540 (254    11) 3564 (324    15) 345 (23
    20               33               30
    ──               ──               ──
    54               26               45
    50               22               45
    ──               ──               ──
    40               44                0
    40               44
    ──               ──
     0                0
```

In illustrating the *Short Division* form, give the same examples, each with only one figure in the divisor, to be worked by both the *Long* and the *Short* forms, taking care to arrange the two modes so that the difference in their lengths shall readily illustrate why *one form* is called "Long Division," and the *other one* "Short Division."

Fourth Step.—Give examples with divisors embracing numbers from 15 to 50. Arrange these examples so that different quotients shall contain naughts in various positions. Each step should be amply illustrated on the blackboard, by the teacher, then a sufficient number of examples given to furnish the practice necessary to enable the pupils to understand it, before proceeding to the succeeding step.

Teachers should aim first to cause their pupils to understand the *processes* of the several rules, then to *use* them in an intelligent manner. The object of the drills, by means of numerous examples, should be *accuracy*, first; *rapidity*, second; never rapidity by neglecting accuracy. Practical examples should be given, in each of the rules, to insure an understanding of their uses.

MENTAL ARITHMETIC.—The forms for answering questions in addition, subtraction, and multiplication in this grade, may be the same as for the Seventh Grade, which see. Questions may also be introduced which will require both addition and subtraction for their solution, as:

Henry had 18 cents; he gave two cents for pencils, and 6 cents for a sponge; how many cents had he left? *Answer.*—Henry spent the sum of 2 cents and 6 cents, which is 8 cents. He then had left the difference between 8 cents and 18 cents, which is 10 cents.

Division.—How many tops at 3 cents each can be bought for 12 cents? *Ans.*—As many tops as 3 cents, the price of one top, is contained times in 12 cents, which is four times; therefore *four* tops can be bought.

If 2 apples cost 4 cents, what will one apple cost? *Ans.*—If 2 apples cost 4 cents, one apple will cost one-half of four cents, which is *two* cents.

Division Tables.—The Multiplication Table may be so reviewed as to enable the pupil to learn the Division Table easily. The following form will illustrate methods for accomplishing this:

```
4 × 7 are 28;   4 in 28 seven times.
7 × 4  "  28;   7 in 28 four    "
6 × 7  "  42;   6 in 42 seven   "
7 × 6  "  42;   7 in 42 six     "      etc.
```

This review, combining Multiplication and Division, should be continued through each of the tables; and subsequently the teacher may review the Division Tables by questions similar to the following:

How many *eights* in 32? How many *sevens* in 56? How many *nines* in 45? How many *twelves* in 108? How many *eights* in 96? How many *fives* in 60? How many *sixes* in 54? etc.

Tables of Weight and Measure.—The tables may be taught as in the Seventh Grade, first, objectively, then memorized in order; and all the tables of both the Seventh and Sixth Grades should be reviewed thoroughly during this grade.

TABLES FOR THE SIXTH GRADE.

Common, or Avoirdupois Weight.

16 ounces make 1 pound.
8 " " 1 half pound.
4 " " 1 quarter of a pound.
100 pounds " 1 hundred weight.
20 hundred weight make 1 ton.
2000 pounds make 1 ton.

Long Measure.

12 inches make 1 foot.
3 feet " 1 yard.
16½ feet " 1 rod.
5½ yards " 1 rod.
40 rods " 1 furlong.
8 furlongs " 1 mile.
320 rods " 1 mile.
3 miles " 1 league.

CLOTH MEASURE.

3 feet make 1 yard.
36 inches " 1 "
18 " " ½ "
9 " " ¼ "
4½ " " ⅛ "
4 quarters " 1 "

SURFACE MEASURE.

144 square inches make 1 square foot.
9 " feet " 1 " yard.
30¼ " yards " 1 " rod.
160 " rods " 1 acre.
640 acres " 1 square mile.

MISCELLANEOUS TABLE.

12 things make 1 dozen.
144 " " 1 gross.
12 dozen " 1 "
12 gross " 1 great gross.
20 things " 1 score.
24 sheets " 1 quire of paper.
20 quires " 1 ream.
32 pounds " 1 bushel of oats.

48 pounds make 1 bushel of barley,
[or buckwheat.
58 " " " 1 bushel of corn.
60 " " " 1 " " wheat.
196 " " " 1 barrel of flour.
200 " " " 1 " " p o r k,
[beef, or fish.
280 " " " 1 " of salt.

Review.—After these tables have been thoroughly learned in order, the teacher may conduct brief reviews of those of both the Seventh and Sixth Grades, by questions somewhat like the following:

How many inches in three-quarters of a yard? How many yards in one rod? How many rods in a mile? How many square inches in a square foot? How many buttons in a gross? How many sheets of paper in a quire? How many in half of a quire? How many pounds in a barrel of flour? Which is heavier, a bushel of wheat or a bushel of corn? How many pounds in half of a ton? How many pecks in two bushels? How many quarts in two gallons? How many days in a year? How many months in half of a year? How many square feet in a square yard? Which is longer, six feet or two yards?

OBJECT LESSONS.

The various topics embraced in Object Lessons furnish far more effective means for thoroughly developing the minds of children than any exercises that pertain exclusively to reading, spelling, arithmetic, etc. Children whose powers of mind have been developed by proper training, so that they observe, compare, classify, and describe intelligently whatever comes within the range of their observation, will learn every subject more easily than they could have done without such training. For these reasons suitable attention should be given in each grade, to all the topics embraced under the head of Object Lessons. And teachers should keep prominently in view the importance of these lessons as a means for proper mental discipline, and not regard the knowledge gained by the exercises as comprising their chief value.

Due attention to these considerations will lead teachers to regard, as of much importance, the *manner of giving* the lesson.

Form.—The character of the instruction in this subject, especially so far as it pertains to learning to recognize and describe the various *forms* and *solids*, need not differ materially in the Seventh and Sixth Grades. However, when the several shapes required have been learned by means of the regular *forms* and *solids* provided for this purpose, the time given to this topic should be chiefly devoted to comparing and describing other objects by their shape, stating wherein those compared resemble each other, and wherein they differ.

Human Body.—The lessons in this grade should be conducted so as to review the facts learned in previous grades, and also so as to extend the pupils' knowledge of the laws of health, especially so far as these pertain to the condition of the skin, habits of cleanliness, and the manner of eating.

Animals.—The manner of conducting the lessons on this topic for the Sixth Grade classes may be nearly the same as that for the Seventh Grade ; but the pupils in this grade should be led to consider a greater number of animals than those in the previous one, and to observe more carefully the peculiarities of structure, etc., with a view to extending their knowledge of classification.

To aid the pupils in making groups of animals, by simple classification, let the teacher write on the blackboard the following and similar names for groups :

Swimming Birds,	*Cud-chewing Quadrupeds,*
Wading Birds,	*Flesh-eating Quadrupeds,*
Climbing Birds,	*Gnawing Quadrupeds,*
Scratching Birds,	*Insects,*
Flesh-eating Birds,	*Reptiles,*
Perching Birds.	*Fish.*

Then request the pupils to give the names of animals to be written under each heading.

These lessons relative to animals should lead the children to make comparisons as to form, structure, habits, size, etc., and to learn in what countries and localities the various birds and quadrupeds may be found.

PRANG's *Natural History Series* will be found adapted to giving this instruction.

Plants.—The lessons on this subject in the Sixth Grade may lead the pupils to consider the parts and uses of leaves, their margins, parts and uses of flowers, as petals, stamens, pistil, etc.; the comparison of pinks, lilies, fruit-blossoms, etc., with a view to noticing resemblances in those of the same family, and differences in others; also kinds of fruits which the pupils have seen—the names to be written on the blackboard, and copied by the pupils on their slates, as a spelling exercise. The names of fruits and grasses used for food, etc., may be written in groups. Like the lessons on animals, these exercises should be so conducted as to lead the pupils to form habits of carefully studying nature, as a means of pleasure and as a source of knowledge; therefore, the time selected for giving the lessons on plants, etc., should be during the seasons when the pupils can personally examine these objects.

The teacher would do well to consult two excellent works by Prof. GRAY—*How Plants Grow;* and *How Plants Behave.*

Objects.—In the Sixth Grade the lessons on objects should include their descriptions as to *form, color,* and most obvious *qualities.* In this connection, it is desirable that the pupils be led to consider what qualities are necessary in the substances used for various tools, utensils, articles of dress, etc. For instance, what quality is necessary for wagon and other springs? What qualities make sponge useful? What qualities render salt and sugar valuable? What qualities give value to India rubber? What qualities give value to glass? What to steel? to iron? Why will not lead make good springs, or knives?

The lessons under this topic should cause the pupils to consider wherein animals, vegetables, and minerals differ from each other. Pupils will understand this subject more thoroughly by presenting the instruction in *three steps.*

First Step.—Request the pupils to observe slate-pencils, pieces of stone, iron, lead, chalk, and various pieces of wood, small plants, etc., and then to tell what can be done with the wood and plants, that cannot be done with stone, iron, etc. Also lead them to consider whether both of these classes of substances are obtained from the same source, and whether the iron and stone grow as the wood and small plants do. When the most obvious differences between these two classes of substances have been perceived by the pupils, give the term *Mineral* as the name for one class, and *Vegetable* as the name for the other.

Second Step.—The teacher may next call attention to the three great classes of substances—mineral, vegetable, and animal—and lead the pupils to observe, and to tell what animals and vegetables can do (as take food, breathe, grow, die), which minerals cannot do.

Third Step.—Let the pupils be led to notice what animals generally can do which vegetables generally cannot do (as move from place to place by their own power); also to observe the differences between the food of plants and that of animals; as that plants feed on minerals, or simple substances from the earth and air, while animals feed on vegetables and other animals.

The pupils might also be taught that substances which once formed a part of an animal, as wool, hair, bone, skin, are called *animal substances;* that wood,

5

bark, gum, sugar, that once formed a part of a vegetable, are called *vegetable substances*.

Occupations.—The exercises on this topic should not only lead the pupils to observe and describe common productions, and manufactured articles, but should also lead them to consider the necessity for buying and selling productions and articles of manufacture; also how these are taken from those who raise or make them to those who want to use them.

GEOGRAPHY.

First Step.—Review the *Points of Compass*, in training the pupils, until they are able to name any direction, as the teacher points, and to point in any direction named.

In connection with and following the instruction relative to the points of compass, lead the pupils to learn the location, and the direction from the school of other streets near the school; also of prominent buildings, as churches, post-office, hotel, railroad depot, etc.; or of villages, lakes, farms, groves, forest, streams, etc., within the range of the children's observation. The teacher should represent on the blackboard the situation of the school-house, and the location and direction from it of the places mentioned, and allow the pupils to copy the same on their slates.

Second Step.—While teaching the definitions relative to the *forms* of land and water, present first the picture, or a drawing upon the blackboard, of the object under consideration, as of an island, peninsula, cape, strait, lake, bay, river, etc.; then show how the same or a similar object is represented on a map. Follow this with a definition to be learned by the pupils. As the characteristics of each form of land or water—as that *an island is land entirely surrounded by water*—is learned, require the pupils to point out on a map several representations of islands, omitting the names of the particular islands in this stage. Proceed in a similar way to teach all the definitions.

Colton's *Geographical Cards* will be found of great assistance as pictorial and map representations to illustrate these definitions.

During this step the instruction has for its chief object training children to recognize the various forms of land and water, by means of their characteristic features, and to describe each by suitable definitions; hence the attention of pupils need not be directed to the names and location of particular islands, isthmuses, straits, bays, etc., at this time.

Third Step.—Commence the instruction relative to the names and location of particular places with the town, village, or city in which the school is situated, and extend it to other places in its vicinity. No fixed limit to the extent of this exercise can be given, since the length to which it can be profitably carried will depend, in some degree, upon the personal knowledge of the members of the class relative to these places. The teacher should aim, however, so to use the knowledge of those pupils whose personal visitations have made them acquainted with the locations of the greatest number of places, as to extend the knowledge of the other pupils.

Such attention should be given to the location upon a map of the town, village, or city in which the school is situated, and to the relative location and direction from it of the chief places in its vicinity, that the pupils will be able to point them out on an outline map. The name of the town, village, or city, of the county, and of the State in which the pupils live, should be taught, and their location shown on a map.

Fourth Step.—In teaching the *shape of the earth* by means of a globe, lead the pupils to compare a marble with an orange, and both the marble and orange with a globe, and thus to notice that each one resembles the other in *shape* only; also that each differs from the other in *size.* By this means prepare them for understanding that the globe represents the earth only in *shape.* Follow this with some simple illustrations as to the comparative size of the earth.

Next lead the pupils to compare the outline forms of the grand divisions of land, water, and of islands, etc., represented on the globe, with their corresponding representations upon hemisphere maps.

Fifth Step.—Talk with the pupils about people of different races and nations, and point out on the globe, also on outline maps, the location of the countries where each may be found: as Africa, the home of the colored men; China, the home of the Chinamen; Germany, the home of Germans, etc. Proceed in a similar manner with the most familiar animals, and the most common productions of different countries. Give the name of the country, and show its location on a globe, also on an outline map. Point out Greenland as the home of the white bear; Africa as the home of the lion, zebra, ostrich and camel; Australia as the home of the kangaroo; Spain as the country where cork and raisins are produced; South America as the country from which brazil-nuts and cocoa-nuts are obtained; West Indies as the place from whence we obtain oranges and bananas, etc.

By means similar to that herein described the pupils may be made to realize that *Geography* teaches them about the homes of the different people, animals, and productions which they have seen, and of which they have heard.

The aim of the teacher should be to give the pupils a good, general idea of the *shape of the Earth,* of the different portions of it as the *homes of races of men,* also as the places where particular fruits grow; and of some parts as having continuous cold weather, and others continuous warm weather. This object must be accomplished chiefly by oral instruction. However, the work may be facilitated by placing in the hands of the pupils suitable text-books on Geography, to be examined by the children *after* the lesson has been given orally by the teacher; but *in no case should the pupils in this grade be required to study a lesson in the book before the subject of it has been presented orally by the teacher,* as above indicated.

Each lesson may be gone over a second time by the teacher, after the pupils have studied the subject in their books. The order of the lessons, the topics presented, and the general character of the facts taught should conform to the directions given here, without regard to the order of presentation in the text-books in common use.

After completing the course of objective instruction in Geography, as indicated in the preceding steps, the pupils will be prepared to commence the study of this subject in an intelligent manner from good text-books.

DRAWING AND WRITING.

The exercises in Drawing and Writing for the Sixth Grade may be continued in a manner similar to those of the Seventh Grade. Pupils should not be simply *allowed* to write, they should be *taught* and *trained how* to write by the teacher. Children need something besides copy-books, to become good writers.

GENERAL SUGGESTIONS.

Reviews.—Such a review of the previous lesson, as an introduction to, and in connection with, each new lesson of the same subject, should be had as will cause the pupils properly to associate together the important facts previously learned with those of the new lesson.

General reviews of subjects should be had at least once during each month. On these occasions the leading facts learned in previous grades, upon that subject, should be included. These remarks are intended especially for the *first five grades* of this course of instruction.

Progress of Classes.—Whenever it is found that a class has advanced further in one or two subjects of its grade than it has in others, the teacher should devote less time to the subject in which the class has thus advanced, and give more time to the subjects in which the class has made the least progress. By this means the grade of the class may be equalized in all its studies.

No study of a succeeding grade should be introduced into a class of a lower grade before that class has completed the requirements of the grade in all its studies.

Time Given to Each Subject.—The pupils belonging to the first five grades of this course should not spend more than forty minutes, at one time, upon the same subject. And in the first two grades they should not spend more than twenty minutes upon the same subject at one time.

The mind, as well as the body, needs rest. Both a change of subject, and a change in the manner of conducting class exercises, are necessary to furnish the opportunities for needed rest during school hours, besides the usual recesses of school.

Vocal Music.—Instruction in vocal music ought to be given to the pupils of all the grades in every school.

Principles of Education Applied.—Teachers who learn to apply principles of Education in the order of presenting knowledge, and in their methods of teaching, will rarely fail of becoming successful in their work. They will early acquire the ability to determine for themselves how to commence the instruction of any class under any conditions, and to proceed surely step by step toward the end in view. The following hints are given as suggestions to young teachers who desire to attain this ability.

Principle.—Commence instruction in each subject with that which the pupils already know concerning it, or with something known which is nearly related to it, and proceed to the kindred unknown which forms the subject of the lesson.

To ascertain the known, or the related unknown, the teacher must consider what previous opportunities the children have had for obtaining knowledge of the subject, and then by questions determine the true attainments of the pupils relative to the matter for the proposed lesson. The next point for the teacher to decide is, how can that which the pupils already know, concerning the subject of the lesson, be used in the best manner to aid them in learning that which they do not yet know of it. For illustration, let this principle be applied to teaching *Reading* to a class of young children that have just commenced going to school.

What is the known to these children, which relates to reading? [See page 23.]

What is the unknown to be first taught as reading? [See page 23.]

How can the known be used to aid in teaching the unknown, which should form the lesson for this stage of the instruction? [See pages 23, 24, 25.]

Suppose a class has made sufficient progress in learning to read to be ready to commence using the first reading book. What then would constitute the unknown which should be taught first? [See page 39.]

How, subsequently, may the known be used for teaching that unknown which forms the main object of the lesson? [See pages 39, 40.]

After this manner the subjects of instruction should be examined by the teacher, in each of the grades; and, as a *most important* part of the process of teaching, the main points of each preceding lesson should be reviewed, before proceeding with the new matter, as a means of connecting the instruction of successive lessons so as to make the knowledge acquired a complete whole, so far as it extends.

FIFTH GRADE.

(LOWEST GRAMMAR SCHOOL.)

Time allowed, about five months.

OUTLINE COURSE.

––––

LANGUAGE.

Reading.—Of the grade of a Third Reader (first half), with a review of punctuation, Roman numbers, and elementary sounds; and with exercises on the subject-matter of the lessons.

Spelling.—From the reading lessons, with miscellaneous words, and words derived therefrom; also exercises in writing words and short sentences from dictation. Particular attention to be given to the use of capitals.

Definitions.—From the reading lessons, to teach the meaning of the words, with illustrations by forming sentences; in no case to be committed to memory and mechanically recited.

Grammar.—Correction of Language.

ARITHMETIC.

Mental Arithmetic.—As far as in written arithmetic, to include exercises in the analysis of operations and examples, and in rapid calculation without analysis.

Written Arithmetic.—Through the simple rules and Federal money, with practical examples.

Tables of weights, measures, etc., completed and reviewed, with practical illustrations and simple applications.

5*

GEOGRAPHY.

First Stage.—Simplest elementary and systematic general outline of the geography of the world as a whole, with definitions and illustrations by means of the globe, of the form, magnitude, motions of the earth, zones, latitude, longitude, etc.

Second Stage.—Outlines of North America and the West Indies, including local and descriptive geography.

ELEMENTARY SCIENCE.

Food, Clothing, and Building Materials—Zoology.
—*By oral instruction,* to develop the powers of observation and reflection, and to cultivate facility in oral description.

DRAWING AND WRITING.

On Slates.—Continued.

On Paper.—Writing in books, with particular attention to position, holding pen, etc., etc., as in Sixth Grade.

1. Words containing easy combinations; as *man, name, noon, soon, etc.*

2. Words containing long and short letters; as *heart, long, youth, etc.*

3. Words with easy capitals; as *Ape, Cold, Ink, Lamb, Time, Useful, Vanquish, etc.*

How to Teach

SUBJECTS OF THE FIFTH GRADE.

—

LANGUAGE.

Reading.—In teaching reading in this grade and in the two or three others immediately succeeding, the chief difficulties to be overcome may be classed under the following heads:

First.—Hesitation over, or the miscalling of familiar words.

This arises from want of practice, and where strongly marked should claim the chief attention.

Second.—Mispronunciation of recognized words, as *stun* for *stone, winder* for *window, theáter* for *théater,* etc.

Third.—New words of which the meaning and pronunciation are not yet known to the pupil.

New and difficult words should be carefully pronounced, and, if necessary, explained, before the piece or paragraph is read by the pupils.

Fourth.—Faulty enunciation. This is in great part a physical difficulty arising from deficient training of the vocal organs and of the ear, though sometimes the result of slight malformation.

Distinctness of articulation and the avoidance of all improper clipping of terminations, and of the omission or slurring of syllables, should receive careful and constant attention.

Lists of common words liable to be mispronounced, such as *length* and *strength*, should be made by the teacher, and the class exercised upon them. The elementary sounds and their more difficult combinations in words and phrases requiring great mobility of the vocal organs, and especially *final consonants*, should receive frequent attention. It should not be forgotten that the difficulty here is chiefly physical, and can be readily overcome by suitable exercises. To show a class the importance of mobility of the muscles of the lips, let the teacher read a paragraph with the lips almost motionless, and then read it again, giving as much play as possible to these muscles. The great contrast in distinctness of articulation will be at once manifest. Among the best exercises for the purpose of improving the enunciation are the well-known "Three gray geese and three gray ganders," "She sells sea-shells." "Saw six slim saplings," " Peter Piper," "Theophilus Thistle," " Amidst the mists," etc., etc. A daily exercise of five minutes would probably be sufficient in most cases. It should be very spirited, the shorter sentences twice or thrice repeated, and with the greatest rapidity consistent with perfect distinctness.

Particular attention should be given to pupils of foreign birth or parentage, so as to insure their mastery of the principal difficulties of English pronunciation. Phonetic drills are very useful for this purpose.

Fifth.—Harsh or unnatural tones. The voice and manner of the pupil should accord with the character and sentiment of the selection. All drawling, sing-song tones should be prevented. This is easily done when the pupils are led to understand and enter into the spirit of the piece.

In the employment of concert exercises in reading, especial care should be taken to prevent any injury to the voice by harsh or unnatural tones.

Sixth.—*Vague or erroneous conception* of the subject-matter of the lesson as a whole, or of the meaning of particular phrases, sentences, or paragraphs.

When the character of the paragraph or of the lesson will permit it, the pupils should be accustomed to state, in their own language, the important facts, principles, and moral lessons therein taught. Words, phrases, or allusions should be briefly explained, whenever necessary for the proper understanding of the piece read.

Seventh.—*Want of rhetorical training.* Should a large number of consecutive lessons in the Reader be of the same general character, a part should be omitted, so as to give variety of style and subject. No selection, other than the best English poetry, should be so long dwelt upon and so frequently repeated as to render the exercise a mere recitation.

As a test of the general condition of the reading, classes should occasionally be called upon to read unfamiliar pieces of the same grade.

Where the *primary* object of the exercise is to teach elocution, it is advisable, quite often, to require all the pupils, except the one reading, to close their books, the teacher also, only using the book for occasional reference. In this way, both the teacher and the class will be better able to criticise, and the criticism will be more just and valuable. Besides, the pupils will all be kept on the alert to listen, and the one reading will unavoidably endeavor to pronounce correctly, enunciate distinctly, and emphasize naturally. Additional effect will be given to the exercise by requiring the pupils to reproduce, in their own language, the substance of what is read to them.

Where a simple system of diacritical marks is used in the Reading Book, the pupils should be taught to understand and apply them. An occasional brief review of the Roman numbers, and of the names and signification of the marks used in punctuation, should be required.

The successful application of these suggestions involves the necessity of carefully grading the exercises and selections, so that the pupils be not required to read pieces which are above their comprehension. This is a point of the greatest importance.

SPELLING.

THE exercises in spelling should be both oral and written, but principally written.

The selections of words from the reading lessons should be so made that the class will not be prevented from advancing from one reading lesson to another with proper rapidity. When a Spelling Book is used, it should be made an auxiliary to the Reader, and not a substitute for it. If the lists of the Speller contain unusual words, these should be deferred until higher grades are reached. No time should be spent in spelling words which the pupil does not understand.

For purposes of review, teachers should keep lists of those words of the lessons in which a large number of mistakes are made by the pupils.

In oral spelling, care should be taken to name each letter distinctly, except in the case of the "doubles," which are to be distinctly pronounced as such, and not as "*d'blee*" for "*double-e*," "*d'blow*" for "*double-o*," etc.

"Miscellaneous words" should include the ordinary proper names of persons (not the surnames), words naturally suggested by those of the reading lessons, and common words of the daily life of the household, the shop, and the street. The derivatives required should be those and those only which are in the commonest conversational use. They may be readily obtained by calling upon the class to suggest them. The modifications of the primitives required in order to form them should be taught.

The written exercises should be as neat as possible, care being taken to train pupils to habits of orderly arrangement of their work. When sentences are given, particular attention should be paid to the ordinary troublesome monosyllables, to the proper use of capitals, the sign of the possessive case, the period, the interrogation mark, and the use of the hyphen in a word divided at the end of a line.

DEFINITIONS.

In selecting words for definition, two leading purposes should be specially kept in view: 1. To impress or illustrate the particular meaning of the word as used in the lesson; 2. To enlarge and correct the pupil's own vocabulary.

Very simple words, such as *father, water, knife, knee, book, child,* etc., the *meaning* of which every child already understands, should not, in the lower grades at least, be assigned for definition. Properly to define such words requires a nice discrimination in the use of language and a minuteness of analysis beyond the power of a young child. Teachers are apt to go astray in this direction. It is principally on this account that the limitation, "to teach the meaning of the words," has been introduced in prescribing this part of the grade. The written exercises will necessarily contain many such words, and thus the child will learn to spell them.

Where a word has, in common use, two or more meanings quite diverse, a separate oral illustration should be required for each ; and where several words differently spelled have the same or a similar pronunciation, a separate construction should be required for each in the written exercises.

Defining one part of speech by giving another part of speech as a synonym, is a common error. It may be corrected or avoided by giving small groups of words, each consisting of a primitive and some of its most commonly used derivatives, and requiring, as an oral exercise, a phrase or a sentence to illustrate the use of each word in the group.

Teachers should be particularly careful to comply with the direction, "in no case to be committed to memory and mechanically recited." The mere committing of dictionary definitions to memory, or the substitution for the word to be defined of another word, perhaps more difficult and unusual, is a perversion of the exercise. It is not only useless but pernicious, for it neither aids in mental development nor adds to the pupil's information, nor does it benefit him in his use of language. For this reason, the lists of words given in a spelling book for the purpose of teaching spelling are not well adapted for teaching the meanings of words, these being most clearly comprehended when the words are put into sentences or phrases.

At this stage of the pupil's advancement, a full exercise on a given word should comprise the following: 1. Pronounce it; 2. Use it in the construction of a phrase or a sentence; 3. Define it; 4. Write a sentence containing it. [For the whole class.]

In the performance of the written exercises required for *definitions* in this grade, the pupils may not only be taught the meaning of the words, but, by a skillful application on the part of the teacher, be prepared for the exercises in *composition* subsequently prescribed. This point should be kept in view. Correctness in the use of words, propriety in the thought, the accurate use of capitals, punctuation marks, etc., should be invariably insisted upon.

ARITHMETIC.

Mental Arithmetic.—The mental arithmetic should both precede and accompany the written arithmetic, step by step. The principal distinction between these two divisions of the subject is, that when the numbers involved are too great or too many to be readily retained in the memory, the slate should be employed as an assistant.

"Exercises in rapid calculation without analysis" should, as far as possible, be of the most practical character. Examples given should be silently wrought by the whole class simultaneously as in written arithmetic, and the results obtained be written upon the slates, promptly, and at a given signal. The analysis can then be separately required of as many pupils as may seem expedient.

Illustration.—One method of conducting such an exercise is subjoined. Teachers fertile in expedients will devise others equally good, and involving the following important elements: 1. The exercise to be simultaneous; 2. Silent; 3. Spirited throughout; 4. All copying, or wrongly claiming the answer prevented. The detail may be greatly varied:

1. Pupils sit silent and erect; slates lying on desk, or held vertically, resting on the knees, the hands being at the upper corners; pencils in right hands.

2. Teacher gives question with distinctness.

3. Pupils work silently, remaining in position until the answer is found, when each silently raises the right hand, or stands.

4. When sufficient time has been given, teacher says "Ready——Write," with a pause between the words. At the last word the answer is *instantly* written in large figures, but only by those standing, or whose hands are up, and the slates instantly turned with the answer toward the teacher. No further working or correction allowed. These movements are better executed, after a little practice, by using four light taps of the pencil, meaning, "Ready," "Write," "As you were," "Show."

5. Teacher calls upon some one to read the answer, usually upon one whose results are frequently wrong. Those claiming the same stand if sitting, or raise the hand or the slate if already standing, the answer being still turned toward the teacher.

6. If thought desirable, an oral analysis may now be demanded of any pupil, whether he obtained the answer or not.

The explanatory or analytic statements made by the pupil should be of the simplest and most direct character consistent with clearness, and all unnecessary repetitions of formulæ be carefully avoided. Where this is not done, the principal effort of the pupil is to recall in due order the set form of words, rather than to form the arithmetical combinations necessary to the solution.

Besides simple examples in the four fundamental rules and Federal money, very simple operations involving practical applications of the selected tables of money, weight, and measure, should constitute a portion of the exercises in mental arithmetic.

In the explanation or analysis of examples in mental as well as written arithmetic, the pupils should generally be called upon, before solving, to state the question.

Mental exercises in arithmetic should be conducted in a spirited manner. They should always have the character of extemporized exercises, and in no case form a part of the home-work of the pupil.

Written Arithmetic.—The slates should be kept in the best condition as to cleanness; the figures should be distinctly and neatly made, and written in lines parallel to the upper edge of the slate. A reasonable allowance should be made for imperfections in the forms of figures in those exercises where haste is required; yet every effort should be made to fix in the pupils habits of care, neatness, and system in all that pertains to the written exercises.

Exercises in adding columns of figures should be given with such frequency as may be found necessary to produce and retain accuracy and rapidity. They should be in both forms—the silent and the oral.

Every form of counting, whether by fingers, dots, marks, or other devices, should be strictly prohibited, and the class should be frequently tested for this special purpose.

The pupil should be allowed to name only the successive results arising from the addition of the several successive figures, avoiding all that oral or mental repetition of the tables which is known as the "spelling process," and all other unnecessary formulæ.

Illustration.

$$789$$
$$457$$
$$632$$
$$178$$

Correct Method.—8, 10, 17, 26 ; 9, 12, 17, 25, etc., etc.

Incorrect Method.—8 and 2 are 10, 10 and 7 are 17, 17 and 9 are 26, set down the 6 and carry the 2, etc., etc. When this method is once fixed, it is difficult to change it. It acts as a clog to the mental activity of the pupil, who finds himself unable to think out the result in any other way. It is as if he should spell aloud every word as he reads.

The above remark, in regard to the oral or mental repetition of the tables, applies to all the fundamental rules and their applications. The processes should be reduced to the most concise form practicable.

When pupils show an ability to add in two or more figures at a time, they should be encouraged to do so in exercises that are wrought out silently.

When the divisor is less than 13, the long-division process is not to be employed or allowed.

Short practical examples, involving two or more of the rules, should frequently be given, and in such a way as to cultivate the intelligence of the pupil.

Examples requiring a very large number of figures

for their solution should be avoided, except as far as they may be necessary in order to give practical expertness.

Examples should be given to test the pupils' accuracy in writing numbers requiring 0's, and their knowledge of the proper methods where the multiplier or divisor contains 0's.

Exercises should be given to insure facility in reading and writing Federal money, and in reducing, by *inspection* and *without analysis*, dollars, or dollars and cents, to cents or to mills, etc., etc., and conversely. This reduction becomes important in certain cases in division of Federal money. (See Analysis B.)

Analogous exercises in Federal money should be substituted for those in the simple rules referred to in the preceding sections, as soon as may be found expedient.

In all practical examples, instead of *telling* pupils to add, subtract, multiply, or divide, give the question in such a manner as to oblige them to exercise their own judgment as to the method and principle to be employed.

No detailed analysis is necessary in addition or subtraction.

Give short examples of bills of purchase or sale involving several items, and similar to those required in daily life. Let them be put into proper form on the slate, with names and date, and occasionally receipted, and the receipt explained.

The following examples involve the points upon which pupils are most apt to fail in the arithmetic of this grade. They are so highly important that a drill upon a series of similar examples is recommended. No pupil should be allowed to proceed further till he has thoroughly mastered them.

Write 30,003,050—700,500,000

Multiply 30850 by 307; by 4070; by 2009.

Divide 732427 by 200; by 40000, etc.—Should of course only be done by short division.

Divide 732427 by 100; by 10000, etc.—Should only be done by pointing off.

Write 3 dollars and 5 cents; 10 dollars and 7 cents, etc.

Bought for $2095.07, sold for $2500. How much did I gain or lose?

Sold 320 bushels for $176. How much a bushel? Analyze.

Spent $42 for tea at 87½ cents a lb. How many lbs. did I buy? Analyze.

Spent $8 for coffee at 40 cts. a lb. How many lbs. did I buy? Analyze.

If 24 yards cost $20.40, what will 17 yards cost? Analyze.

If 24 yards cost $20.40, how many yards can be bought for $14.45? Analyze.

NOTE.—If fractions arise in the first stage of examples similar to the last two, they may be rejected in the second stage in this grade.

The following are all the forms of arithmetical analysis necessary to the fifth grade:

FORMS OF ARITHMETICAL ANALYSIS

FOR BOTH MENTAL AND WRITTEN ARITHMETIC.

A. (*Fundamental*)—*Multiplication.*

Question.—If one yard cost $3, what will 4 yards cost?

Analysis.—If one yard cost $3, 4 yards will cost 4 times $3, which are $12.

NOTE.—Avoid the too concise form, " will cost 4 times 3, which are 12."

B. (*Derived*)—*Division.* (1.)

Question.—If one yard cost $3, how many yards may be bought for $12?

Analysis.—If one yard cost $3, $12 will buy as many yards as $3 are contained times in $12, which are 4 yards.

NOTE.—Avoid the too concise form " as many as 3 are contained in 12."

Question.—Spent $42 for tea, at 87½c. a pound. How many pounds did I buy?

Analysis.—$42 are 42000 mills, and 87½ cents are 875 mills. I can buy as many pounds as 875 mills are contained, etc.

See preceding "Suggestions" for remark about reducing Federal money without analysis.

C. (*Derived*)—*Division.* (2.)

Question.—If 4 yards cost $12, what will one yard cost?

Analysis.—If 4 yards cost $12, one yard will cost ¼ of $12, which is $3.

NOTE.—Avoid the very faulty forms "as much as 4 is contained in $12," or " times in $12," or "4 is contained in 12."

Question.—If 5 lbs. cost $3, what will 1 lb. cost?

Analysis.—If 5 lbs. cost $3 or 300 cents, 1 lb. will cost ⅕ of 300 cents, which is 60 cents.

COMBINATIONS OF A, B, AND C.

C and A. Division and Multiplication.

Question.—If 4 yards cost $12, what will 9 yards cost?

Analysis.—First by C for price of 1 yard, then by A for price of 9 yards.

C and B. Division. (2) and (1).

Question.—If 4 yards cost $12, how many yards may be bought for $27?

Analysis.—First by C for price of 1 yard, then by B for number of yards.

NOTE 1.—*Avoid set forms of giving questions.* Vary the order of statement as far as is consistent with perfect clearness. For instance, the last question might have been put thus: Spent $27 for cloth. How many yards did 1 buy, if $12 bought 3 yards; or, How many yards for $27, if 4 yards cost $12? etc., etc.

NOTE 2.—In this grade avoid examples in which fractions form a part of the quotient.

NOTE 3.—It is frequently an assistance to some pupils to have them divide each question into *conditions* and *demand*—as in C and A. "The condition is, that 4 yards cost $12. The demand is, what is the price of 9 yards." Such devices should be sparingly used.

NOTE 4.—Analysis A and B apply to questions in the tables, substituting the word *since* for *if.* Examples: How many quarts in five pecks? Since one peck contains eight quarts, five pecks contain, etc., etc. How many feet in 84 inches? Since 12 inches make 1 foot, 84 inches contain as many feet, etc., etc.

TABLES.

In this grade, the tables of the preceding grade should be thoroughly reviewed, with the following additions :

Time.—Teach about leap-year.

Avoirdupois Weight.—7000 grains = 1 pound; 2240 pounds = 1 old ton ; 62¼ pounds, or 1000 ounces = 1 cubic foot of water.

Troy Weight.—Explain its use, the great difference between its pound and ounce, and those of Avoirdupois Weight, the grain being the only identical element. 24 grains = 1 pennyweight; 20 pennyweights = 1 ounce ; 12 ounces, or 5760 grains = 1pound.

Apothecaries' Weight.—Explain its use. Show that it differs from Troy Weight in nothing but the method of subdividing the ounce. Teach that the fluid ounce is a measure, and not a weight. 20 grains = 1 scruple; 3 scruples = 1 dram ; 8 drams = 1 ounce; 12 ounces = 1 pound.

Long Measure.—Add the following : Explain the use of each term. 4 inches = 1 hand ; 3 feet = 1 pace; 6 feet = 1 fathom ; 1⅛ miles = 1 knot.

Surveyors' Long Measure.—4 rods, or 66 feet, or 100 links = 1 chain ; 80 chains = 1 mile.

Surveyors' Square Measure.—Explain the local use of *section* and *township*. 16 square rods = 1 square chain ; 10 square chains = 1 acre ; 640 acres = 1 square mile or *section ;* 36 square miles = 1 township.

Solid or Cubic Measure.—Explain its use, and the *difference in kind* between the linear, superficial, and solid units of the *same name.* 1728 cubic inches = 1 cubic foot; 9 cubic feet = 1 cubic yard ; 128 cubic feet = 1 cord of wood ; 2150 cubic inches = 1 bushel ; 231 cubic inches = 1 gallon.

Angular Measure.—Teach the following terms : *Circle,*

circumference, quadrant, radius, diameter. Teach the notation. Give examples in reading, as 16° 17' 45". 60" = 1 minute; 60' = 1 degree; 90° = 1 quadrant; 360° = 1 circle; 360° = circumf. of the Earth; 69¼ miles = 1 degree of latitude; circumference of a circle = 3¼ times the diameter.

English Money, etc.—The usual table. Teach the value of a *pound sterling*—$4.866¼. Teach the value of a *franc*—18 cents 6 mills.

If any foreign dollar is taught, let it be the *thaler* of Germany = 69 cents.

GEOGRAPHY.

General Suggestions for all Grades.—It is of the first importance that geography should be so taught and reviewed, as not to leave in the mind of the pupil a mere collection of facts, without mutual relation or dependence. On the contrary, he should, from the first, be led to consider the *earth* as man's dwelling-place—its *motions* as bringing him the necessary vicissitudes of day and night, and the changes of the seasons—its *land-surface* as the chief theater of animal and vegetable life—the *ocean* as the world's broad highway, and the exhaustless source of clouds and rains, so necessary to every form of life on the land-surface— the great permanent *air-currents* as carrying to the land this moisture from the sea—the *mountains* as its condensers, as well as the chief source of mineral wealth —the *springs* and *rivers*, with their branches, as carrying back again, and over the land, the ever-circulating water of the ocean—and of *cities* and *towns*, not as black dots on a map, in colored patches, which he has learned to call countries, perhaps near some crooked black streaks which he has learned to call rivers, but as the centers of social life and development, the seats of government, and the crowded, busy hives of human industry and intelligence.

When geography is thus taught, it is one of the most interesting, important, and practical of studies; but if it is taught chiefly as a description, by unvarying formulæ, of long lists of rivers, capes, peninsulas, boundaries, etc., supplemented, perhaps, by a precise, verbatim repetition of the descriptive geography, as contained in even the very best text-book, it is one of the dullest and most unprofitable of studies.

The text-book is a most important, and even indispensable *auxiliary*, but there is no more common and pernicious error, than that of *substituting it in place of the teacher*, who thus is degraded into a mere stupid, profitless, and mechanical *hearer of lessons*. The requisites for successful teaching are a globe, a blackboard, an outline map and pointer, and a good text-book. The pupil's first impressions should be formed from the globe, rather than from the flat and distorted representation of the map. When the text-book is to be used, and important and comprehensive lessons given, such as the presentation of the general outline of the world as a whole, or of a continent or grand division, or of the United States as a whole, the subject should first be gone over orally, in outline, by the teacher. If this be done in a spirited manner, and the results carefully tested, the detailed study of the text-book will be greatly assisted and unified by the comprehensive view thus imparted, and the important details more surely remembered.

Geography of the Fifth Grade.—In the preceding grade, the pupil has been taught the leading elementary ideas upon which geography is founded; in the present grade, these are to be reviewed, explained, and systematized, beginning with a general view of the world. The following is a syllabus of the points which should claim attention :

Syllabus for the Fifth Grade. Part 1st.—The form of the earth, its magnitude, the continents and grand divisions, their relative positions, their connecting isthmuses, and a few of their most important projections—the *oceans,* their positions, and principal arms and islands—five or six of the great *mountain systems* of America, and from eight to ten in the rest of the world ; three or four well-known *volcanoes*—about a dozen each of the chief *rivers* and *straits,* and about half as many great *lakes*—from ten to a dozen of the most important *cities* of the world, and, in a very general way, the location of the most important countries, such as the *United States, Great Britain, Germany, Japan, China,* etc. With each of these cities and countries some interesting or important *fact* should be at once associated.

Part 2d. (To be taught as facts, in the simplest outline, and without attempting to explain according to any of the hypotheses of scientific physical geography, using the map and globe, whenever necessary, to impress any particular statement on the pupils' minds.) A *brief* notice of the *ocean currents,* their direction, temperature, and use, pointing out only the equatorial current, one Arctic current, one Antarctic current, and the Gulf stream—the *trade winds* (very briefly), their location, direction, use in commerce, and their influence (in assisting to produce the great South American rivers, the Nile, etc.)—a general notion of *climate,* as affected by distance from the equator, and by elevation—the *motions of the earth,* and the *inclination of its axis*—the *zones,* their limits, and a very few of their well-known and characteristic plants and animals, and, in a very general way, the location of the *chief races* of mankind.

"Outlines of North America."—First : Treat the continent *as a whole,* pointing out its separate countries, most important capes, peninsulas, islands, and arms of the sea ; its divisions into mountains, plateaux, and lowland plains, naming only a few of the most important of each.

Iceland, Greenland, Alaska, and all other *Arctic Geography* to be treated very briefly, and chiefly with reference to climate, resources, and people.—*Newfoundland;* the *Dominion of Canada,* its surface, its provinces and territories, with their climate, resources, and people, and our trade with them; the form of government; the capital of the Dominion and those of the provinces, and the other most important towns; the commercial and international importance of the St. Lawrence River and the Great Lakes, and the small importance of the other rivers, of which three or four will be enough.

United States.—A simple outline will embrace the following:

Local Geography.—The boundaries of the country as a whole; its dimensions in round numbers; the location of the great mountain systems; the western plateaux [a section of the country roughly drawn in chalk upon the blackboard will be found efficient]; the high western plain; the low central plain; the eastern slope, and the California basin; about a dozen of the chief rivers, with the great branches; about five or six each of the great lakes, bays, and capes; about twenty of the principal cities.

Descriptive Geography will include a very brief description of the highlands, lowlands, and drainage system already pointed out; the climate and its gradual modifications by latitude, elevation, and distance from the sea; and a general statement of the leading agricultural staples in the order of their latitude—rice, sugar, cotton, tobacco, corn, and wheat.

Mexico.—Its surface, climate, resources, and people; their language, government, and social condition; about five or six of the principal cities.

Central America very briefly; the names of its states and their capitals, and their general similarity to Mexico.

West Indies, the principal groups, about ten or a dozen of the most important islands; five or six principal ports; the climate, resources, and people; their colonial relations, and their commerce with the United States, if important.

LANGUAGE.

Correction of Language.—In all the grades
the pupils should be trained in the *correction of language*, and taught to avoid common errors of speech.
This is best accomplished in connection with the *dictation exercises* required in the several grades; also by oral
exercises specially adapted to this purpose, and by *incidental instruction* during the recitations and lessons in
other subjects, as in the definition exercises, the lessons
in elementary science, etc. Indeed, every exercise in
which the pupils are required to use their own language,
either orally or in writing, should be made a vehicle for
this instruction, the object being to impart the *habit of
using correct language.* It is of the greatest importance
that this habit should be acquired at an early age, for
without it, the technical study of grammar will scarcely
prove adequate to impart fluency in the correct use of
language. The old habits, in spite of the knowledge of
principles and rules, will be always apt to show themselves.

On this account, teachers cannot be too careful themselves in the use of language. Their *words* as well as
their *acts* should present a model for the imitation of
their pupils; and example in this, as in other things,
will prove far more potent than precept. For special
exercises in this department of the instruction, the following suggestions are made :

Write on the blackboard such faults in expression as
are liable to be committed, including—1. Ungrammati-
cal expressions: as *I haven't no book ; I haven't got my
pencil ; I seen him do it,* etc. 2. Slang: *This is an awful
easy lesson,* etc. The faulty expressions written in this

c

way should, however, consist of such as may have been committed by some of the pupils of the class, lest those who have acquired good habits of speech be contaminated by having their attention called to such errors.

Award premium marks, or some other kind of reward, to those who succeed in pointing out improper expressions on the part of their classmates; but let this be done in the right spirit, and not for the purpose of subjecting any of the pupils to jeers or ridicule. The fact that their language may be made the subject of criticism by their fellow-pupils, will put all on the alert to use the best modes of expression in their power, and then correction will have a permanent effect in improving them in the use of language.

Sometimes one or more pupils may be selected by the class to act as censors for a definite period (say a week), and to call attention to errors made by any of the pupils of the class. The object of this and the previous suggestion is to make the pupils critics on themselves and others, most of the inaccuracies committed resulting rather from carelessness and inattention than from a want of knowledge. The teacher will, of course, often find it necessary to give direct instruction in relation to certain expressions.

Of course, no instruction in technical grammar, or in any grammatical rules, is required until the next grade.

ELEMENTARY SCIENCE.

(By Oral Instruction.)

GENERAL SUGGESTIONS FOR ALL GRADES.

The *leading object* in this branch of instruction is to cultivate habits of *observation and reflection*, and to give

facility in oral description. Avoid everything tending to convert these lessons into recitations of set forms
of words, however these forms may have been obtained,
however well they may be understood by the pupils, and
however important the facts thus stated.

" *Familiar objects,*" and familiar animals, plants, and
minerals take precedence of all others in the selection
of topics.

It is neither possible nor desirable to attempt to teach
all, or even the greater part of the topics that might be
classified with the requirements of any grade. No topic
should be treated exhaustively, nor should the topics
selected be so few, or so frequently reviewed, as to narrow down or suspend the discipline of the observing
faculty. The selection and limitation must be left to
the good sense of the teacher.

The *objective method* of teaching presents two distinct, though intimately related departments. *Perceptive* teaching, in which the object, as an acorn or an egg,
is directly presented to the pupils' senses ; and *conceptive
teaching,* in which impressions previously received are
recalled, arranged, and utilized, the objects themselves
not being presented to the senses during the lesson.
An oak, an elephant, or a thunder-storm, would fall
under the latter department.

The use of pictures, models, or other sensible representations of objects, constitutes an important combination and modification of the two principal methods,
and should be often employed.

Definitions should be very sparingly introduced, and
never in the first stage of a subject. *If given at all,*
they should sum up knowledge already attained. The
terms *organic, inorganic, vegetable, animal,* and *mineral,*
are prominent among the very few terms requiring defi-

nition. Such definitions should be prepared for by a process at once inductive and objective.

No fact which the teacher can *readily* lead the pupil to discover for himself, should be imparted by the teacher. *Important* facts not readily derived from the pupil's own observation, must, of course, be supplied by the teacher. Avoid overloading a topic by details. No topic should be selected in which the number of *facts to be told* bears a large proportion to those which the pupil may be *led to discover* for himself.

The language used by the pupil should be entirely his own, excepting, of course, the few indispensable definitions.

The *process employed* will present two distinct stages: *First*, the analytical or preparatory, in which the teacher leads the pupil by questions to discover or to remember the properties or peculiarities of an object, or to state any other important facts associated with it. The responses by the pupil will be, of course, in his own words; and the additional statements which the teacher himself may find necessary to make, will be given in the form of conversations. This stage gives the principal discipline of the powers of observation and reflection.

The points thus considered, and the facts thus stated should be written upon the blackboard in the briefest possible synoptical form, but each only *after* it has been considered. While some such synopsis is *indispensable* to the *teacher* as the first step of *preparation* for giving the lesson, it should never be presented to the *pupil* except by the *gradual* process above indicated.

The *second* or *review stage* of the process is based upon the results of the *first*, and furnishes the principal discipline of the powers of description or oral statement. The facts already considered should be re-arranged, if necessary, into an orderly synopsis upon the blackboard, the pupils being called upon to assist in this arrangement. They should then be required, in turn, to state what they can recall of each item of the synopsis, then of each group of items, and, lastly, of the whole subject. Then the synopsis may be wholly or in part removed or hidden, and the oral process of review repeated. *As a final stage*, and before dismissing the subject, an extempore *composition*, with or without the aid of the synopsis upon the board, should be written by each pupil upon his slate.

OUTLINES OF ZOOLOGY.

In relation to this part of the fifth grade, the following suggestions are made:

Zoology being a science of *classification*, it is indispensably requisite to teach the distinctions upon which the classification depends.

Only the *simplest outline* need be taught, with such facts and details as seem most naturally appropriate to illustrate the subject.

The process of classification being naturally *objective*, that is, animals being classified by their obvious peculiarities, the pupil should be led, by an exercise of the observing faculties, to discover the leading peculiarities himself.

For instance, suppose the teacher wishes to lead to the perception of the basis of the classification into the four great types or sub-kingdoms. Write upon the blackboard the names of a sufficient number of familiarly known animals without classification. If he have their pictures in books, or on charts, let each be shown before asking and writing its name. Let the

6 *

pupils spell each name before the teacher writes it. Suppose them to be *lobster, ox, oyster, dog, beetle, starfish, snail,* and *coral.* Lead the pupils to see and decide for themselves which two or three most resemble each other. Adroit questioning, and a little patience, will soon make them group together the lobster and the beetle on account of their hard, jointed rings, and their many equally hard limbs; the ox and the dog, from their four legs, and their similarity as to eyes, ears, and other organs; and the oyster and the snail, from their hard shells and soft bodies. The remaining starfish and coral will present difficulties, because not so familiarly known; but these may readily be overcome by the use of pictures or even rough sketches on the board.

Having thus grouped the names upon the blackboard, a few questions will lead to the perception that the animals of one group have a *backbone,* composed of many pieces, and an internal bony skeleton; those of another are made up of *distinct rings and joints ;* and so on of the other groups, each of which may now be readily expanded, by asking the pupils for the names of other animals, and the reasons for assigning them to a particular group.

Then, AND NOT TILL THEN, the teacher should give and explain the terms *vertebrate, articulate,* etc., carefully reviewing and questioning the class, to see that all is understood.

In the same manner, the classes of the vertebrates, and the principal orders of the mammalia, etc., may easily be drawn from the pupil's own observations of resemblances and differences.

The terms *mineral, vegetable, animal, organic,* and *inorganic,* should be previously taught or reviewed in a similar manner, through the perceptions of the pupil, guided by the questions of the teacher.

Remember that the skillful use of interrogation is the teacher's chief means of awakening thought, and producing lasting impressions.

Well-known typical animals should be taken as the *objective basis* of the classification; such as *man, monkey, bat, cat, rat, horse, deer, cow,* and *whale ;—eagle, parrot, canary, rooster, ostrich, snipe,* and *duck ;—turtle, alligator, rattlesnake,* and *frog;—perch, cod, shark,* etc.;—*bee, butterfly, beetle,* etc.;—*spider, cray-fish,* and *crab ;—squid, snail,* and *oyster ;—starfish, jellyfish,* and *corals.*

The simplest names should be used, where possible, in preference to the more scientific, or, at least, as preparatory thereto; thus, it is better to use the term *four-handed* than *quadrumana; gnawers* than *rodentia; scratchers* than *rasores ; two-winged* than *diptera,* etc. A few scientific terms, such as *mollusc* and *bivalve,* are in such common use that they may be readily explained and applied.

Associated facts not strictly scientific—such as the uses of animals, anecdotes concerning them, their peculiarities and habits—which the pupils themselves may have observed, will form a valuable part of these exercises, and a means of increasing the interest of the lessons.

The pupils should be encouraged to acquire as many facts as possible by their own observation and research out of school.

The exercises should be *conversational,* the reviews frequent ; the instruction should also embrace exercises in classifying well-known animals from a miscellaneous list, giving the reasons in each case. Too much ground should not be attempted at first.

Some system of *diagrams,* roughly sketched in chalk, will be found of great service in assisting the pupils to remember the classification. The best and simplest is, probably, that used in the ordinary " genealogical tree." The diagram should be gradually developed as the lessons proceed, and not the whole of it given in the preliminary stages.

No teacher can give such a classified " outline" without having first, by careful study, acquired it. This can be readily accomplished by means of any good school manual on the rudiments of Natural History.

Excepting in important instances, it is not expected that the classification should extend to *species* and *variety*, sometimes not even to *genera*. It is desirable that the pupils should have some definite ideas as to the relations of the following terms used in zoology: *kingdom, branch* or *type, class, order, family, genus, species, variety, individual*. These can be best exhibited by a diagram, but they should in no case be presented by formal definition. All but the last four should be mentioned in describing any given animal.

The exercises should include a portion, at least, of the topics suggested in the following synopsis, which is here presented for the guidance of the teacher. This synopsis comprehends three successive outlines, each complete in itself, or taken with that preceding it:

First General Outline.

Distinction of organic and inorganic objects taught objectively. Differences between animals and plants. What is an *organ?* An animal? Four great *types* of animals (Cuvier's, and omitting the *protozoa*). Exercises in classifying, by *types* only, such animals as the *dog, lobster, clam, coral, shad, wasp, goose, starfish, garter-snake, shrimp, toad, tortoise, oyster*, etc. The reasons for the classification should be given in each case. Each type to be then briefly defined. Why vertebrates are placed first.

Second General Outline.

Classes of Vertebrates.—(Tenney's arrangement is here selected as being brief and simple, but any other may be taken.) Illustrate, as by types, by mentioning animals belonging to the several classes, mammals (those which feed their young with milk), birds, reptiles, batrachians (frog kind), fishes; brief description of each class to be given. Name common vertebrates to be classified, occasionally mentioning an animal not a vertebrate, in order to test the attention and accuracy of the pupils; for example: *alligator, robin, mouse, worm, herring, toad, lion, jelly-fish, rattlesnake, elephant, flea, hawk, turtle,* etc., etc.

Classes of Articulates to be treated very briefly, but in the same manner as the vertebrates. Simplest division, as *insects, crustacea,* and *worms,* to be employed.

Classes of Molluscs.—Treat also briefly, by referring only to their general characteristics. Teach the meaning of the terms *univalve* and *bivalve.* Specimens of shells will be useful for illustration; but it must be remembered that the structure of the animal itself is far more interesting and important than that of the shell which incloses it. A living oyster or clam, opened and carefully examined, a living snail, and a tumbler of water containing a few of the small molluscs found in every pond, will give clear ideas. A small aquarium will be found very useful.

Classes of Radiates, probably treated with sufficient fullness in connection with types. Review if necessary.

Here it would be well to mention the grouping of animals as *herbivorous, carnivorous,* and *omnivorous;* also the general relations of the *teeth* of animals to other peculiarities, such as *feet, forms, food, digestive apparatus,* and *habits;* also, as far as may be possible, illustrations of the importance of their several functions in nature.

Third General Outline.

In this outline some orders should be omitted, or but briefly considered, because not readily treated objectively. If all the prescribed classes cannot readily be taught, owing to the limited available time, selections sufficiently complete in themselves may easily be made, as of the class mammals, or birds, or of the type articulates.

MAMMALS.

Two-handed (Bimana).—To be treated briefly. The five races of men, with their characteristic peculiarities. The geographical distribution of each to be also briefly referred to.

Four-handed (Quadrumana.)—A few examples, according to the experience of the pupils. Refer to the geographical distribution.

Hand-winged (Cheiroptera).—Use a drawing, or a dried, or a living specimen, if one can be procured. Any interesting facts about bats, and their nocturnal habits.

Insect-eaters (Insectivora).—Treat very briefly. The *mole*, its habits—refer to its small, hidden eyes, etc.

Flesh-eaters (Carnivora).—To be treated more fully. Refer to general structure of teeth, feet, and stomach. Refer to *cat family*, using common cat as type; *dog family*, using dog as type; *weasel family*, their form, habits, etc., naming *sable, marten, ermine*, and *mink*, and referring to the value of their furs; *bear family ;* also briefly to *seal family.*

Pouched Animals (Marsupials).—Refer to the geographical distribution. The exception of the opossum.

Gnawers (Rodents).—Use the *rat* or *squirrel* as a type. Refer to peculiarity of teeth, and the provision for their continued growth. Teach about the *rat, mouse, squirrel, beaver, rabbit*. Refer to the *woodchuck, porcupine*, and *guinea-pig.*

Thick-skinned (Pachyderms).—Treat briefly of the *elephant*, the *rhinoceros*, and *swine* families ; more fully of the *horse* family, including *horse, ass*, and *zebra*. Geographical origin of the horse, its dispersion, and its influence in human affairs.

Cud-chewers (Ruminants).—Relations of food to teeth, stomach, feet, etc., etc. Teach three families : 1. *Deer family*, horns solid, deciduous; 2. *Hollow-horned family* (horns permanent); 3. *Camel family* (hornless). Refer to *llama* and *vicuna.*

Whale-like (Cetacea).—Refer to the fish-like character of the whale ; how it differs from a fish ; its uses. The *porpoise* and the *dolphin.*

Note.—Two of the preceding orders (8th and 9th), are sometimes classified under the following arrangement, which may be readily substituted for the above if thought desirable.

Hoofed (Ungulates) into two sub-orders : *A*, cud-chewers (Ruminants), and *B*, (Non-Ruminants). These are again divided into the following groups of families :—

   A. (Hollow-horned) ox, sheep, and antelope families.
     (Solid-horned) deer, giraffe families.
     (Hornless) camel family.
   B. (Solid-hoofed) horse family.
   (Thick-skinned or Pachyderms) elephant, swine, hippopotamus, rhinoceros, and tapir families.

Birds.

Birds of Prey (Raptores).—Vulture, falcon, owl, condor, hawk, eagle.

Climbers (Scansores).—Parrot, woodpecker, etc.

Perchers (Insessores).—Humming bird, swallow, kingbird, thrush, sparrow, canary, etc.

Scratchers (Rasores).—Gallinaceous birds and dove family.

Runners (Cursores).—Ostrich ; its habits.

Waders (Grallatores).—Crane, stork, snipe, etc.

Swimmers (Natatores).—Duck family : Swan, petrel, penguin, albatross, etc. Refer to *nests* of birds, also their *migrations*, *instinct*, etc.

Reptiles and Frog Family.

Treat very briefly, teaching something of turtles, crocodiles, and alligators ; serpents and their fangs ; the frog and its transformations.

Fishes.

Treat the classification very briefly ; show distinction between the two groups, bony and cartilaginous fishes, with the orders spine-finned and soft-finned ; also the shark and the sturgeon.

Articulates.

These present many advantages for the school-room. They are small, and easily procured for perceptive teaching. A simple microscope is of great assistance in awakening an interest. Of *insects*, collections of type specimens can easily be made. Only the simplest and most interesting facts, however, need be taught. The general characteristics of this class of animals should be explained—their structure and the functions of their chief organs. Their wonderful *transformations* should be explained and exemplified; also the difference between *insects proper, spiders*, and *many-footed articulates* (*myriapods*).

The following orders should be taught and exemplified:

1. *Membrane-winged* (*Hymenoptera*).—Including the *bee family*, the *ant family*, the *wasp family*, the *ichneumon family*, their peculiarities, habits, and *instinct*.

2. *Scale-winged* (*Lepidoptera*).—Moths and butterflies, how distinguished; caterpillars, etc., clothes-moth, geometer.

3. *Two-winged* (*Diptera*).—Mosquito family, wheat-fly, house-fly, etc.

4. *Case-winged* (*Coleoptera*).—Beetle, fire-fly, weevil, etc.

5. *Half-winged* (*Hemiptera*); or bugs, cicadas or harvest-flies, tree-hopper, cochineal, boat-fly, etc.

6. *Straight-winged* (*Orthoptera*).—Cricket, katydid, locust, grass-hopper.

7. *Net-winged* (*Neuroptera*).—Dragon-fly, May-fly. Refer to the white ants.

Spiders (*Arachnida*).

Many-footed Insects (*Myriapods*).—Centipedes.

Crustacea.—Crab, lobster.

Worms.—Earth-worm.

NOTE.—It is important to distinguish carefully the three terms, *insect* (i. e., six-footed [hexapod], or true insects), *arachnids*, or eight-footed spiders and scorpions, and *myriapods*, or many-footed millipeds and centipedes. In using a representative of one of these groups as an object, it should be the primary aim to establish the obvious characteristics by which they are distinguished firmly in the pupils' minds. Thus, in the insect proper, the body is divided into three divisions—the head, the body (or thorax), and the hind-body (or abdomen). The head is furnished with feelers, (*antennæ*) ; the body supports three pairs of legs, and generally one or two pairs of wings ; the abdomen shows more or less clearly a number (seven) of rings or joints. In the arachnids, the head and body are consolidated into one division, which has no antennæ, supports four pairs of legs, but no wings. In the myriapods, the entire body consists of a series of very similar joints, not grouped into divisions separated (insected) from one another, but of which the first serves as a head, whilst each of the others, however numerous, supports either one or two pairs of more or less imperfect legs.

FOURTH GRADE.

Time allowed, about five months.

LANGUAGE.

Reading.—Of the grade of a Third Reader (latter half), with exercises as in the preceding grade.

Spelling and Definitions.—From the reading lessons, with exercises in miscellaneous words and sentences, as in the preceding grade. Also easy exercises on the prefixes and suffixes, and their applications.

English Grammar.—To include the analysis, parsing, and construction of simple sentences, and with such definitions *only* as pertain to the parts of the subject studied.

ARITHMETIC.

Mental Arithmetic.—As far as in written arithmetic, with exercises as in the Fifth Grade, including practice in the simple applications of the tables of weight, measure, money, etc.

Written Arithmetic.—Common and Decimal Fractions, with their simple practical applications, and their conversion one into the other. Also, practice in the simple rules and Federal Money, for the purpose of securing rapidity and accuracy.

GEOGRAPHY.

Geography.—Of the United States in detail. Local and descriptive geography treated as in the Fifth Grade.

ELEMENTARY SCIENCE FOR ORAL INSTRUCTION.

Botany.—An outline knowledge of Botany, including the general structure and common uses of such plants as most pupils may readily observe.

This should, if possible, be taught during the spring and summer months, in order to make it in the highest degree objective by the use of specimens.

Mineralogy.—A simple outline knowledge of Mineralogy, illustrated by specimens.

This may constitute the fall and winter course, the specimens being previously collected. When the time permits the teaching of only one of these branches, the season of the year should determine the choice between them.

WRITING.

On Slates.—Continued with practice, to give expertness and fluency.

On Paper.—Review of the elementary forms; their combination in words containing long and short letters, without capitals; next, in words containing both capitals and small letters; an explanation of the elements involved in each.

Instruction as to proper position, holding the pen, etc., as in the preceding grade.

DRAWING.

On Slate or Paper.—Review of the Fifth Grade as far as may be necessary, and drawing curve lines, and figures formed from them, as the circle, ellipse, etc.

How to Teach.

LANGUAGE.

Reading.—See directions and suggestions given for the Fifth Grade.

The latter half of a Third Reader usually comprises selections appropriate to this grade. Particular attention should be given to clearness of articulation, to naturalness of intonation, and to general style.

Spelling.—The exercises in spelling, both oral and written, should be the same as in the previous grade, with the following additional suggestions. The names of important cities, states, and countries, which occur in the geographical lessons of the class, and especially such as are in frequent use in post-office addresses, or are liable to be mis-spelled, should form a part of the *miscellaneous words* taught in this grade; also, familiar personal names. An excellent occasional modification of this exercise is, to have the pupils draw the outline of a letter-envelope upon the slate, or use a neatly-trimmed piece of writing paper of the same shape, and direct it to some person whose address is given by the teacher. The ingenuity of the teacher will suggest many other similar modifications of the exercise.

Definitions.—These should be as in the previous grade, with the following additional exercises designed to lead to the study of etymology.

"The easy exercises on the prefixes and suffixes" should be with *English primitives* at first, without regard to the etymology of those primitives. The affixes of Anglo-Saxon origin will therefore be taught first; afterward the meaning of such as *ab, con, pre, pro, sub, ion, ent,* etc., may be taught as illustrative of the diversity of meaning of such words as *abstract, subtract, concede, accede, precede,* etc. Also as showing that, for example, all words having the prefix *sub* convey the signification of *under,* and all having the suffix *ion* mean the *act of.*

2. Each group, with its common radical or primitive, after being written on the slate or blackboard, should be made the subject of an oral exercise in definitions, in order to impress upon the pupils' minds the modifications of meaning produced by the affixes. The exemplification of the words in sentences should be also carefully attended to.

English Grammar.—The instruction in this subject required for the Fourth Grade includes *analysis, parsing,* and *construction,* and in the order mentioned. Grammar is the *science of the sentence ;* and, therefore, the fundamental idea to be imparted is, *what constitutes a sentence.* Oral lessons should precede the study of the text-book, as a preparation for it. The ideas involved in the *definitions* should first be developed, before the pupils are required to commit these definitions to memory. The contrary practice, once so common, is very discouraging and injurious to the pupil, since it compels him to learn by rote a mass of verbiage which is perfectly unintelligible to him.

Let a short sentence be written on the slate or blackboard; and then, by analysis, let the pupils be made familiar with the relations of the words used as *subject, verb* or *predicate,* and *adjuncts,* or *modifiers.* The distinctions comprehended in the *parts of speech* can all be successively taught in this way, and the pupil enabled readily to point them out, before he is required to say what a noun, or pronoun, or verb, etc., is. The learning of the definitions will be easily accomplished as he proceeds.

The object of the *analysis* is to find out in what relation the words used in the sentence stand to one another (general grammar); the object of the *parsing* (only another kind of analysis) is to apply the principles and rules proper to these relations (particular grammar); the object of the *construction* is to impart practical skill in applying these rules and principles, as well as to give thereby clearer ideas of their nature and use. Thus, when the teacher presents the sentence, " Industrious pupils learn very rapidly," the pupil is made to discover, first, the principal parts—*subject* and *verb,* or *simple predicate ;* next, that *industrious* is added to *pupils, rapidly* to *learn,* and *very* to *rapidly.* The pupil then knows that *industrious,* being an adjunct of a noun, is an adjective; that *rapidly,* being an adjunct of a verb, is an adverb; and that *very,* being an adjunct of an adverb, is also an adverb. This instruction can be supplemented by requiring the pupils to construct sentences of a similar kind; as, sentences containing a simple subject and predicate,—sentences containing a subject and adjuncts with a simple predicate,—sentences containing a subject and predicate, with adjuncts of both. Some of these sentences may be required to be *declarative*, some *interrogative*, etc. In this way the ingenuity or invention of the pupil is brought into play in connection with his knowledge of grammar; and the exercises glide progressively into extended composition.

The sentences presented should at first be carefully classified, so that no difficulties may be presented which are beyond the pupils' ability or actual attainments to solve. In grammar, especially, should the instruction be systematic and logical.

Etymological exercises should be interspersed, especially in the use of the *apostrophe* as the sign of the possessive case—in the proper plural termination of nouns—the proper forms of the pronouns, etc. This is a point of considerable importance.

The sentences required to be studied in this grade include :

1. Sentences with a simple subject and a simple predicate; 2. Those with simple word adjuncts of either subject or predicate, or both; 3. Those with simple phrase adjuncts (so as to teach the *preposition*); 4. Those with compound subjects or compound predicates, or both, but of an easy character; as, " John, William, and Samuel are diligent boys,"—" The animals turned, looked, and ran away." This class of sentences will serve to introduce the *conjunction*.

It is especially requisite in all the lessons given on this subject, that the instruction should not be allowed to degenerate into the repetition of formulæ, and instead of being made a means of developing the analytic and reasoning faculties of the pupils, become a piece of worse than useless mechanism. Grammatical instruction has a distinct office as an educational agent,—an office that can be performed by no other subject. It is addressed to faculties that probably cannot be trained in any other way; and, therefore, no educational curriculum would be complete without it. It should, however, be carefully kept within proper limits, both as to time and place, and should not be permitted to encroach upon other branches of equal importance. Each department of it should also have its due share of attention.

Of course the study of grammar as prescribed in this grade does not supersede the "exercises for correction" required in all the grades. These exercises, however, by degrees lose their *empirical* character, and become scientific. They should not be exclusively either etymological or syntactical, according to the technical discrimination followed in most text-books on English Grammar. Indeed, nothing has done more to bring upon this study an unmerited depreciation, as being a senseless waste of time, than the unwise separation of these correlated departments of the subject.

For instance, instead of teaching the declension of the pronouns *I*, *thou*, *he*, and *she*, long before the application of any syntactical rule, the diversities of inflection and their proper use may be observed and studied by the pupil in connection with the ordinary analysis of simple sentences, and consequently at a quite elementary stage of the study. The transformation of "John can see James" into "*I* can see him," will teach him the nature of a pronoun, how to *distinguish* it, and then how to *define* it. An attempted change of places, as in "Him can see I," when taken in connection with the analysis, will show him the reason of the change of *form* from *he* to *him* and from *I* to *me*.

Similar exercises upon the other pronouns, used in

both numbers, will lead him to see that each of them takes one form when used as the *subject* of a sentence, and a different one when used as the *object*. He will then be ready to use intelligently the terms *singular, plural, nominative,* and *objective,* as applied to varied inflections, and to correct such errors as, "Who saw him? *Me.*" " Me and her saw him," etc., as well as to give the reason for such corrections. Then, and not till then, can he be profitably required to *construct,* re*peat,* and *explain* the declensions of the pronouns. A similar plan should be followed in the comparison of adjectives and the conjugation of verbs.

A few common errors are subjoined as a further illustration of the kind of work proper to this grade.

ERRORS IN ETYMOLOGY.—1. *The Possessive Sign.* A goos'es foot. Three geeses' heads. Two fox's tails. A mans hat.

2. *Improper form of tenses.* They done it. We seen him. He would have went. If I had have seen it.

3. *Improper use of verbs.* He must set still. The book lays on the desk. He laid still.

ERRORS IN SYNTAX.—1. *Subject.* Me and her can sew 2. *Predicate.* We was there. He don't know. She dare not do it. 3. *Object.* He struck my brother and I. Who did you see? *Attribute.* If I were him. She looks beautifully.

ARITHMETIC.

Mental Arithmetic.—The character of the examples to be given in this grade is suggested by the exercises in Written Arithmetic. The same processes and forms of analysis should be employed in both. In connection with the commonly-used tables of weight, measure, etc., should be given such questions as, "In ⅜ of a pound of sugar, how many ounces?" "18 quarts are what part of a bushel?" etc., etc.

Written Arithmetic.—Federal Money should also form a part of the regular work of this grade at least once a week, and should be frequently reviewed.

Particular care should be taken in the selection of examples that no one of them be so intricate and prolix as to consume a large amount of time, without affording sufficient exercise of thought in the application of arithmetical principles.

Too much importance, nevertheless, can scarcely be given to the requirement of "practice for *rapidity* and *accuracy*" in Federal money, as well as the simple rules of Arithmetic. To this should invariably be assigned a brief portion, at least, of the time given to every lesson in this subject. No part of the arithmetical discipline has a higher utilitarian value, whether for the purposes of practical life, or for progress in the more advanced portions of the study; for nothing is more discouraging to the pupil than to find that, in any exercise involving other than a few figures, his results are almost always incorrect, from a want of habitual accuracy in performing the simple combinations involved in the elementary rules. Teachers are, therefore, especially advised to employ every variety of proper stimulus to make the exercises for this purpose thorough and effective.

For general suggestions see the preceding grade.

Common Fractions.—No part of the study of arithmetic is of more importance than the subject of fractions. When properly taught, their value, as a mental discipline, is of the highest order. When taught merely, or chiefly, by memorized formulæ, called "rules," they are, for the greater part, a waste of precious time.

No principle should be presented until the pupil is

about to make use of it, and no definition should be given or required before the ideas which it embodies have been deduced, and clearly presented by preliminary illustration and questioning.

No rules should be given until a sufficient number of examples for practice have made them a succinct statement of principles previously understood, or the results of the application of principles, rather than mere mechanical formulæ for working.

In teaching the fundamental principles of fractions the objective process is indispensable.

The most effective method of treating the subject as a whole, is to give first a very simple *outline course* of exercises, covering all the essential principles, but by means of examples requiring only small numbers for their solution. Such examples, though readily solved mentally, after some practice, should, in *the first stages,* be wrought upon the slates, in order to secure correctness in notation, and to allow the pupil more easily to give the necessary analysis without the additional mental tax required by the effort to retain the numbers.

In the written exercises pupils should use the signs of operation, $+ - \times \div$, and the sign of equality, to indicate the work performed, and its result.

This outline should then be followed by a *full course,* in which the substance of the first constitutes the exercises in mental arithmetic, while the written arithmetic comprises the more difficult portions of the general subject, as well as a systematic statement of definitions and rules, and practical examples, involving numbers too large to be readily retained in the memory. Such a plan, though apparently long, is in reality the most expeditious. The pupil soon obtains a clear, comprehensive, and connected view of the essential principles, and the expanded review which constitutes the second course will then require but little time.

Syllabus of Topics for Outlines of Common Fractions.

(WITH SUGGESTIONS AND EXAMPLES.)

I.—The *idea* of a fraction developed *objectively*.

The *equality* of the parts to be very carefully illustrated.

The *relative value* of various fractional parts, *as greater or less,* as $\frac{1}{4}$, $\frac{1}{6}$, $\frac{1}{20}$, etc.

The *definition* of a fraction. One or more of the equal parts of a unit.

The *terms* of a fraction *defined* and the *order of statement.*

The *notation* of fractions and *location* of terms, or *order* of *writing.*

Exercises in writing and explaining fractions.

Fractional expressions *less* than a unit.

Proper fractions defined, and examples. A proper fraction is one that is less than a unit.

Fractional expressions *equal to* or *greater than* a unit.

Improper fractions defined and illustrated. An improper fraction is one that is equal to, or greater than a unit.

Exercises in writing proper and improper fractions.

II.—Fundamental Axiom $1 = \dfrac{n}{n}$

Reduction of units to improper fractions.—*Analysis* A. (Page 152.)

Reduction of mixed numbers to improper fractions.—*Analysis* A.

Definition of mixed numbers.

Exercises in mixed numbers, *limited to small denominators.*

Reduction of improper fractions to mixed numbers.—*Analysis* B. (Page 152.)

III.— Reduction of fractions *to greater denominators*—or higher terms. [What may halves, thirds, etc., be changed into ? ⅓'s? etc.] To be illustrated objectively.

Examples with greater denominators than can readily be solved by *inspection*.

Analysis C.   (Page 152).   (Begin with fundamental axiom.)

Term *Divisor* or *Factor*, with exercises in finding, by *inspection only*, a *Common Divisor* or *Common Factor*. Definition to be given.

NOTE.—Too great importance can hardly be given to this exercise of inspection. The application of the principle is indispensable in many of the arithmetical exercises in every succeeding grade. With proper training, it will become, within reasonable limits, a fixed mental habit, requiring no conscious effort.

Reduction of Fractions to Lower Terms or *Less Denominators*— Examples—*Analysis* D. (Page 152). Definition of " Lowest Terms."

Examples in finding what part one whole number is of another —corresponding examples in tables.

IV.—Multiple—term illustrated and defined.
Common Multiple   "   "   "
Exercises, to be solved by inspection.

Reduction to Common Denominator—use two fractions only.
Application of common multiple in reducing to common denominator.
Distinction between common multiple and common denominator.
Definition of common denominator.
     "   " least common denominator.
Examples in reducing to least common denominators.— *Analysis* C.
Examples involving previous reduction to lowest terms, by inspection. Reduce $\frac{34}{35}$ and $\frac{16}{18}$ to their least common denominator.
Use of common denominator as the simple but indispensable basis for the working and explanation of Addition, Subtraction, and Division of Fractions.

V.—Impossibility of adding quantities with unlike names, illustrated : Add 3 elms and 4 oaks; add 3 trees and 4 trees = 7 trees.

In teaching the elementary principles, the subject of fractions should, as far as possible, be divested of technicalities, and be made to coincide with the acquired experience and simple notions of a child.

On this account it is much better at first, to say, *find* $\frac{2}{3}$ of $\frac{5}{8}$, than to say, *multiply* $\frac{5}{8}$ by $\frac{2}{3}$, or *find* $\frac{2}{3}$ *times* $\frac{5}{8}$.

Adding things of like names.

Adding fractions of the same denominator—Examples.

Adding fractions of different denominators—Examples—*Analysis* C. (Page 152).

Necessity of reducing to common denominator.

The numerators *only* added; why?

NOTE.—In no example give more than two fractions. The common denominator to contain not more than two digits.

Addition of small mixed numbers—Examples—*Analysis* C.

NOTE.—See that the *sign of operation* and the equality sign are not omitted. Avoid reducing to improper fractions.

Rule.—1st. See that the fractions are in their lowest terms ; 2d. Reduce to common denominator ; 3d. Add their numerators, etc.

Subtracting fractions of different denominators—*Analysis* C.

Rule.—1st. See that the fractions are in their lowest terms ; 2d. Reduce to common denominator ; 3d. Subtract the less numerator from the greater, etc.

The same examples may be used as in addition.

Questions should be occasionally varied by asking: "Which is the greater?" or "What is the difference?"

NOTE.—In mixed numbers avoid { 1st. Reducing to improper fractions. 2d. The difficult case, $7\frac{1}{3}-2\frac{7}{8}$ (deferred to review.)

VI.—"Multiplication of fractions" and "compound fractions" identical.

Such expressions as $\frac{1}{2}$ of $2\frac{2}{3}$, $\frac{3}{4}$ of $\frac{7}{8}$, etc., only involve the finding of a *fractional part*, and should be treated at first as such, rather than as a special kind of fractions.

It must not be forgotten *by the teacher* that from the nature and definition of a fraction, every example in fractions must involve or relate to division in some way.

There are two cases in the so-called multiplication of fractions:

1st. Where a fraction or mixed number is to be actually multiplied. In this case the multiplier must be a *whole number*—as 3 *times* $\frac{2}{7}$, or 3 *times* $4\frac{2}{7}$.

2d. Where a *fractional part* is to be taken of *either a whole number*, or of a *fraction*, or of both; as $\frac{2}{3}$ of 17, or $\frac{2}{3}$ of $\frac{5}{7}$, or $\frac{2}{3}$ of $7\frac{1}{2}$.

NOTE.—Mutliplication by a mixed number is a combination of the 1st and 2d cases.

Only in the first case should the expression "*times*" be used.

In the second case the expression "*of*" only should be used.

In the case of multiplying by a mixed nnmber, the expression "*times*" is used for conciseness, though not logically correct. The proper expression is too cumbersome in practice—" 4 *times the number and ⅔ of the number.*"

Only the two varieties of the first case, and the first two varieties of the second case should be required until the subject is reviewed.

Examples :	
Multiplication OF Fractions	7 times $\frac{3}{8}$——Analysis as in simple ×, then B. (Page 152). 7 times $4\frac{2}{3}$——Analysis as in simple ×, then B. (Page 152).
Multiplication BY Fractions = taking part = division :	$\frac{1}{8}$ of 24; $\frac{12}{36}$ of \$24. No analysis, except reducing to lowest terms. $\frac{3}{8}$ of 25; $\frac{24}{36}$ of \$25. *Analysis* E. (Page 152). $\frac{3}{8}$ of $\frac{5}{7}$; $\frac{12}{18}$ of $\frac{4}{5}$. *Analysis* F. (Page 152).

For rule and its origin, see *Analysis* F.

Examples to be given in the *practical form* at as early a stage as can be made expedient.

Find how many cents, or cents and mills, in a given fraction of a dollar.

Occasional examples involving preliminary reduction to lowest terms.

Rule.—1st. See that the fractions are in their lowest terms ; 2d. Multiply the numerators for new numerator, and the denominators for a new denominator.

Solutions by direct *cancellation* should not be required until the review.

VII. There are, theoretically, two cases in the *Division of Fractions:*

1st. Division OF a FRACTIONAL NUMBER by an integral number, as $\frac{3}{8} \div 7$, and $4\frac{3}{8} \div 7$; evidently identical with $\frac{1}{7}$ of $\frac{3}{8}$, and $\frac{1}{7}$ of $4\frac{3}{8}$ in the so-called multiplication of fractions.

2d. Division of any number, integral or fractional, BY A FRACTIONAL NUMBER, as $5 \div \frac{7}{8}, \frac{5}{6} \div \frac{7}{8}, 8\frac{5}{6} \div \frac{7}{8}, 8\frac{5}{6} \div 9\frac{1}{8}$.

The form of putting the questions should be varied as much as possible, so as to train pupils to select and apply the right principle and method. Sometimes the divisor, sometimes the dividend, should be first named.

" *How many times* are $4\frac{3}{8}$ contained in 9 ?" Use this form of questioning at least as frequently as the more technical form, Divide 9 by $4\frac{3}{8}$.

The two varieties of the first case, and the first two varieties only of the second case, should be required before the review.

Examples in Division of and by Fractions—Analysis:

The method and analysis to be by *common divisor*. The first case may also be analyzed by *Analysis* F (page 152), if desired.

The *method by inverting the divisor* is deferred to the review. See Note 1 under *Analysis* G (page 153.)

Rule.—1st. See that the fractions are in their lowest terms ; 2d. Reduce to a common denominator ; 3d. Divide the numerator of the dividend by the numerator of the divisor.

Examples in finding what part one fractional number is of another. Begin with integers : 5 are what part of 8 ? 3 what part of 11 ? (Analyze from the unit, 1 is $\frac{1}{8}$ of 8, 5 are $\frac{5}{8}$ of 8, etc., etc.)

$\frac{3}{8}$ are what part of $\frac{7}{8}$? $\frac{3}{8}$ are what part of $\frac{1}{8}$? etc., etc.

Practical Examples : { If 7 yards cost $2, what will a yard cost? }
1st Group.   { " 8 yards " $4½, "   "   "   " }

2d Group. { If a yard cost $⅔, how much can be bought for $8?
If a yard cost $⅞, how much can be bought for $⅚ ? }

3d Group. { If ¾ yard cost $5, what will a yard cost?
" ⅜ " " $⅚, " " " " }

FORMS OF ANALYSIS FOR THE OUTLINES OF COMMON FRACTIONS.

Analysis A.—*Example.*—Reduce $5\frac{1}{2}$ to halves, or to an improper fraction :—$1 = \frac{2}{2}$; $5 = 5$ times $\frac{2}{2} = \frac{10}{2}$; $\frac{10}{2} + \frac{1}{2} = \frac{11}{2}$.

Analysis B.—*Example.*—Reduce $\frac{15}{2}$ to units, or to a mixed number :—$1 = \frac{2}{2}$: hence, in $\frac{15}{2}$ there are as many units as $\frac{2}{2}$ are contained times in $\frac{15}{2}$, equal to $7\frac{1}{2}$.

Analysis C.—*Example.*—Reduce $\frac{2}{3}$ to *ninths :*—In a unit there are $\frac{9}{9}$; hence $\frac{1}{3} = \frac{3}{9}$, and $\frac{2}{3} = 2 \times \frac{3}{9} = \frac{6}{9}$.

NOTE.—Avoid saying "a whole number," or "one whole number," when speaking of a *unit.*

Analysis D.—*Example.*—Reduce $\frac{12}{18}$ to its lowest terms :—By inspection the greatest common divisor is 6, hence it may be reduced to *thirds ;* $\frac{6}{18} = \frac{1}{3}$; hence there are as many *thirds* as $\frac{6}{18}$ are contained times in $\frac{12}{18}$, or *two*-thirds—$\frac{2}{3}$.

Analysis E.—*Example.*—Find $\frac{3}{8}$ of 25. $\frac{1}{8}$ of 25 is $3\frac{1}{8}$; $\frac{3}{8}$ of 25 are 3 times $3\frac{1}{8} = 9\frac{3}{8}$; or (using as a basis the *Axiom* $\frac{3}{4}$ of a unit $= \frac{1}{4}$ of 3 units ; $\frac{3}{4} = \frac{1}{4}$ of 3, first *illustrating* objectively by lines divided into parts), $\frac{3}{8}$ of $25 = \frac{1}{8}$ of 3 times $25 = \frac{1}{8}$ of $75 = 9\frac{3}{8}$. The former process is, in many respects, preferable.

Analysis F.—*Example.*—Find $\frac{3}{4}$ of $\frac{5}{7}$. (First, as a basis, show OBJECTIVELY that $\frac{1}{2}$ of $\frac{1}{2} = \frac{1}{4}$; $\frac{1}{2}$ of $\frac{1}{3} = \frac{1}{6}$; $\frac{1}{3}$ of $\frac{1}{4} = \frac{1}{12}$, etc., etc.) $\frac{1}{4}$ of $\frac{1}{7} = \frac{1}{28}$; $\frac{1}{4}$ of $\frac{5}{7} = 5$ times $\frac{1}{28} = \frac{5}{28}$; $\frac{3}{4}$ of $\frac{5}{7} = 3$ times $\frac{5}{28} = \frac{15}{28}$.

NOTE 1st.—Make the same question "practical," and apply the same analysis. If a yard cost $\frac{5}{7}$, how much will $\frac{3}{4}$ of a yard cost? It will cost $\frac{3}{4}$ of $\frac{5}{7}$ of a dollar, etc., etc., as before.

NOTE 2d.—*After* a few simple examples have been carefully analyzed, point out the numerical relation of the numerator and the denominator of the product to those of the factors, and *then, not before,* deduce or give the following

Rule for *the Multiplication of Fractions :*

1st. See that the fractions are in their lowest terms ; 2d. Multiply the numerators for the numerator of the product; and multiply the denominators for the denominator of the product.

Analysis G.—*Example.*—If a yard costs $\$\frac{3}{8}$, how much can be bought for $\$\frac{7}{9}$?

(See *Analysis* B, 5th Grade, to be combined with reduction to Common Denominator.)

If a yard cost $\$\frac{3}{8}$, $\$\frac{7}{9}$ will buy as many yards as $\$\frac{3}{8}$ are contained times in $\$\frac{7}{9}$, or, reducing to Common Denominator, $\frac{3}{8} = \frac{27}{72}$, $\frac{7}{9} = \frac{56}{72}$, as many yards as $\frac{27}{72}$ are contained times in $\frac{56}{72}$, or $2\frac{2}{27}$ yards.

Note 1st.—To "invert the divisor and proceed as in multiplication," is much more concise as a method, but it is not in any sense an *analysis*, but a condensed and valuable *rule*, which is to be both taught and analyzed in the review. When this concise rule is taught before the analysis by reducing to a common denominator, the teacher will usually find three undesirable results: first, the pupils are as likely to invert the wrong fraction as the right one, unless the question is always put in one particular way, and even then, until after much practice; thus showing that they are not guided by any principle: second, they cannot explain the process; and third, it is then much more difficult to teach the analysis, because their minds are preoccupied by the brief rule, which naturally seems to them so much more desirable, as it costs little or no mental effort.

As the study of fractions is an important mental discipline, any course which practically excludes the fundamental principle of division by a fraction should be carefully avoided.

Note 2d.—It will be perceived that the analysis of the division of one fraction by another by the process of reducing to a common denominator, is essentially identical with the analysis of reducing an improper fraction to a whole or mixed number.

Analysis H.—*Example.*—If $\frac{4}{7}$ of a yard cost $\$\frac{3}{5}$, what will a yard cost?

(See *Analysis* C, in 5th Grade, with which the following is essentially identical.)

If $\frac{4}{7}$ of a yard cost $\$\frac{3}{5}$, $\frac{1}{7}$ of a yard will cost $\frac{1}{4}$ of $\$\frac{3}{5}$ (note that this division by the numerator is the vital step in the process), which is $\$\frac{3}{20}$; and a yard or $\frac{7}{7}$ will cost 7 times $\$\frac{3}{20}$, or $\$\frac{21}{20}$, equal to $\$1\frac{1}{20}$.

Note 1st.—This is one of the most important analyses in the entire range of the arithmetic of the grammar-school grades. If neglected, or badly taught, it seriously deranges the work of the teachers of more advanced grades, where it must be so frequently applied. If the teacher will present it immediately *after*, and then *in connection with*, a review of *Analysis* C, in the Fifth Grade, and dwell particularly upon the *step noted in parenthesis*, a great part of the difficulty in fixing the entire process will disappear.

NOTE 2.—It is, of course, understood that the examples given to the class will not be confined to yards and dollars. Even the order of these should be at times inverted ; as, in the problem last treated, we might have—

If $\frac{2}{5}$ purchase $\frac{4}{7}$ of a yard, how much will a dollar buy ?

SYLLABUS OF TOPICS FOR EXPANDED REVIEW OF COMMON FRACTIONS.

I. Systematic *Review of Definitions* of terms used in fractions, *with illustrative examples.* Omit complex fractions having fractions in the denominator. Complex fractions having an integral denominator, such as $\dfrac{2\frac{1}{3}}{5}$, read 2½ fifths, are to be "reduced to higher terms." See *Analysis* C, page 152. The multiplier to be used is evidently the denominator of the fraction found in the numerator. All other cases of "complex fractions," so called, should be treated as *indicated division.* Such expressions as $\dfrac{7\frac{1}{4}}{9\frac{1}{3}}$ are not to be explained as fractions. A unit cannot be divided into 9⅓ *equal* parts.

Examples in finding the Greatest Common Factor of numbers by inspection.—Mental.

Examples where the factor *cannot* be readily found by inspection, as 292 and 365 ;—315 and 572. The SPECIAL METHOD required is too difficult for *analysis* in this grade. It is one of the few points to be taught *empirically.*

The result always should be tested or proved in accordance with the definition of Common Factor or Common Divisor.

II. *Reduction of Fractions to their Lowest Terms.*

Examples to be reduced by inspection ; $\frac{1408}{1500}$, $\frac{420}{750}$, *Analysis* D, page 152.

Examples involving the special method of finding the Greatest Common Factor; as $\frac{292}{365}$, $\frac{315}{572}$, etc., etc. Not too long.—*Analysis* D, page 152.

Reduction of Improper Fractions and Mixed Numbers.

1st. Examples solved mentally or by inspection.

2d. Examples with larger numbers.—*Analyses* A and B.

Examples in finding the Least Common Multiple of two or more numbers—and definition.

1st. By inspection, as 5, 3, 2; 10, 20, 30.

2d. When not readily solved by inspection, as 28 and 39; 72, 25, 88; 6, 12, 18, 24, 36, and 48.

Statement of Method or rule.

Relation of Least Common Multiple to Least Common Denominator.

Distinguish carefully between the two, and define each.

Examples in reducing to Least Common Denominators.— *Analysis C.*

Give occasional examples involving preliminary reduction to lowest terms by inspection.

III. *Analysis C. Examples in Addition of Fractions and of Mixed Numbers.*

Say " *Reduce to Least Common Denominator,*" rather than, "*Find the Least Common Multiple of the Denominators.* Of course the latter forms a *part of the process* of the former.

Examples in Subtraction; as $\frac{7}{15}$—$\frac{4}{17}$; $87\frac{1}{5}$—$29\frac{10}{15}$. Do not allow reduction to improper fractions.

Make both kinds of examples as practical as possible.

Practical Examples (not too long), each involving both addition and subtraction.

NOTE.—Teachers should remember, that arithmetic is not only a *science,* but also a practical *art;* that this art involves important *devices,* many, or most, of which have been already taught, and their principles explained. These devices, such as reducing to lowest terms, cancellation, rejecting terminal 0's of a divisor, should not be at any time lost sight of. Examples should be occasionally given of such a character as to require these devices. The omission or neglect of these important matters would be a serious defect in the character of the instruction given.

Principle of *Cancellation.*—Show its *identity* with dividing by *common factors,* and with *reducing to lowest terms.* Show this by examples in fractions.

Examples of simple applications of cancellation to whole numbers.

IV. *Multiplication of Fractions*

Give examples where cancellation cannot be applied.— *Analysis F.*

$\frac{4}{9} \times 3\frac{7}{15}$; $\times \frac{4}{9}\frac{2}{7}$; $\frac{17}{25} \times 144$; $16\frac{3}{8} \times 12\frac{1}{4}$; abstract and *practical.*

Give examples that should be done by cancellation.— *Analysis.* Lowest terms.

125 × $\frac{4}{15}$; $\frac{3}{4}$ of \$17.38 ;—if 39 barrels cost \$84, what will 26 barrels cost ?

If a ton of hay cost \$17½, what will $\frac{3}{4}$ ton cost ?

If 1 acre cost \$23½, what will 19$\frac{1}{4}$ acres cost ?

Pupils should be made familiar with the following principle and its applications. It is frequently the most convenient method of solution. See *Analysis* E, page 152. $\frac{3}{8}$ of a number are equal to $\frac{1}{8}$ of 3 times the number, etc., etc.

$\frac{3}{8}$ of 40 = $\frac{1}{8}$ of 3 times 40.

V. *Division of Fractions.*

1st. Review and apply the method by *common denominators.*

2d. Review thoroughly its analysis. *Analysis* G, page 153.

3d. Teach carefully the following analysis, giving a variety of short examples to fix it thoroughly. See *Analysis* I, page 157.

4th. Teach the brief and useful device of *inverting the divisor*, but in no case let the analysis of the rule be forgotten. Let it be given by the pupils as often as may be found necessary to insure its retention. The teacher is again reminded of the importance of the proper application of the principle of repetition of mental effort.

Examples in finding what part of one number is of another; as 7½ are what part of 9½ ? \$4¾, what part of \$7¾ ? $\frac{1}{5}$ what part of $\frac{2}{5}$?—See *Analysis* I, page 157.

Give examples where cancellation cannot be applied :

$\frac{11}{13} \div \frac{25}{19}$; 13½ ÷ 1¾.

At \$1¾ a yard, how many yards can be bought for \$13½ ?

If 5¾ bushels cost \$18½, what will 1 bushel cost?

Give examples where cancellation is to be applied :

23½÷12$\frac{8}{11}$; 21¾÷2$\frac{19}{2}$, etc.

Give short examples involving simple combinations of the multiplication and division of fractions ; also addition or subtraction, with multiplication or division, like the following :

Bought 7¾ yards and 3½ yards at \$1¾ a yard ; what is cost of the whole ?

Bought 36 yards ; kept 9½ yards, sold the remainder at \$¾ a yard ; how much did I get for it ?

If I had sold it for \$7½, how much a yard would that be ?

If $\frac{3}{4}$ yard cost \$$\frac{4}{5}$, what will $\frac{1}{7}$ yard cost?

If $\frac{2}{3}$ yard cost \$$\frac{4}{5}$, how much can be bought for \$5¾ ?

FORMS OF ANALYSIS.

The following is the simplest form of the analysis of the important practical rule of "inverting the divisor," etc. The introductory step of using a unit as the dividend, is only a case of dividing one fraction by another.

Analysis I.—*Example.*—Divide $\frac{3}{8}$ by $\frac{5}{7}$.

(*Begin with a unit for the dividend*, and apply the principle of *common divisor.*)

1st Step.—A unit divided by $\frac{5}{7}$, or $\frac{7}{7} \div \frac{5}{7} = \frac{7}{5}$ (which quotient, it will be observed, is the *divisor inverted*).

2d Step.—Therefore $\frac{3}{8}$ of a unit divided by $\frac{5}{7} = \frac{3}{8}$ of $\frac{7}{5} = \frac{21}{40}$.

Condensed form.—$(1 \div \frac{5}{7}) = (\frac{7}{7} \div \frac{5}{7}) = \frac{7}{5}$; therefore $(\frac{3}{8} \div \frac{5}{7}) = \frac{3}{8}$ of $\frac{7}{5} = \frac{21}{40}$.

Example.—If $\frac{4}{7}$ of a yard cost \$$\frac{3}{8}$, how much can be bought for \$$\frac{7}{8}$?

Analysis.—Combination of H and G. Page 153.

Example.—If $\frac{4}{7}$ of a yard cost \$$\frac{3}{8}$, what will $\frac{9}{11}$ of a yard cost?

Combination of H and F.

NOTE.—Give a thorough review of analyses F, G, and H, before attempting the above combinations.

Decimal Fractions.—The exact nature of decimal fractions should be explained and illustrated; also the meaning of the word *decimal.* Show that decimal fractions may be used like common fractions by writing the denominator. Illustrate by the decimal notation, showing that whole numbers greater than 9 are also expressed *decimally.*

Show also that decimal fractions are really only a kind of common fractions, the two having the relations of species and genus. The methods of writing, and the various analyses are essentially identical, case for case, as shown by the following syllabus.

The illustrations may embrace the following :—1. How to write decimals, as 7-tenths, 7-hundredths, 7-thousandths, 7-ten-thousandths, etc. 2. Show that the *numerator* is FIRST written, as in common fractions. 3. Show that the "decimal point" and the ciphers, when used, are only required to *indicate* the *denominator.* 4. In *reading* decimal fractions, the pupils should be cautioned to avoid such expressions as "tens of thousands" for *ten-thousandths,* "hundreds of thousands" for *hundred-thousandths,* etc., etc. In connection with the reading of such fractions, pupils should be trained to recognize readily the comparative value of different fractions; as that .3 is greater than .0987 or .01 than .009596, etc. They may also be made to perceive readily the *approximate value* of decimals as compared with simple common fractions; as, that .7634 is a little more than $\frac{3}{4}$; that .8741 is somewhat less than $\frac{7}{8}$, etc. Previous to this, however, it is well to teach the exact value of certain decimal expressions: as .75 = $\frac{3}{4}$, .125 = $\frac{1}{8}$, .375 = $\frac{3}{8}$, etc. These exercises will serve to render the subsequent work of the pupil intelligible.

Syllabus of Topics.

I. Exercises in READING decimal fractions.

Exercises in telling how many places are necessary for a given denominator, and *vice versa.*

Exercises in *writing* decimal fractions.

Reduction of decimal fractions :

1st. *By Inspection,* with analysis as in common fractions.

Examples, mental, oral, and written.

.3 to .00's, to .000's, etc.; .15 to .00000's. To higher terms, *Analysis* C, common fractions. Page 152.

3 to .0's, to .00's, to .000's, etc.; 7.3 to .0's, to .000's, etc.; to improper fractions, *Analysis* A, Page 152.

Reduce .700 to *lowest* DECIMAL *terms.* Give *Analysis* D, Page 152.

Note.—Avoid saying "the ciphers to the right are crossed off because they are of *no use*." The statement that "they do not affect the value," is not satisfactory unless the pupils show why they do not.

II. *Reduce common fractions to decimal fractions.* Give *Analysis* E.

Use axiom—$\frac{3}{4}$ of a unit $= \frac{1}{4}$ of 3 units; $\frac{3}{4} = \frac{1}{4}$ of 3.

Make this definite by objective illustration, using lines divided into parts.

Example.—$\frac{3}{4}$ to tenths; to hundredths; $\frac{3}{4}$ of $1 = \frac{1}{4}$ of $3 = \frac{1}{4}$ of 30 tenths $= 7\frac{1}{2}$ tenths $= .7\frac{1}{2} = .75$.

Note.—Pupils should be accustomed to read decimal fractions, especially hundredths (in subsequent grades applied to per cent.), so as to include outstanding fractional parts, where there are any.

It is generally better to state what denominator is required, instead of the more indefinite requirement to "reduce to a decimal fraction."

Example.—Reduce $\frac{4}{11}$ to a decimal fraction of two places, or reduce $\frac{4}{11}$ to hundredths.

Ans. Two places will give hundredths for the denominator.

$$\frac{4}{11} = \frac{1}{11} \text{ of } 4 = \frac{1}{11} \text{ of four-hundred hundredths} = 11\overline{)\begin{array}{l}4.00 \\ \hline .36 \ \ 4\text{-}11\end{array}}$$

Reduce $\frac{240}{320}$ to a decimal : $\frac{240}{320} = \frac{24}{32} = \frac{3}{4} = \frac{3}{4} \text{ of } 3 = \frac{3}{4} \text{ of 300 hundredths} = 4\overline{)\begin{array}{l}3.00 \\ \hline .75\end{array}}$

Rule 1. 1st. Reduce the numerator, considered as a whole number, to an improper fraction with the required denominator. 2d. Divide by the given denominator. Or,

Rule 2. *Divide the numerator by the denominator.*

Note.—Give examples to show what common fractions in their lowest terms *can be made entirely decimal*, and which *can not*. In the general work of the class, pupils should rarely be required to continue the division beyond three or four places.

Reducing Decimal Fractions to Common Fractions in their Lowest Terms.

Rule.—Write the fraction as a common fraction and reduce to lowest terms. *Analysis* D, common fractions.

Examples : .625   .4125   .87500   14.125

"   .07$\frac{1}{2}$ .3$\frac{1}{3}$ .66$\frac{2}{3}$ 5.11$\frac{1}{9}$ .87$\frac{1}{2}$

Note.—Pupils should be made thoroughly familiar by rapid mental exercise, usually without analysis, with the decimal expressions for halves, 3ds, 4ths, 5ths, 6ths, 7ths, 8ths, 9ths, 11ths, 12ths, and *vice versa*, using preliminary reduction to lowest terms whenever possible, as in $\frac{9}{12}$, $\frac{6}{9}$, etc., etc.

III. *Addition of Decimal Fractions.*

Examples : Add .2, .05, .008, .7283.　Add .0005, .97, .0101, etc.
　　"　　　Give mixed numbers.

Analysis as in common fractions, by principle of reducing to lowest terms.　The necessary additional ciphers may be "understood" in the solution, but not in the oral analysis, which should be *as brief as possible.*

IV. *Subtraction of Decimal Fractions.*

Examples : .1 — .075; 1.001 — .01009, etc.

Explain as in common fractions, with the same analysis.

V. *Multiplication of Decimal Fractions.*

NOTE.—Do not give large denominators. *Use the brief rule of common fractions. Cases* as in common fractions.

1st.　When a fraction or a mixed number is to be *multiplied,* as :
　　4 times .75, 17 times 8.047.
　　Value of 13 barrels at $8.375 a barrel.

2d.　When a *fractional part* is to be taken, as :
　　.4 of .83, .4 of 75, .4 of 8.75.
　　How much is .7 of $38.45 ? .079 of $120 ? .90¼ of $160.48 ?
　　Value .179 of ton @ $92 a ton ? at $92.87½ a ton ?

3d.　Combinations of the 1st and 2d cases, as :
　　3.4 lbs. at 79 cts. a lb. ? $.79 × 3.4.
　　8 cwt. 75 lbs. @ $2.47 a cwt.　$2.47 × 8.75.

NOTE.—As preliminary to 2d and 3d cases, give mental exercises in finding the *product* of two decimal denominators, as "10ths by 10ths, how many places ?" "1000ths by 100ths, how many places ?" etc., etc.

Examples of cases involving reduction :

.024 × .15 = ?　Product of numerators, 24 × 15 = 360, the new numerator, 1000ths by 100ths = 100.000ths, or 5 decimal places for denominator.　*Ans.* .00360 = in lowest decimal terms .0036. Why cross off the last 0 ?　To divide both terms by 10.

NOTE.—Many questions are as well solved by the application of principle (E) in common fractions.　See *Analysis* E, page 152.
　　　.079 of $14.83=.001 of 79 times $14.83, etc., etc.
Use or not as may be judged expedient.

VI. *Division of Decimal Fractions.*

There are two cases, as in common fractions :

1st. When the divisor is *an integer :*

7 ÷ 8, 8 ÷ 7, 6÷5, 6 ÷ 120, 7.2 ÷ 6, 3.6 ÷ 120, etc. Put question in several ways : 1st, Divide 7.2 by 6; 2d, How much is ⅙ part of 7.2? 3d, How many times is 6 contained in 7.2? . etc., etc.

This simple case does not require the principle of the common denominator.

2d. When the divisor is or contains a *decimal fraction :*

6 ÷.03 ; .8 ÷ .005 ; .004 ÷ .8 ; .0036 ÷ .024 ; 7.2 ÷ .009 ; 8 ÷ 5.45 ; 3 ÷ 7.203 ; .2 ÷ 8.75 ; .3006 ÷ 7.4 ; 8.5 ÷ 9.78 ; 8.638 ÷ 9.5 ; 8.638 ÷ 4.3, etc., etc.

Solution and analysis by the principle of common denominator. There are two forms of applying this principle :

1st. Where the denominator of the divisor is the *greater,* (.003).6,) INCREASE the denominator of the dividend to .000's.

2d. Where the denominator of the divisor is the *less,* (.12).17286,) DIMINISH the denominator of the dividend to .00's (hundredths) by cutting off the last three figures.

A General Rule.—1st. Reduce the denominator of the dividend to the denominator of the divisor ; 2d, Divide the numerator of the dividend by the numerator of the divisor.

The quotient will then be a whole number. Other decimal places either added to the dividend or cut off from it, are to be " brought down " in the further division, and will give the fractional portion of the quotient.

Applications.—The applications of decimal fractions will be principally found in Federal Money. Simple combinations with common fractions should occasionally be used ; also simple combinations of two or more of the rules of decimal fractions.

Use the principles of *cancellation* and *reduction to common fractions* whenever they will simplify the operation.

Examples in finding what *decimal fraction* one decimal fraction is of another ; especially how many *hundredths*—use ONLY small amounts or very simple examples :

8 cents, how many hundredths of 64 cents?

$7.25, how many hundredths of $9.75 ?

SUPPLEMENTARY NOTE TO THE ARITHMETIC OF THE FOURTH GRADE.

Particular attention is directed to the three following elementary and mutually related problems, and to their importance as the essential preparation for the commercial arithmetic of the higher grades.

1st. To take a fractional part of a given number: Fundamental.

Common Fractions.	*Decimal Fractions.*	*Percentage.*
How much are $\frac{3}{4}$ of 15?	How much are .75 of 15?	Find 75 per cent. of 15?
How much are $7\frac{1}{3}$ times $9\frac{1}{2}$?	How much are 3.48 times 7.53?	Find $62\frac{1}{2}$ per cent. of 8.75?
Value of $4\frac{2}{3}$ yards @ \$$5\frac{3}{7}$ a yard?	Value of 8.47 tons @ \$3.45 a ton?	Find $87\frac{1}{2}$ per cent. of \$$48.37\frac{1}{2}$?

2d. To find what (fractional) part one given number is of another given number: Derived.

6 is what com. fract. of 15?	6 is what dec. fract. of 15? 6 is how many 100ths of 15?	6 is what per cent. of 15?
$7\frac{1}{3}$ is what com. fract. of $9\frac{1}{2}$?	$7\frac{1}{3}$ is what dec. fract. of $9\frac{1}{2}$? $7\frac{1}{3}$ is how many 100ths of $9\frac{1}{2}$?	$7\frac{1}{3}$ is what per cent. of $9\frac{1}{2}$?
\$$4\frac{2}{3}$ is what com. fract. of \$$5\frac{1}{4}$?	\$$4\frac{2}{3}$ are what dec. fract. of \$$5\frac{1}{4}$? \$$4\frac{2}{3}$ are how many 100ths of \$$5\frac{1}{4}$?	\$$4\frac{2}{3}$ is what per cent. of \$$5\frac{1}{4}$?

3d. To find the number of which a given number is a given fractional part: Derived.

85 is $\frac{5}{8}$ of what number?	85 is .625 of what number?	85 is $62\frac{1}{2}$ per cent. of what number?
$2\frac{1}{8}$ is $\frac{7}{9}$ of what number?	18.75 is 1.3 of what number?	$8\frac{2}{3}$ or 8.45 is 11 per cent. of what number?
\$$8\frac{1}{4}$ are $\frac{4}{5}$ of what sum?	\$9.25 are 1.25 of what sum?	\$12.60 are $87\frac{1}{2}$ per cent. of what sum?

GEOGRAPHY.

Geography of the United States in detail.—IN teaching the geography of the United States, it is particularly important that the time of the pupil be not exclusively taken up with the study of mere local details—with learning the several courses, etc., of long lists of rivers, and the exact situation of still longer lists of towns. A certain, but carefully limited, amount of local geography is indispensable as a basis for the more important descriptive geography.

The necessary *local geography* embraces the names of the several States and Territories, and their division into several groups, as New England, Middle, States etc., etc.; their boundaries or relative positions; their important rivers, lakes, bays, capes, islands, mountain ranges, and peaks; the capital of each State, and a few of its other leading cities or towns, if of any importance. All these should be carefully learned as a basis for the subsequent portions of the study.

The descriptive geography should include the simplest physical outlines of the country as a whole; the *elevations*, the great mountain ranges, plateaux, and plains; the *drainage* by single rivers on the Atlantic slope, and by extensive complex river systems in the remainder of the country; the *climate*, with its modifications in the several sections, as cold or hot, wet or dry; the leading industries and the staple agricultural, mineral, and manufactured productions, with their dependence upon the physical conditions.

Add to this a simple and very brief outline of the general and State governments, the population, its four races and their distribution; the great commercial routes, natural or artificial, and the cities, as the centers of manufacturing and commercial industry.

The descriptive geography of *individual States or Territories* may then, in great part at least, be deduced from a consideration of these general facts. All tiresome sameness and repetitions will thus be avoided, and the pupil will be made to appreciate the real importance of the study.

ELEMENTARY SCIENCE.

(By Oral Instruction.)

BOTANY.

THE general suggestions relating to the object of this branch of instruction, given in connection with the subject of zoology, in the preceding grade, and the remarks there made in regard to the extent of classification, the terms employed, etc., are equally applicable to the subject of botany. As a science of observation, this subject has a decided advantage over zoology, especially for educational purposes, inasmuch as the objects of which it treats are examined, dissected, and analyzed with more facility. They also possess more obvious beauty, and are devoid of the repulsiveness which attaches to so many objects of the animal kingdom. An insect, apparently disgusting at the first view, when closely examined, often shows more beautiful properties and more striking evidences of design than the most elegant blossom ; but the natural aversion to handle it, or come in contact with it, must first be overcome.

The *classification* of plants, being based upon distinctions often very minute, must, for the purposes designed to be accomplished in these simple lessons, be carefully limited. Only common plants need to be classified. The limitations of the classification to be taught are indicated below.

The first *few* lessons should show the *structure* of plants and the general functions of each of their parts, —the *root,* the *stem,* the *leaf,* the *flower,* the *seed;* the *growth* of the plant from the seed, both as to root and stem, the food of plants, buds and branches,—how a plant grows from them ; the distinction between *herbs, shrubs,* and *trees;* also between *annuals, biennials,* and *perennials.* Examples of each to be given.

Classification of leaves—a beautiful and very useful department of the subject, especially as a means of training the powers of observation—may then be taught, the children being encouraged to gather specimens for careful scrutiny. The vocabulary employed to indicate the peculiarities is very interesting, and will serve to teach something of etymology—as *ovate, cordate, palmate, digitate, serrate,* etc., etc. Give the pupils *formulæ* for methodical examination and description. (*See Miss Youmans's "First Book of Botany."*)

Classification of roots and stems, to be taught in a similar manner, but much more briefly. Next, that of *blossoms.* First, show the parts of a blossom, taking a regular one to begin with—as of a *lily,* a *morning-glory,* or a *butter-cup.* Analyze so that the pupils can see the parts, showing the *calyx* and *sepals,* the *corolla* and *petals,* the *stamens* and the *pistil with its ovary.* Give a sufficient number of exercises to make this familiar, and let the pupils analyze for themselves. The *principal forms* of flowers, as *bell-shaped, wheel-shaped, salver-shaped, cross-shaped, butterfly-shaped,* etc., etc., may then be shown. The *arrangement* of the blossoms on the stem (inflorescence), as far as it can be exempli-

fied by actual specimens, as *head, raceme, spike, umbel,*
etc., may also be learned.

The following outline of classification may be
taught:—

A. (Series.) Flowering (*phænogamous*) plants.

B. (Series.) Flowerless (*cryptogamous*) plants.

At first use only the *familiar* terms. The scientific
may often be dispensed with entirely. Give examples
of plants in each series; as—

Rose, Lily, Geranium ; Fern, Moss, Mushroom.

A, including *a* (class). Outside-growing (*exogenous*)
plants

  b (class). Inside-growing (*endogenous*)
plants.

Illustrate by *stems,* showing the rings or annual lay-
ers of growth in the former, with *bark, wood,* and *pith,* ·
and their absence in the latter. Teach the coincident
peculiarities of the leaves, as *netted-reined* and *parallel-
reined,* affording a ready method (approximate) of distinguishing these plants, and thus giving opportunity
for useful exercises ; also those of the seeds, as of two
seed leaves (cotyledons) or only one (*dicotyledonous*
and *monocotyledonous*).

Familiar examples to be found by the pupils; such
as Rose, Buttercup, Geranium, Pea, Potato, Grape-vine,
· etc., etc., and Lily, Indian Corn, Common Grass, etc.

(*a*), Including 1. Orders or families of plants, with
blossoms of many petals (*polypetalous*) ; and, 2. Orders,
or families, of those, with blossoms of one petal (*mono-
petalous*). The pupils will readily find specimens of
each, the names of which they have already learned.

The orders of (*b*) should not be taught. Nor need
any instruction be given in relation to the classification
of cryptogamous plants, *ferns, mosses,* etc., this being

too difficult, and depending upon distinctions not sufficiently obvious for the purpose of these lessons. Attention, however, may, if occasion offers, be called to the
fructification of ferns.

Such of the *orders* or *families*, should be taught as
are very familiar, and depend upon quite obvious distinctions, familiar names being exclusively used. Thus
the *Mustard Family*, the *Pulse Family*, the *Crowfoot
Family*, the *Rose Family*, the *Lily Family*, etc., etc.,
may be taught as far as the collection and presentation
of specimens render it desirable ; that is, not the mere
fact that there are such families, but in connection
with an actual object, and when the *inquiry* is, to what
family does it belong ? If the season permits, and there
is an opportunity for the pupils to seek for specimens,
this part of the instruction may be extended. Here the
judgment of the teacher (never to be superseded) must
be carefully exercised, it being constantly in view that
the object of these lessons is not to make the pupils
botanists, but to create a basis for the study of natural
objects, and to develop the faculties of perception and
reflection. *Species* need not be taught, although the
pupils may, as occasion offers, be made to perceive the
diversity presented by different individuals of the same
family, so as to learn what is meant by species.

The *common uses of plants* may be taught to some
extent incidentally with some of the above instruction,
but more fully at this stage. This will embrace their
uses for *food, clothing, medicine*, etc. Take our own
plants first. Show that the *roots* of some plants are
useful ; of others, the *seeds ;* others, the *leaves;* others,
the *fruit ;* others, the *bark*, etc. Some few plants of
other climates and countries may then be referred to,
as *cotton, rice, sugar, tea, coffee*, etc., etc. The relation-

ship of these plants to our own may then be shown; that is, the *families* to which they belong.

MINERALOGY.

Before commencing instruction in this branch, the teacher should again read the general remarks on teaching elementary science in the Fifth Grade. This subject presents some peculiar advantages for attaining the special object of oral instruction—the discipline of the observing faculties. In no other department of natural science, is it so completely within the power of the teacher to present the facts to be acquired to the immediate perception of the pupils in the class-room, and in no other is more delicacy of discrimination required in the exercise of the senses upon which the perceptions are based. But while the *objective method* is thus seen to be peculiarly applicable to this branch of science, it must, at the same time, be remembered that no other subject perhaps requires so large a share of *imparted information*. This, however, should be given not arbitrarily, but as something needed to supplement the knowledge gained by the pupil in the exercise of his own faculties, and, as far as possible, in answer to his inquiries, the determination of the mind to *self-activity* being the great *desideratum* in this kind of teaching; hence, the important principle should be kept steadily in view that nothing should be done for the pupil which he can be made to do for himself.

The teacher should also bear in mind that it is utterly impossible to teach the subject without *special preparation* for it—without being practically familiar with at least the outline facts of the science. This preparation may readily be made with the assistance of even a small cabinet of minerals, properly labeled (*Day's Grammar School Cabinet*, for example), and any of the smaller manuals of Mineralogy (Dana's, for instance).

What has been said in the preceding grade, as to the propriety or necessity of attempting only a part of the subject, is equally applicable here. What is done should, however, be systematic—not miscellaneous and unrelated. Do not attempt to treat any of the topics exhaustively. A large part would not be understood or remembered, and valuable time would be misapplied.

The investigations made by the pupils in relation to each mineral should be guided by the teacher by means of a regular formula, considering in a fixed order its *form, structure, cleavage, fracture, hardness, weight, color, luster, etc., etc.* These special characteristics and their proper order will be readily remembered after a little practice. Each term thus used should be carefully illustrated and explained as soon as its introduction becomes necessary.

Begin with *Minerals*—*Rocks* to be afterwards considered as mineral aggregates. A clear conception of the general properties of minerals may readily be given by commencing with ice—water—steam.

As a preparatory step, lead the pupil to form some definite idea of the variety of forms of crystals, by briefly comparing coarse salt, alum, borax, quartz, mica, rock-candy, etc. Use only the term *crystal, without* giving the *names* of substances.

In treating of ice, draw attention, not by telling, but by proper questioning, to its transparency, color, luster, weight, solidity, hardness, fracture, and to the needle-like crystals which can be so readily shown in ice-films when water begins to freeze, and in the frost-flowers on the window-pane. Lead him now to see that a block of

8

ice, or a snow bank, must be made up entirely of such crystals, even though their individual forms are no longer perceptible. Show next that many other fluid substances, like water, upon losing their heat, crystallize into definite solid forms, under favorable conditions, as in melted sulphur, and in the beautiful zinc crystals which cover the surface of so-called galvanized iron. Dwell somewhat upon these phenomena of crystallization, and draw attention to the mysterious and indestructible force which somehow rebuilds the atoms of the water into the same forms, no matter how often the ice may be melted.

The next step in this preliminary lesson will be to show that crystals may also be formed from substances in solution. Alum, salt, borax, etc., will furnish ready means of illustration. Lead the pupil further to notice, that, as in the case of the ice, so with the sulphur, zinc, alum, etc., the crystals may become so massed as to be no longer individually distinguishable.

The principal points to be fixed in such a lesson are that there are many kinds of crystals, some formed from liquids which have become solid by a loss of heat, and others deposited from solution. These facts will be found of great importance in further treating the subject.

The pupil is then prepared to compare ice with a *quartz crystal,* which should be presented but *not at first named,* and should be compared first as to the resemblances, then the differences. When the pupils can be made to furnish no more ideas, the teacher should state where it is found, its relative abundance, geological importance, economic uses, etc., etc. Be particular *not to introduce* an unexplained term—such as the *name* of any rock or mineral, as gneiss, or gypsum. The name means nothing until explained as quartz has been. Other forms of quartz may then follow, each treated in the same way, and each in its turn compared with those that have preceded it. This will constitute an excellent review, and will thoroughly fix what has been already taught. Encourage the pupils to look for and bring in specimens which they think to be of the same character as those studied. *Let them tell* why they think they are the same. *Let others tell* why they think they are not.

Having thus treated of *quartz*, next consider, in the same way, *feldspar* and *mica*. The pupils will now be ready to consider a *rock*.

Let it be gneiss or granite. Let the pupils look for the minerals in it [a cheap single lens as a magnifier will often be of service]. Then consider the texture, structure, where found, uses, etc. The mineral *hornblende* and its important varieties may then follow, and after that the rock *syenite.*

All needful information may be obtained from any of the manuals in use.

It will not be necessary here to follow out in detail all the minerals and rocks of which it is desirable that pupils should have some knowledge. A list of the more important, mostly from Dana, is subjoined, from which the teacher can make such selections as will conform essentially to the above plan.

MINERALS.

Water; carbon, diamond, coal and coal-mining, anthracite, bituminous, jet, plumbago, amber, petroleum, asphalt; sulphur; saltpeter, salt, borax; lime, gypsum, alabaster, selenite, calcite spar, chalk, stalagmites, limestones (crystalline and compact), marbles, quicklime, hydraulic lime, dolomite; alum; talc, soap-stone, (French chalk), meerschaum, pyroxene and hornblende, corundum and emery, feldspar, albite, orthoclase, garnet, mica.

METALS.

Mineralized [ores] or native—Ores of tin, iron, nickel, zinc, lead, mercury, copper, gold, silver, platinum. Enter into no *details* of Metallurgy ; a few simple facts in regard to smelting, fluxes, etc., will not be out of place. The economic uses of these metals and the poisonous properties of some of them should receive very careful attention.

ROCKS.

As single minerals—example pure limestone. As compounds—granite or conglomerate. Rocks as crystalline and uncrystalline, stratified and unstratified, aqueous, igneous and metamorphic.

The relative position of important rocks—granite, syenite, gneiss, mica-slate, steatite, trap, basalt, lava, pumice, slate, shale, schist, quartz-rock, burr-stone, sandstones, grits, conglomerates, limestones, marbles, sand, clay.

Such of these rocks as are found in the vicinity of the school, or are frequently seen by the pupils when used for paving, flagging, building, etc., should receive particular attention.

WRITING.

Penmanship and Slate-Writing.—Penmanship should be carefully taught in each grade of the Course, in addition to the constant practice which is required in *slate-writing*. By means of the latter, if a due attention is given to it, much may be accomplished in aiding the pupil to acquire readiness and fluency in the exercise of this art; but if he be allowed to fall into careless habits, his style of writing, both with pen and pencil, will be almost incurably vitiated.

The exercises in spelling from dictation, etc., should be performed with punctilious accuracy, even if some sacrifice of rapidity be at first required. Of course, there should be a constant effort to improve both in rapidity and accuracy—*quantity* as well as *quality* being made a criterion of merit and success.

The slate-writing should, as far as it is practicable, exemplify the principles and methods formally taught in the lessons in Penmanship. Pupils should not be permitted to violate in the one class of exercises the rules and precepts taught and practiced in the other. This caution is especially applicable to the holding of the *pencil,* which should be sufficiently long to be held as a *pen.*

The lessons in *penmanship* should be methodical and ·progressive, whatever system may be employed. In this, as well as the preceding grade, the exercises should be rudimentary, but the pupil should be advanced as fast as possible. He should be permitted to *write* as much as is practicable,— making *strokes* and *curves* is not writing, although it may be valuable as leading to it. A few of such exercises will suffice.

Neither should the use of *trial papers* be carried to the extreme of withholding the pupil for a considerable time from the use of his copy-book, so that months are required to finish the latter. The pupil should be taught the necessity of doing everything as well as he can do it; but perfection ·in details should not be expected in the rudimental stages. It should, *from the first,* be deemed essential (at least *meritorious*) to execute the work prescribed with dispatch, provided there is no want of care or attention. *Festina lente,* however, is a motto that applies to the acquisition of this art, as well as others, in its first stages.

A proper distinction should be made between the lessons given to show the pupils how to write and the exercises designed to practice them on what they have thus learned. In the former, the whole class should invariably be occupied in the same work, the teacher explaining and illustrating from the blackboard the principles and methods which form the subject of the lesson ; in the latter, practice being the object in view, it is not so essential that all the pupils should be doing the same thing at the same time, although even here it is a convenience to the teacher, since it facilitates supervision.

It should be carefully kept in view that the *hand* and the *eye* as well as the *mind* of the pupil are to be trained in this branch of instruction,—the *hand* to execute, the *eye* to discern, the *mind* to judge. These are not to be educated separately and successively, but simultaneously. The pupil must be taught to. know what is the correct form of every letter, and his hand must be so trained by correct practice, that it will execute the dictates of mind and eye.

Hence a correct method of holding the pen, a proper position of the body while sitting at the writing-desk, and a suitable placing of the book or paper, are all indispensable pre-requisites to the acquisition of a good hand-writing. The first of these demands especial attention, and every lesson should, for some time, be introduced by distinct directions as to the proper method of holding the pen, and these the pupils should not be permitted to violate. With regard to the latter —position of body and position of book—a few simple directions will be all that are requisite.

THIRD GRADE.

Time allowed, from eight to ten months.

LANGUAGE.

Reading.—Of the grade of a Fourth Reader, with attention to the elocutionary *principles*, *rules*, and *exercises* required to teach expression; also special exercises in *vocal culture*.

Spelling.—From the reading lessons, with additional exercises, both oral and written; careful attention to *syllabication*.

Definitions.—In connection with the reading lessons; also a review of the *prefixes* and *suffixes* taught in the preceding grade, and exercises in their combination with various easy roots.

English Grammar and Composition.— Continued, with the analysis, parsing, and construction of easy complex and compound sentences; also the writing of short compositions under the inspection of the teacher.

ARITHMETIC.

Mental Arithmetic.—Through denominate numbers and fractions, with their practical applications; also a review of the preceding grades by exercises in both calculation and analysis; and a careful review of the tables.

Written Arithmetic.—As far as in mental arithmetic, with similar processes and methods of analysis; also with exercises to give practical expertness in simple computation.

GEOGRAPHY AND HISTORY.

Geography.—Of *South America* and *Europe*, both local and descriptive; the topics of the preceding grades to be occasionally reviewed in outline.

History.—Of the United States, including an account of the early discoveries, and the outlines of the Colonial History to 1763, only such dates to be taught as are essential to a clear understanding of the narrative.

ELEMENTARY SCIENCE
(FOR ORAL INSTRUCTION.)

A review, as far as possible, of the topics of the preceding grades, and, in addition thereto, the simple outlines of Physiology and Hygiene.

WRITING.

On Slates.—Continued as in the preceding grades.

On Paper.—Words containing difficult elementary forms; also phrases and short sentences. Instruction and practice in the elementary forms, continued.

DRAWING.

Review of the work of preceding grades, to which add *scrolls*, and simple geometrical solids in outline, such as the cube and parallelopiped, in various positions; also the cylinder, cone, pyramid, and prism. The drawings of simple objects, domestic utensils, etc., may also, occasionally, be copied from cards.

How to Teach.

SUBJECTS OF THE THIRD GRADE.

LANGUAGE.

Reading.—In the preceding grades, due attention is required to be given to *emphasis* and *modulation;* but in this grade the exercises should take the *special* direction indicated by these departments of elocution, so as to lead to the higher stages of this art, required in the more advanced grades. It is not enough that the pupils should be accustomed to read with clear articulation and proper inflections of the voice; they should be taught *expression*—to comprehend the character of the piece read, to enter into its spirit, and, to some extent, at least, communicate it justly and forcibly.

Considerable attention should also be given to *vocal culture.* For this purpose exercises should be employed with the view to impart the *physical* as well as *mental* capabilities required for this purpose. The pupils should be taught the proper position of the body, and the right mode of using the lungs and the vocal organs so as to make their utterance effective. This kind of discipline has a most important bearing upon the general physical development of the pupils, as well as on the invigoration of the organs specially concerned in vocalization.

For the attainment of the special objects of this grade, the elocutionary rules, principles, and exercises contained in the Reader, should be made available; a

8*

portion of each reading-lesson being devoted to this kind of instruction and practice.

It is essential that the pupils should be required to stand while engaged in these exercises—either the whole class, or the particular pupil called upon to read. The other pupils, in a proper manner and in the right spirit, may be permitted to criticise the performance of the one called upon to read, and to exemplify the criticism by reading the same passage.

Lessons, especially such as involve a difficulty, should not be hurried over; they should be read and re-read, until an approximation, at least, to correctness has been attained by one or more pupils.

Concert reading and declamation may be resorted to occasionally, with very beneficial results.

Spelling.—Oral spelling, except for the purpose of teaching *syllabication*, should be discontinued. The proper division of words into syllables is an important matter, and should receive due attention. In this connection the correct use of the *hyphen* in compounds should be taught, and the pupils exercised therein.

The *written exercises* should be correctly performed, with care not only as to penmanship, but as to capitals, punctuation, etc. These exercises should be carefully inspected, and after the errors have been pointed out, should be revised and corrected by the pupil himself. The sentences used for dictation should contain a sufficient number of *common test-words*, including proper names, both of persons and places, so as to impress the orthography of such terms firmly on the pupils' minds.

Definitions.—For suggestions, see the preceding grade.

English Grammar.—*Analysis, parsing* and *construction* are to be continued in this grade, the class of sentences employed being of a more difficult character, but still carefully kept within the assigned limits of " easy complex and compound sentences."

By these are meant such as involve: 1. Complex sentences, containing simple adjunct clauses, or brief clauses used as subjects, objects, or attributes,—those containing long and involved or intricate phrases being reserved for the next grade; 2. Compound sentences, formed by the union of simple clauses, or of complex clauses, such as those above described. The analysis should be sufficiently minute, to keep before the pupil's mind the relations upon which grammatical distinctions are based. The *simplest phraseology* should be used.

The exercises in *construction* should be made to correspond with the advanced character of the analysis; and the pupils, in the " short compositions" required to be written, should, as far as possible, exemplify the instruction in the other portions of the subject. They should be required to analyze and parse the defective sentences which occur in their own compositions, so as to discover the inaccuracies and to apply the necessary principles and rules for their correction.

The exercises for the special purpose of accustoming the pupils to care and criticism in the use of language should be continued.

Composition.—The compositions should, as far as possible, be *impromptu*, and written under the immediate inspection of the teacher, so that the pupil may be made to depend upon himself in performing what is required. Much practice of this kind is needed before the formal writing of compositions is assigned as a *home task*. To many pupils this very essential part of school education is made utterly repulsive by the impossible requirement that they should, with scarcely any previous training, write out at their homes, long compositions on difficult themes assigned by the teacher.

The compositions proper for this grade should be *brief*, and on *simple subjects*, which should be either selected by the pupils themselves, or, when prescribed by the teacher, should be of such a character as to interest the mind of a child. Those which require the pupils to relate the incidents of their own experience—what they have seen, heard, or enjoyed, are chiefly to be preferred, since they are thus required to make use of their own language, while their attention is given rather to the thought than to the expression. And this is an important consideration; for exercises of this kind should not be designed to teach the use of language simply, but language as the *vehicle of thought*.

ARITHMETIC.

Mental Arithmetic.—For the purpose of review, brief examples in fractions, both common and decimal, should be employed, both as a test, and more thoroughly to fix in the pupil's mind a knowledge of the principles and applications of fractions as taught in the preceding grades. The improvement made by the pupils in accuracy and rapidity, as well as in the ready application of arithmetical principles to particular cases, involving an exercise of the judgment and reasoning powers, should be progressive from grade to grade, and therefore should be carefully tested in the mental work.

The *special* province of this grade being *Denominate Numbers,* the exercises, both in mental and written arithmetic, should deal largely with the applications of fractions to that class of numbers, including Federal money, and should, of course, combine/ practice in all the essential tables of weight, measure, etc.

The teacher need not, perhaps should not, conform himself to the order or kind of examples presented by any particular text-book. If the questions given out to the pupils to be solved *instanter* are spontaneously constructed by the teacher, they will be more appropriate to the special needs of the pupils, and the exercise will have far more spirit, and be of much greater value. It is among the dullest of all the occupations of the class-room to read from a book questions in mental arithmetic, of little variety, hackneyed in form and character, and which the pupils have previously been required to con over. To expect an uninterested, drowsy class to perform any intellectual "exercise, is absurd; but the absurdity is greater, perhaps, in mental arithmetic than in any other subject. For suggestions in relation to this point the teacher is referred to the statements made under the fifth grade.

The review of the analysis previously taught should be systematic and thorough, but should not consume a large part of the time of the pupils.

Written Arithmetic.—The arithmetic specially prescribed in this grade, both mental and written, is of a practical character, perhaps more generally so than in' any other grade of the course. All that precedes has been, to a considerable extent, a preparation for the work of this grade, and will be found involved in it.

The whole subject of compound denominate numbers

is strictly *utilitarian*. Practical utility should, therefore, be the controlling element in all the exercises employed. The daily necessities of the house, the shop, the market, etc., indicate the general character of the selections to be made. These will furnish at least as good mental discipline in calculation and analysis as those of a less severely practical character.

It is usually the case, that pupils who have reached this grade can spend but little more time in school. In view of this fact it is important to attend first to the more practical, and therefore more essential, parts of the arithmetic of the grade. To this end, the tables, its indispensable basis, should be thoroughly reviewed, and not only memorized, but understood. Pupils should be trained to work with reasonable rapidity, and all long and complex examples, as well as those involving obsolete weights, measures, or money, should be carefully avoided. Reduction should not be so long dwelt upon as to lead to the omission of important practical points in other rules. It is desirable that a record of the points covered by the class-work should be methodically kept to be used as a basis of the necessary reviews.

SYLLABUS.

Reduction Descending.—Show why it is so called. The denominations should always be written with the exam‚ Pupils should not be allowed to "add in" by a separate line; it greatly increases the work, absorbs the time unprofitably, and indicates mental feebleness. The explanation or analysis should be given by processes which make the multiplier an *abstract number*. The impossibility of multiplying by a *concrete number* should be carefully shown.

As an illustration of the above, suppose the question to be,

" How many pints in 75 gallons, 3 quarts ? "   There are at least two correct methods of analysis for this question.

Analysis 1.—Since 4 quarts make 1 gallon there are 4 times as many quarts as there are gallons (75), which are 300 quarts ; 300 quarts and 3 quarts are 303 quarts ; and since 2 pints make 1 quart, there are twice as many pints as there are quarts (303), which are 600 pints.

gals.   qts.
75   3
4
———
303 qts.
2
———
606 pts.

In this analysis the work done on the slates is *directly* explained, the multipliers 4 and 2 used in the slate-work and in the analysis being *identical*.

Analysis 2.—Since in 1 gallon there are 4 quarts, in 75 gallons there are 75 times 4 quarts, which are 300 quarts ; 300 quarts and 3 quarts are 303 quarts ; and since in 1 quart there are 2 pints, in 303 quarts there are 303 times 2 pints, which are 600 pints.

In this analysis, which is concise, and perhaps more clear than the other, the work done on the slate is *indirectly* explained, the multipliers 75 and 303 not being those actually used. When this method is employed, an illustration of the following principle should be occasionally required : " The product of two or more abstract numbers is the same, whatever may be the order of the factors." Also the modification of this principle, in the case where one of the numbers, as in the given instance, is *concrete*.

The following errors are frequently heard and should be avoided : " I multiply 75 gallons by 4 quarts, etc." *Four quarts times* 75 gallons is, of course, absurd.

I multiply 75 gallons by 4, etc. Four times 75 gallons is of course 300 *gallons*, not 300 quarts.

It will be seen that the above analyses and that required for Reduction Ascending are identical with those already given in the preceding grades. The " adding in " is the same as in the reduction of mixed numbers.

Reduction Ascending.—This is best taught and understood in immediate connection with Reduction Descending, at first by reviewing the same example.   Long division by divisors less than 13 should not be allowed, nor if cutting off 0's will change to short division.

Explanation may be by any process which will clearly account for the denominations of the successive quotients and remainders.

Weights.—Teach briefly by examples the relations of Avoirdupois and Troy weights, and the essential identity of Troy and Apothecaries' weights. Let most of the examples in Reduction be in the first of the three. They should be few and very short in the last.

Remember that the quarter of a hundredweight is seldom used now, excepting in text-books—the Avoirdupois dram nowhere else.

In addition and subtraction, give only Avoirdupois weight. Remember that in things sold by the ton, the ounce is not taken into account. Review the principle of carrying, if that plan is used ; of its better substitute, if not. A short question in Troy weight may be written upon the board or read from the text-book if pupils have one. Then require them *to state succinctly* what process will be required in working it, omitting detailed analysis.

NOTE.—To avoid repetition, it may here be stated, that the plan just mentioned may be taken in multiplication and division as well as in reduction, addition, and subtraction, with those portions of the weights, measures, etc., practice in which is of less general utility. Many practical examples in multiplication and division will arise under Avoirdupois weight, such as finding values at so much a pound, hundredweight or ton, or *vice versa*. Such examples may involve preliminary addition or subtraction, or both

Linear Measure. — Reduction. — Employ the denominations most in use—the inch, the foot, the yard, the rod, and the mile —very rarely, if ever, all in the same example. Omit cloth measure, or if briefly referred to, use only $\frac{1}{2}$s, $\frac{1}{4}$s, $\frac{1}{8}$ths and $\frac{1}{16}$ths. Give a very few examples to show the use of the chain and its subdivisions. Measuring-tapes usually have feet on one side and chains and links on the other. One may be employed to advantage in the class-room. To convert feet or yards into miles, and *vice versa*, use only 5,280 and 1,760 ; for instance, so many miles of railroad track having so many lbs. of iron to the yard, at so much a ton, etc., etc. Omit addition and subtraction, multiplication and division.

Surface Measure.—(Of very great practical importance.)—Treat briefly, in reduction. When $30\frac{1}{4}$ is used as a divisor let it be in very short examples. Give examples in addition and subtraction. In multiplication and division give examples in finding areas of rectangular figures, in feet, in yards, etc. Give the feet, or the chains, on the sides of rectangles, to find acres and value ; acres and hundredths the most usual form. Omit roods. Simple questions may be given occasionally, involving cost, in estimating for plastering, bricks, carpets, dress-linings, etc. ; also very simple questions in finding the area, circumference, or diameter of a circle *when square root is not involved,* using $\frac{2 ?}{ }$ or 3.1416 for ratio.

Solid Measure.—Employ only the inch, the foot, the yard, and the cord ; use the last but little. See that pupils understand the mutual relations of linear, surface, and solid measures, and that they are not convertible, the units being of totally different natures. Reduction—a few simple questions. Omit addition and subtraction. Give examples in finding cubic inches, feet, or yards, in boxes, bins, cellars, cylindrical cisterns, etc., etc. Some knowledge of *board measure*, giving very simple practical examples involving cost.

Dry and Liquid Measures.—Use no obsolete denominations. Omit beer measure. Remember that the barrel and the hogshead are not often measures in commerce. Simple examples in reduction. Omit addition and subtraction. Give the simplest possible examples, in connection with solid measure, in finding bushels or gallons in bins, vats, cisterns, etc., using 231 and 2150 cubic inches, and omitting fractions. No other multiplication or division should be required.

Circular Measure.—Treat briefly ; explain the terms and their use ; omit signs. Reduction—Short examples of two or three terms. Addition and Subtraction—Questions in difference of latitude and longitude. Geographical and statute miles on the meridian, on the equator, on parallels of 60°.

Time.—(In part very important.) Treat reductions very briefly. Do not involve more than two or three denominations in one example. Leap-year. Addition and subtraction. Difference of dates—by days, and by years, months and days. Relations of difference of longitudes to time. Explanations and examples. Conversion of longitude into time and *vice versa.*

Miscellaneous.—Practical examples in values, involving dozen, gross, quire, ream, quintal, barrels of flour, fish, etc., making out simple bills, receipts, etc.

Money.—Reduction and other simple exercises in Federal money are always in order from the Fifth Grade. Give but few examples in each rule in sterling money. Reduction of sterling to Federal and *vice versa*, omitting, of course, all reference to the percentage of exchange.

Pupils should know something of the money of Canada—identical with our own—the value of the franc, and the dollar of the Zollverein.

Fractional Compound Numbers.—The consideration of this subject has been deferred to avoid complicating it with simpler and more important matters. Reject all examples in addition, subtraction, multiplication, and division. In reduction *there are but two cases,* and the second of these is simply the converse of the first. Each divides into two varieties, in one of which the fraction is common and in the other decimal, but the principle applied in working is the same.

Be careful to select only those denominate numbers in which such fractional quantities are likely to need consideration, chiefly sterling money.

Examples : Case 1st.
{
A. $\frac{3}{7}$ of a bushel to pecks, quarts, etc.
B. .673 of a £, how many shillings, pence, etc., or dollars and cents.
}

" Case 2d.
{
A. 7ft. 95 in., what common fraction of a cubic yard?
B. 15 cwt. 38 lbs. are what decimal fraction of a ton?
£8 14s. 9½d are how many dollars and cents (at $4.866⅔)?
}

GEOGRAPHY.

SOUTH AMERICA.

Local Geography.—Begin with the continent of South America, as a whole, its boundaries, the names and relative positions, or boundaries, of its political divisions—a few of the chief capes and islands, the position and direction of the great plateaux and mountain ranges [use chalk sections roughly drawn on blackboard]—five or six of the most famous volcanoes. In the drainage, only two or three lakes, the courses of the Orinoco, the Amazon, the San Francisco, and the Parana described, and their great branches named and pointed out as systems, but not described.

The *local geography* of the several countries taken separately should be very brief, and should include a *review* of the matter previously considered in the study of the continent—that is, the relative positions or boundaries, the positions of the mountains and plateaux, the principal rivers, etc., etc., together with the capitals of the several countries, and about twenty-five of the other principal interior cities and seaports of the continent.

Descriptive Geography.—It will also be found most expeditious and effective to teach the descriptive geography of the continent first as a whole. From this, that of the several countries may be very easily deduced and distinctly remembered. It should include the *surface* of the country as mountain, plateau, or plain; the *zones;* the *climate* as modified by latitude, elevation, and the prevalent winds; the leading characteristics of the great plains and plateaux; a brief notice of *volcanoes* and *earthquakes;* a few of the principal *plants* and *animals;* the three *races*, their distribution, and their principal occupations, and the influence of the physical geography thereon; the European *languages* spoken; the chief *productions* and *exports*, vegetable, animal, and mineral, and the forms of *government*.

EUROPE.

Local Geography.—The geography of Europe should be so taught as to avoid the presentation of a large amount of minute detail. In local geography the boundaries of the continent, the names and relative positions or boundaries of its states; the position of its principal peninsulas, capes, gulfs, bays, seas, and straits; its chief highlands and lowlands; from twelve to fifteen principal mountain systems, the famous volcanoes, the great islands and groups of islands, seven or eight important lakes, including two or three in Switzerland; from twenty to twenty-five of the important rivers, specifying those which are important as commercial waterways; the names and positions of the capitals of the several countries, and from fifty to seventy of the other important cities.

Descriptive Geography.—The descriptive geography to be on the same plan as for North and South America. It should include the general surface, climate, and productions, the people and their industries, together with their relations of blood, language, commerce, etc., with the people of the United States. In reviewing the chief cities, state any important or interesting facts in relation to each.

Review.—The topics of the preceding grades should now be reviewed in outline.

This important requirement may best be met by making the exercise a comparative one. It should not be a home-lesson, but a vigorous class-room exercise, discarding for the time the text-book, and using the outline maps, the pointer, and the globe. For instance, a rapid pointing out and naming of all the countries of America and Europe, and their capitals, might constitute one lesson; all the mountain systems, plateaux, plains, and volcanoes, another; the climate and productions, a third; and so on.

HISTORY OF THE UNITED STATES.

General Suggestions.—The *leading purpose* of this study is that the pupil may understand the origin, character, and condition of the nation of which he is a part, and that he may be fitted for an intelligent exercise of his duties and responsibilities as a citizen.

It is obviously impossible to treat so comprehensive a subject exhaustively. The immaturity of the pupil's mind and the pressure of other studies alike forbid. Yet the leading facts and principles may be readily comprehended and remembered, and the outline which he is to retain be made from the first coherent and definite. To this end a simple *preliminary outline sketch* should be carefully fixed in the minds of the pupils of this grade, and frequently reverted to in the reviews of all the grades in which the subject is taught. The geography already learned will greatly simplify the process. This outline can be given most expeditiously and efficiently by means of oral instruction and the use of the map. It should be very brief, and, if it be thought expedient, should be reduced to writing by the pupil for reference. All detail should be reserved for the study of the text-book.

The following sketch is presented only as illustrative of this suggestion. Its modification by re-arrangement or otherwise, or the substitution of another in its place, may be found desirable.

OUTLINE SKETCH.

1st. The people of the United States are of European descent, excepting the negroes.

2d. Less than 400 years ago our ancestors knew nothing of the existence of this continent.

3d. Spain, guided by Italian genius, led the way to its discovery, exploration, and colonization.

4th. The first permanent English settlement within our limits was not effected until more than a century after the voyage of Columbus. In the interval, Spain and Portugal had possessed themselves of the shores and islands of the Mexican Gulf and of nearly all South America.

5th. For a century and a half the English colonies were confined to a narrow strip east of the Alleghanies.

6th. Spanish slavery exterminated the Indians of the West Indies. This led directly to the opening of the African slave trade, and indirectly to the introduction of slaves into our own country.

7th. The colonies had wars with the Indians in whose country they had settled, and with the neighboring French colonies. The French were subjugated and their territories occupied.

8th. Less than a century ago all European settlements were still dependent colonies.

9th. The necessities of distant colonial settlements had developed in the English colonies a spirit of self-reliance and political freedom, and a system of local and elective self-government.

10th. The expenses of the French wars left a heavy debt and led to unusual taxation. A tyrannical system of taxation led to the War of Independence, which fixed the national boundary at the Mississippi. The colonies had become States.

11th. The present form of government (the Constitution) was established soon after the close of the war, about eighty-three years ago.

12th. The number of States has been greatly increased by immigration and emigration. The population and wealth have increased many fold.

13th. By purchase and otherwise the national territory has been expanded to the Gulf of Mexico and to the Pacific and Arctic oceans.

14th. Since the War of Independence there have been three important wars: 1. A *war with England* in defense of naturalized citizens and in vindication of the rights of neutrals; 2. A *war with Mexico*, resulting from our annexation of Texas; 3. A *great civil war,* arising in part from questions originating in our colonial history and in part from more recent causes.

· *Lessons and Recitations.*—Lessons i n ni..ory should be assigned by topics and not by pages.

All verbatim recitations of sentences and paragraphs should be strictly forbidden, and the pupils should be required to state the facts in their own language.

Only such dates should be committed to memory as are indispensable as landmarks in history. The *sequence* of events, rather than the precise date of each, is what is chiefly necessary.

Maps, especially those of the text-books, snould be used whenever the subject may require it.

Historic episodes, however interesting, should not receive the careful study given to the essential narrative. The stories of Juan Ponce de Leon, the Conquest of Mexico, De Soto's Expedition, John Smith, Pocahontas, the Salem Witchcraft, etc., should indeed be carefully read, and, as far as may be necessary, explained; but, unless great care be taken by the teacher, the pupils will be apt to conceive that these are the most important portions of the history.

Important incidental allusions to European history, such as the rise of the English Puritans, the expulsion of the Stuarts, the French Revolution, etc., should be carefully but briefly explained. Great caution should be exercised throughout these lessons to state the facts in such a manner as not to wound the religious or political sensibilities of any.

Reviews.—Reviews of the portion already taught, with frequent references to the preliminary sketch, are of the highest importance. These reviews should take three distinct forms: the *Chronological,* the method usually followed in the text-book; the *Biographical*, requiring the pupil to state all that has been learned in regard to particular individuals; and the *Geographical*, requiring a statement of all important facts relating to the history of a locality. Many of the topics treated by the second and third of these methods necessarily become cumulative. For instance, the facts relating directly to George Washington will be gathered from at least three distinct and important periods in our history. A connected statement of the important events that have taken place in Philadelphia, or in the valleys of the Hudson and of Lake Champlain, or in the State of Virginia, will necessarily cover a large part of the general subject in the higher grades. Such statements must, of course, be brief, and will often be a mere chronological table.

Many of these reviews and certain parts of the regular recitations may be made spirited general exercises for the whole class by the use of the slate or of paper. The writing of the few essential dates, the sequence of important events, the names of important individuals, etc., are instances. The narrative reviews will necessarily be, for the most part, oral.

It will be observed that the system of reviews above suggested must, if faithfully carried out, result in a thorough unifying of the general subject in the mind of the pupil.

Suggestions for the Third Grade.—The essential points requiring careful study and frequent review in the history assigned to the Third Grade are given below. Other interesting facts usually stated in text-books should be carefully read, but should receive a less proportionate share of attention. In no other grade is a frequent reference to the maps so important.

Syllabus of Topics.

The voyage of Columbus; the naming of America; the occupation of the West India Islands and all the neighboring portions of the continent by the Spaniards; their enslavement of the Indians and its results (the last very briefly).

The discovery, exploration, and occupation of the St. Lawrence and Nova Scotia by the French.

Virginia.—Th settlement of Jamestown and the events directly leading to it. The cultivation of tobacco; the introduction of slavery; the navigation acts and Bacon's rebellion.

Maryland.—The Calverts; religious freedom; Clayborne.

New England.—The Plymouth Company and the settlements under their patent. The Puritans; their previous history and why called Pilgrims. The settlement of Plymouth; of Boston; of Dover; the Massachusetts Bay Colony. The settlement of Connecticut; of Rhode Island; provisions for religious freedom. The Union; Indian Wars (*read* only, and do not commit the details to memory). Andros; King William's War, its causes and results. The Salem Witchcraft (*read*). Queen Anne's War, its causes and results. King George's War, its causes and results.

New Netherlands.—Henry Hudson; the settlement on the Delaware; at Fort Orange; at Manhattan Island; the Dutch Governors; Kieft's conduct: Stuyvesant.

New York.—Changes of name; reconquest by the Dutch and final restoration to England. Andros; the extent of his rule. Dongan; Leisler; the burning of Schenectady; the Negro plot.

New Jersey.—Its name; its division; union with New York; final separation.

Delaware.—Its settlement by Swedes; its conquest by Stuyvesant.

Pennsylvania.—William Penn; his grant; his objects. The settlement of Philadelphia; the relations of Pennsylvania to Delaware.

North Carolina.—The grant of Charles II.; its geographical limits; John Locke.

South Carolina.—Charleston settled; Carolina divided into two separate governments in 1729.

Georgia.—Savannah settled; character and purposes of Oglethorpe.

9

The general condition of the English colonies in 1752. Their population ; their national derivation ; their industries, social condition, planters, patrons, and proprietors ; the causes which were developing a love of liberty.

Review *chronologically* under heads of the following sovereigns of England : Elizabeth ; James I.; Charles I.; Cromwell ; Charles II.; James II.; William and Mary ; Anne ; George I.; George II.; also, *biographically,* referring to Columbus, De Soto, Cortez, Cartier, Raleigh, etc., etc.

The French and Indian War.—This should be taught in outline, the principal points being :—The gradual extension of the English and French settlements leading to conflicting claims ; the explorations and posts of the French in the valleys of the Mississippi, the St. Lawrence, and the Lakes ; Marquette and La Salle ; the debatable land on the upper Ohio ; relatively small population of Canada ; the building of Fort Du Quesne, 1754 ; Colonial Congress at Albany, 1754 ; Braddock's and Johnson's Expeditions, and their results, 1755 ; Monckton's Expedition in 1755 ; cruel expulsion of the Acadians ; capture of Oswego, 1756 ; Fort William Henry, 1757 ; siege and capture of Louisburg, 1758 ; repulse at Ticonderoga, 1758 ; concentration of French forces at Quebec, by abandoning nearly all other posts ; battle of Quebec, 1759 ; results ; Treaty of Paris, 1763 ; its conditions.

In teaching the French and Indian War let the ten dates marked be studied by the *years* only. Read, but do not memorize, the *details* of military movements and events ; fix the sequence of events ; *use the map.*

In the biographical review, let the pupil tell very briefly of Washington, Braddock, Johnson, Monckton, Amherst, Abercrombie, Howe, Wolfe, Dieskau, and Montcalm.

ELEMENTARY SCIENCE.

(For Oral Instruction.)

PHYSIOLOGY AND HYGIENE.

The chief purpose of this study as a branch of Common School instruction is, to give useful practical knowledge of the laws of health. As the subject can receive, at most, but a small part of the time assigned to a single grade, it is the more important that only those parts of the study should be considered that are essential to the main purpose. Anatomy, which occupies so much space in many text-books, should not take up the time of the pupil, excepting so far as it may be absolutely necessary in order to teach the physiology and hygiene. It is a matter of little consequence to the pupil to know exactly the number of bones, or of pairs of muscles in his body, or to repeat their scientific names. Only those terms and facts should be introduced that are actually necessary in order to deal intelligently with the main subject. *Oral description* of structure or function should take the place of *definitions.*

The appliances necessary for teaching this branch are, the blackboard and charts. The teacher should carefully consider, at every step, to what extent the subject can be treated objectively. This can, in part, be done by drawing the pupil's attention to his own body, as in the case of the pulse, the veins, arteries, respiration, etc. For several very important parts of the subject, there is no better apparatus than that which can be procured without expense at any butcher's stall, such as the lungs and windpipe of a sheep; the diaphragm, the heart and part of the great tubes leading to and from it; the brain and the bony cavity which contains it; the eye; portions of the spinal cord and nerves; small glands; and portions of limbs, showing the relations of muscles, tendons, ligaments, and joints. None of these need present anything offensive or disgusting. Add to these a small knife, and reasonable preparation on the part of the teacher, and the instruction given will be both interesting and profitable. Where it would not be expedient to resort to this means of illustration, preparations (similar to those manufactured by Auzout) could be used, if procurable, and in their absence, diagrams and charts.

A *syllabus* of leading points is subjoined. It should not be expected that all these can be taught in one class, though all are important, nor that any point should be treated exhaustively.

Syllabus of Topics.

The pupil should be led to look upon the body as a complex apparatus for the use of his mind. To know that it consists primarily of—

First, a bony frame-work (the skeleton); *second,* a motor apparatus attached to the frame (the muscular system); *third,* a directing apparatus by which the mind controls the body (the brain, the nervous system, and the sensory organs); *fourth,* a general envelope protecting all the preceding, as well as serving other purposes (the skin).

He should then be led to see that every motion of the body or of its minutest part, however slight, and whether voluntary or involuntary, requires the *destruction* of a minute part of the organism and the removal of the destroyed part from the system; that this constant destruction and removal make necessary a corresponding *reconstruction* and *renewal,* by means of new material; and that for these purposes there are provided, *fifth,* a circulatory apparatus (the blood-vessels), to carry away old material and to distribute the new; *sixth,* an aerating apparatus (the respiratory system), to purify, warm, and enliven the circulating fluid; *seventh,* a system of drainage (the skin and the kidneys), to take from the blood a large part of the worn-out material; and *eighth,* an apparatus to prepare and supply the new material (the digestive and assimilative organs).

Under each of these heads a few points are noted:

1. The *bones,*—their composition and various uses; *joints* and their lubrication; important peculiarities of the spinal column; cautions as to injuring the large bones of an infant; the repair of broken bones, how effected.

2. The *muscles and tendons,*—their uses; their arrangement in

pairs, and why; how attached; how able to contract; effects of exercise; use of calisthenics.

3. The *nervous system*,—the means of becoming conscious of the external world; the spinal cord; its importance and protection; its ramifications; effects of severing or injuring the spinal cord; care of infants in this respect. The sympathetic system; the nerves as telegraph wires; the brain and its principal functions; uses of sleep; late hours, stimulants, etc.

The organs of the *special senses*,—touch, papillæ; taste; smell; the ear, its mechanism, hearing; the eye, its mechanism, sight; abuse of the eyes; myopy, its causes and prevention.

4. The *skin,*—its structure and uses; the perspiratory glands and tubes; uses of perspiration; importance of bathing; the proper time for bathing; proper clothing; sympathy of the skin with the lungs, with the digestive organs; caution against the exposure of the limbs, arms, or chests of little children; the skin as an absorbent; danger of cosmetics and hair-dyes; treatment of burns and scalds, etc.

5. The *circulatory system*,—the general relations of the heart, arteries, veins, and capillaries; the valves; the pulse; its rate; the rapidity of circulation. Effects of fresh air and exercise on the circulation; limits of exercise; dangers of excessive rope-jumping, etc. Effects of sleep on the circulation; effects of tight garments; of insufficient or improper food; wounds; how to know when an artery is wounded, and what to do.

6. The *respiratory system.*—(Practically the most important part of hygienic knowledge). The apparatus; how protected; arrangement of the ribs for flexibility, and for the expansion of the lungs; the muscles of the chest and the diaphragm; importance of the diaphragm; (show its positions at the beginning and at the end of an inspiration;) the trachea; the vocal chords; structure of the lungs; its air cells, and their membrane; exosmosis and endosmosis as concerned in respiration; intimate relations of the capillaries and air vessels; frequent full inspirations a means of increasing the capacity of the lungs; pernicious effects of tight lacing on the capacity and action of the lungs. The *air,*—its composition; relations of oxygen to the carbon and the hydrogen introduced with the food; products of respiration all invisible excepting watery vapor; the poisonous nature of carbonic acid; danger from it in wells, and in vats;

the effects of smaller quantities; the other substances thrown off by the lungs and the skin; the ventilation of class-rooms and of sleeping-rooms; effects of foul air from cellars, sewers, sinks, water-pipes, garbage, gas-lights, stoves, etc.; simple and cheap disinfectants; chloride of lime; chlorine; sulphate of iron; carbolic acid, etc. Respiration as affected by position, in standing, or in sitting, and especially in sitting to write or to draw.

7. *The digestive apparatus,*—the teeth, their uses, structure, and hygiene; a brief notice of the salivary glands, their position and uses; of the gullet; of the structure and function of the stomach; a brief notice of the duodenum, the intestines, and the lacteals; the importance and functions of the liver; the thoracic duct as the link between the digestive and the circulatory systems. Dyspepsia, its preventable causes and terrible consequences; common errors to be avoided in the preparation of food; common poisons and their antidotes.

SECOND GRADE.

Time allowed, about ten months.

LANGUAGE.

Reading.—Of the grade of a Fifth Reader, with instruction and exercises in elocutionary principles, and in vocal culture, as in the preceding grade.

Spelling.—Continued as in the preceding grade.

Definitions.—As in the preceding grade, with *word analysis*, or etymology.

English Grammar.—Analysis, parsing, and construction continued; also the correction of false syntax.

Composition.—Continued.

ARITHMETIC.

Mental and Written.—Commercial rules, through percentage, including profit and loss, commission, insurance, stocks, interest, discount, etc.; with carefully graded exercises in analysis and calculation.

The problems, to teach and illustrate the methods of computation employed in ordinary business transactions.

GEOGRAPHY AND HISTORY.

Geography.—Of Asia, Africa, and Oceanica, both local and descriptive; an outline review of the topics of the preceding grades.

History.—Of the United States, from 1763 to the present time, including the outlines of the Revolutionary War, the formation of the Union, the chief events of the national history, including also a brief outline of the great Civil War of 1861–5, and its results.

ELEMENTARY SCIENCE.

BY ORAL INSTRUCTION OR WITH A SIMPLE TEXT-BOOK.

Natural Philosophy.—The outlines of mechanics, hydrostatics, and pneumatics.

Astronomy.—Elementary astronomy, to include an explanation of the ordinary phenomena, and a brief account of the bodies constituting the Solar System.

WRITING AND DRAWING.

Penmanship.—Instruction and exercises of a similar character to those of the preceding grade, but more advanced.

Drawing.—Continued practice in the work prescribed for the preceding grades, to which should be added the sphere, the oblate and oblong spheroids, the hemisphere, with first lessons in shading ; also the drawing of rectangular solids from blocks in various positions, with a few simple directions as to perspective.

How to Teach

LANGUAGE.

Reading.—In this grade, the simple principles of elocution, taught in the preceding grades, should be carefully reviewed, and exercises to cultivate the voice, and confirm habits of distinct articulation should be continued to some extent. The *rationale* of good reading should, as occasion offers, be more fully explained, particularly as regards emphasis and modulation. Emotional reading should receive a fair share of attention. In classes or schools for males, exercises in declamation and recitation will be useful as an auxiliary.

The pieces read, being of a higher order of style and subject, should receive a more careful analysis on the part of the teacher, so as, by interrogation, to lead the minds of the pupils to a proper understanding of their subject-matter, and enable them to obtain all the *information* and *culture of mind* which they may be made the vehicle of imparting. Much time is apt to be misspent in this grade by simply permitting the pupils to read mechanically and listlessly pieces of difficult prose and poetry, which by earnest teaching might be made to fix in the minds, and often in the hearts, of the pupils so much that is valuable. Few tests of the earnestness and skill of a teacher are so thorough as the teaching of reading in this grade and the next. The subject, the style, the difficult or unusual words, the allusions, the course of reasoning, mode of treatment, etc., may all be made the basis of useful investigation by the pupil or of comment by the teacher.

The pieces read should comprehend a sufficient variety, both as to style and subject, to afford scope for what is above suggested. They should include didactic, narrative, argumentative and oratorical selections; extracts from distinguished writers in history, biography, popular science, etc., as well as the various departments of poetry; an important object of the instruction being to give a taste for reading more fully the works or compositions from which the extracts are made. Some account of the authors should be given in connection with the lessons.

Definitions and Word Analysis.—The *prefixes* and *suffixes* learned in the preceding grades should be reviewed by means of appropriate exercises involving the application of *easy roots*. For this purpose such words as the following may be used: — Drunk*ard*, Thrall*dom*, Dep*th*, *Ab*duct, Ver*sion*, Loc*al*,—involving English, or Anglo-Saxon, and Latin affixes only.

Next, the exercises should involve the use of easy *Latin* roots, such words as the following being used: A*vert*, Ad*vert*, Con*vert*, Per*vert*, etc.—*verse*, *ver*sion, di*verse*, etc. The application of various affixes, so as to form several words from the same root, will serve to impress the meaning of the root, *in its various forms*, on the mind of the pupil, as well as to review the affixes. Latin *words* need not be taught.

After a few exercises of this kind, words containing miscellaneous roots may be used; as, Pre*dict*, Sub*mit*, Re*ject*, In*vade*, etc.; then words containing prefixes and suffixes, as, Sub*mission*, Ob*ject*ion, Con*fluent*, Pro*cedure*, etc.; care being taken at first to select such words as are *regularly* formed, and the literal signification of which exactly or nearly agrees with the actual meaning as used.

The following form of *analysis* is suggested: *Abduct*, —formed from the root *duct* which means *to lead*, and the prefix *ab*, which means *away*. Hence, *abduct* means *to lead away*. Actual meaning, *to take away by stealth;* as, "They tried to *abduct* the child from his parents."

In this form of analysis, the *root* and its meaning are first stated; next, the *suffix;* then, the *prefix*, and then the literal meaning of the word, to be followed in all cases by the actual meaning, which is to be exemplified in a sentence.

After the pupil is sufficiently initiated in the method so as to analyze words with some degree of facility, the principal *Latin roots* should be taken up and taught exhaustively, alphabetically, or in the order of their difficulty. These should be followed by a few of the *Greek roots*, suffixes and prefixes, to be followed by the French or other foreign roots. The Anglo-Saxon or English roots should, if taught at all, follow these. All beyond the Latin roots, and if necessary some of these, may be reserved for the First Grade.

Exercises in the *formation of words from given roots* should form a prominent part of the exercises used to familiarize the pupils with the meaning of the *roots*, as well as the meaning of words derived from them. For the purpose of this instruction the English form of the root is all that needs to be taught. In this way the subject will be freed from much complexity. Thus, after analyzing the word *dentist*, the pupil gives, as far as he can recall to mind, the words derived from the root *dent ;* as *dent*al, *dent*ate, *dent*oid, *dent*ition, *denti*-frice, *dent*iform, in*dent*, etc. Words such as *dentistry* are to be considered as of *secondary* formation, and to be analyzed by considering *dentist* the primitive. In this way the analysis of a very large class of words will be greatly simplified.

The analysis of words is, of course, etymological ; but it is rather introductory to the study of etymology than, properly considered, a part of that study. The science which treats more directly and specially of the origin and relation of verbal forms, their primitive meaning, their combinations, and the varied significations with which their derivatives have been used from time to time, is scarcely appropriate at this stage of the pupil's progress. The instruction derived from such exercises as are above indicated is exceedingly valuable for its practical usefulness ; but such facts as that *half* is the Anglo-Saxon *healf, home* the Anglo-Saxon *hám,* and the German *heim,* etc., etc., are interesting and useful for a very different purpose, and should occupy a more advanced place in an educational scheme.

English Grammar.—In this grade, the pupils should be exercised in the *analysis* and *parsing* of sentences of a higher grade of difficulty ; but those of anomalous or peculiar construction should be avoided. The analysis, except for review, should be only in outline, so as to show the "general structure of the sentence," and enable the pupil to see clearly the relation of the clauses or members. This is essential to a correct and definite understanding of the *meaning* of the sentence, as well as for the application of rules having reference to the construction of sentences. Some knowledge of *punctuation* should be imparted in this connection.

The following sentence analyzed will illustrate the requirements of this grade in this respect:

"Pay the debts which thou owest; for he who gave thee credit relied upon thy honor, and to withhold from him his due is both mean and unjust."

Analysis.—This sentence consists of two members: 1. *"Pay the debts,"* etc., to *" owest ;"* 2. *" He who gave thee,"* etc., to *" unjust."* These members are connected by *"for."*

The first member contains the clause *"which thou owest,"* used as an adjunct of *" debts."*

The second member consists of the two clauses: *"He who gave thee,"* etc., to *" honor,"* and *" To withhold,"* etc., to *" unjust."*

This should be followed by the *parsing* of the most important words, which will show whether a more minute analysis of the sentence should be required of the pupil or not.

As far as may be necessary, the *structure* of the sentence, discovered by analysis, should be made the subject of rhetorical criticism, with reference to its *clearness* in expressing the meaning intended to be conveyed, its *propriety, unity, harmony,* etc. The thought itself may be, to some extent, analyzed, and subjected to critical remark.

The *parsing*, as an application of the rules and principles peculiar to our own language, should also, as far as possible, be so conducted as to have a *critical* end in view. This will greatly improve the pupils in their use of language, by rendering them more alert in discovering inaccuracies, as well as by impressing more deeply upon their minds a knowledge of the rules by which they should be guided in expression.

Exercises in the *correction of false syntax* should be abundantly used in this grade.

Composition.—The construction of sentences should assume the character of extended composition, the themes being selected by the pupils themselves or assigned by the teacher. Of course, care should be taken that the themes are of a simple character—appropriate to the mind of a child, and calculated to awaken thought, not to repress it, as is too often the case when difficult subjects, of an abstract or too comprehensive character, are chosen for the exercise.

ARITHMETIC.

The commercial arithmetic of this grade differs from that taught in the preceding grades, chiefly in the introduction of the various forms of percentage. The divisions of percentage should be presented in the following order: First, *simple percentage*, in four cases—one fundamental and three derived; second, the *applications* of simple percentage, technically known as *Commission, Brokerage,* and *Profit and Loss,* following the same order and with the same analysis as in the four cases of simple percentage.

Those who prefer to do so may readily combine these divisions under the general head of "percentage not involving time."

The third division of the subject is *interest,* or "percentage involving time." It has five cases—one fundamental and four derived.

In treating the percentage rules many skillful teachers prefer to introduce algebraic formulæ, in which the initial letters of the several terms employed in percentage are the elements. To this course there is no objection, *provided* that the formulæ be not employed in the mental arithmetic, and that they accompany the usual *analysis* and be not used as a *substitute* for it. With this exception, the processes and explanations of the mental arithmetic should not differ from those of the written arithmetic, the chief distinction between the two being, that in the latter the numbers are too large to be carried in the mind.

The subject of arithmetic being necessarily to a great extent cumulative, the teacher of this grade is especially advised to read over the directions given in the preceding grades, and in particular the table on page 162. For the sake of brevity, the terms base, percentage, etc., are employed in the following syllabus of topics in the usual technical sense of the text-books.

SYLLABUS OF TOPICS.

The term *percentage*—exercises in reading per cent.

Examples—Read the following, exemplified and defined first as decimal fractions, and then as per cent.: .75, .8, .605, .003, $.08\frac{1}{2}$, $.00\frac{3}{4}$, etc.

Exercises in changing common fractions to per cent. and *vice versa*:

Examples—$\frac{3}{4}$, $\frac{7}{8}$, $\frac{450}{900}$, $\frac{33}{88}$, $2\frac{1}{5}$, $1\frac{2}{11}$, $\frac{14}{7}$, etc., how many hundredths? what per cent.?

Examples—25 per cent., 75 per cent., $33\frac{1}{3}$ per cent., $14\frac{2}{7}$ per cent., $88\frac{8}{9}$ per cent., 325 per cent., $137\frac{1}{2}$ per cent., etc., are equivalent to what common fractions?

NOTE.—The common business fractions, halves, thirds, etc., to twelfths, inclusive, should be reduced to per cent., and the pupils made thoroughly familiar with them.

SIMPLE PERCENTAGE.

1ST CASE (*Fundamental*).—To find the *percentage*, the *base* and rate *being* given.

See table, page 162.—To find a given fractional part of a given number.

Examples—How much is 9 per cent. of 750? Had $750 in the bank; drew out 9 per cent. How much was it?

Analysis as in the multiplication of decimal fractions.

NOTE.—When this form of the case has been taught, its *modifications* should immediately follow.

Example—Had $750; paid out 9 per cent. How much had I left?

Example—Had $750; earned 9 per cent. more. How much had I then?

2D CASE (*Derived*).—To find the *rate* when the *percentage* and *base* are given.

See table, page 162.—To find what fraction one given number is of another given number.

Examples—140 is what per cent. of 400?

"   Had 400 sheep; sold 140. What per cent. did I sell?

Analysis as in reducing a common fraction to a decimal fraction whose denominator is hundredths.

Modifications of Case 2d:

Example—I had 400 sheep; I now have 540. What is the per cent. of increase?

Example—I had 400 sheep; I now have only 260. What is the per cent. of decrease? or, what per cent. have I left?

3d. CASE (*Derived*).—To find the *base* when the *percentage* and the *rate* are given.

See table, page 162.—To find the number of which another number is a given fraction.

Example—140 is 35 per cent. of what number?

"   Sold 140 sheep, which was 35 per cent. of my flock. How many had I at first?

Analysis as in simple fractions—140 is $\frac{35}{100}$ of what number?

Modifications of Case 3d:

Example—Sold 140 sheep, which was 35 per cent. of my flock. How many had I left?

Example—Sold 140 sheep, and have 65 per cent. of my flock remaining. How many had I at first?

4th CASE (*Derived.*)—To find the *base* when the *amount* (or difference) and *rate* are given.

To find a number which differs by a given fractional part of itself from a given number.

Example—What number is by 8 per cent. of itself more than 351? or 351 is 8 per cent. more than what number?

Example—My flock of sheep increased 8 per cent.; I then had 351. How many had I at first?

Example—I lost 8 per cent. of my sheep, and had 299 remaining. How many had I at first?

Note.—Axiom.—The *base* is 100 per cent. of itself. This is only a form of the fundamental axiom of fractions, $1 = \dfrac{n}{n}$

Analysis of last two examples.

> First, find the per cent. of the base, represented by the given number; 100 per cent. + 8 per cent. = 108 per cent. of the base; 100 per cent.—8 per cent. = 92 per cent. of the base.
>
> Second, proceed as in 3d case—351 is $\frac{108}{100}$ of what number?—299 is $\frac{92}{100}$ of what number?

As a part of the general review, give an example in the fundamental case, and let the pupils derive the other three cases from it, and then their modifications.

Commission and Brokerage and Profit and Loss are but applications of simple percentage. Each presents itself under all the four cases, but requires no special additional teaching, except in regard to the technical terms employed.

INTEREST.—Teach the definitions of the terms employed; the distinction of simple from compound interest; the legal rate of U. S. and of the State in which the school is situated.

Note.—In classes of an average character, *one* good method, in solving examples in interest, will be found to give better results than *two or more*. Whatever method be employed, the pupils should, from the first, be carefully guarded against considering and calling the multiplier a concrete number. For instance, multiplying $15, the interest for 1 year, *by* 3 *years*, etc., is, of course, an absurd statement.

If the six per cent. method be employed, it should be carefully analyzed, and the pupils should not be allowed to sacrifice sense to conciseness by such statements as "the half of 7 months is 3 cents-and-a-half"—one-sixth of 24 days is 3 mills, etc., etc. As a preliminary to applying this method, the class should have a thorough training on such questions as the following: Find .207 of $185.75; find .0685 of $36.25; (see preceding grade).—In 2 years, 3 months, and 20 days, at 6 per cent. per annum, *what decimal fraction of the principal* is equal to the interest? at 7 per cent? at 5? at 8? at 7½? etc.

Give examples involving the various forms of the difference of dates—the application of the six per cent. method to a given or ascertained number of days. Example : Interest of $340 from Jan. 5th to July 2d, at 6 per cent. Examples involving the method when the year is estimated to consist of 365 days, should also be given.

Give examples in Bank Discount, and explain its similarity to Compound Interest in being the interest on the *amount*.

NOTE—(On the derived cases of simple Interest.)—In teaching the four derived cases of simple interest, begin with an easy example in the fundamental case, and from that derive the others in their order, being particularly careful to teach that, being derived, they all require division ; that, to find the *rate*, the given interest is to be divided by the interest of the given principal at 1 *per cent.;* to find the *time*, by the interest of the given principal for 1 *year;* to find the *principal*, by the interest of a *principal of $1 ;* and that, in the fifth case, the given *amount* is to be divided by the *amount of $1.*

Give examples in True Discount, distinguishing carefully its difference in principle, and therefore of method, from Bank and Commercial Discount

Partial Payments and Compound Interest should be very briefly treated, and with very simple examples.

The form and nature of a promissory note, and the meaning of the several terms applicable to it, and the form of bills and receipts are included in the work of this grade.

GEOGRAPHY AND HISTORY.

Geography.—Complete the local and descriptive geography of one continent or grand division before beginning that of another. The same general plan should be pursued as in the preceding grades. If the prominent physical features of Asia, for instance, be first taught as a whole, including the climate, the pointer and the outline map being used to expedite the process, the descriptive geography of the individual countries will involve but little labor, and will be easily remembered.

The geography of Asia is by far the most important and interesting; that of Africa and Oceanica is comparatively simple, and should be reduced, in teaching, to the narrowest limits that will give a clear view of the general physical conditions of surface and climate, and of the social conditions of the various races, together with a knowledge of the leading productions and exports, and the location of the principal cities.

Review.—The review should be as in the preceding grades. One of the most comprehensive and important elements of a *general review* of the entire subject is, to show the relations of Europe to all the other grand divisions of the globe, as to conquest, settlement, colony, language, etc. This may be taught in a very brief and general way, and is indispensable to a correct outline knowledge of the present condition of the human race,—one of the most important objects of the study of geography.

History.—The teacher is particularly referred to the General Suggestions in regard to U. S. History, in the preceding grade.

The Outlines of the Revolutionary War.—(Teach as in the French and Indian War.)

Causes of the Revolution.—Navigation Acts—Restriction of Colonial manufactures—effects of war on the national debt of England—taxation without representation—the Stamp Act, 1765; its nature—causes which led to its repeal—the Tea Tax—riot in Boston, 1770—the Boston "Tea Party," its immediate causes, and its consequences—nature of the Port Bill, 1774—first Congress at Philadelphia—its measures—*Lexington, April* 19, 1775—its effects upon the country—Bunker Hill—siege of Boston—Washington appointed Commander-in-Chief—evacuation of Boston,

and subsequent general drift of military events towards the west
and south—*Declaration of Independence, July* 4, 1776—battle of
Long Island—its purposes and results—retreat to the Delaware
—capture of the Hessians at Trenton—Princeton—La Fayette—
British move on Philadelphia, 1777—Chad's Ford—its consequences—Burgoyne's invasion, its route and purpose, 1777—
Schuyler—Burgoyne's disasters—Gates—the two battles of Still-
water—Clinton's movements—*Burgoyne's surrender, October,*
1777—its far-reaching consequences—the French alliance and
assistance—British retreat from Philadelphia—Battle of Mon-
mouth, 1778—New York the base of the British—destruction
along the coasts of Connecticut and Virginia—Wyoming—battle
of the Chemung, 1779—it breaks forever the power of the Iro-
quois—Paul Jones—Charleston captured, 1780—large numbers of
Tories in the south—consequent years of guerrilla warfare—Sumter—Marion—Gates at Camden—destruction of his army, and of
Sumter's force—Arnold's treason—the mutiny at Morristown,
1781—its causes—condition of the army—Robert Morris—Arnold's ravages—Greene's retreat—battles in Carolina and their
consequences—Cornwallis at Yorktown—combination of the
French and American forces—*Surrender of Cornwallis, October,*
1781—its effects in America and in England—Treaty of Paris,
1783—its terms—condition of the country at the close of the
war.

Articles of Confederation, 1776-1777-1781—the government
before 1781—after 1781—Shays's rebellion, 1786—leads to a convention to revise the Articles—a new *Constitution* devised instead,
1787—adopted by the States—*goes into operation,* 1789.

In the biographical *review* include a brief notice of Henry,
Hancock, Franklin, Lee, Jay, Livingston.

1789-1797.—*Washington's Administration—Domestic* history;
the cabinet—leading measures—States admitted—their former relations. *Foreign* relations—Trouble with France, and its causes.

NOTE 1.—*Read* the Indian war. The teacher will give a brief statement concerning Boone, Clark, the original extent of Virginia, and the Ordinance of
1787.

NOTE 2.—Give, orally, a very brief outline account of the French Revolution,
the resulting relations of France and England and of Europe generally; the
continuance of these wars to 1815. Refer particularly to the fact that political
differences in the United States were, to a great extent, based upon our foreign

policy, and that we were at last drawn into the vortex of the great European wars in 1812.

Refer also to Washington's Farewell Address, and give, briefly, a very few of its leading points.

1797–1801.—*Adams's Administration.* — *Foreign* relations ;—continued troubles with France.—*Domestic* history ;—unpopular measures—the death of Washington—removal of the Capital.

1801–1809.—*Jefferson's Administration.*—*Domestic* history ;—admission of Ohio—its previous relations—the Louisiana purchase—its immediate and subsequent importance—Hamilton and Burr, 1804—a sketch of the history of each—Fulton's first steamboat, 1807.—*Foreign* relations;—Tripolitan war, 1801–1805, its causes and results.—(*Read* the detail.) The state of Europe, and the importance of our carrying-trade—extraordinary measures of France and England in relation to the rights of neutrals—English claims of right of search and impressment—bearing of the impressment claim upon our naturalized citizens, and our national honor—" Once a subject, always a subject "—affair of the Leopard and Chesapeake, 1807—Orders in Council and the Milan Decree, 1807—Embargo, 1807–1809—Non-intercourse Act, 1809.

1809–1817.—*Madison's Administration.*—The entire interest centers in the *Foreign* relations—they control the *Domestic* history. Berlin Decree abolished, 1810.

NOTE.— *Read* the affair of the Little Belt—Indian War.

War declared June 19, 1812—its two chief causes.

NOTE.—*Read* the detail of the military and naval operations ; show briefly, in outline, first, the several aggressive expeditions into Canada, from Detroit to the St. Lawrence—their general failure ; second, the smallness of the navy—its brilliant success, but little direct influence on the fortunes of the war, excepting on the lakes—utter destruction of American commerce ; third, the aggressive expeditions of the British, the Americans being chiefly on the defensive after 1812—Indian war in the West and Southwest—invasions from Canada—blockade of all important ports—naval and military expedition against Washington and Baltimore—invasion by the way of Lake Champlain—expedition against New Orleans, and its purposes—final repulse of all these attempts, and similar fate of renewed aggressions of the Americans against Canada—destruction of the Indian power.

Give the sequence of leading events, omitting the dates, except as to years.

The Hartford Convention—its alleged purposes—its effects—treaty of peace, December, 1814—a part of the general pacification of Europe upon the fall of Napoleon—the causes of the war not even alluded to in the treaty—have these questions ever been settled? If so, when and how?

NOTE.—*Read* the second Barbary war, 1812-1815—its causes and results.

In the biographical review include a brief notice of Hamilton, Burr, Randolph, Fulton, Whitney, De Witt Clinton.

1817-1825.—*Monroe's Administration.—Domestic* history;—Missouri Compromise, 1820—formation of new parties on questions of commerce and finance—Whigs and Democrats—the leading questions until 1845.—*Foreign* relations;—purchase of Florida—the Monroe Doctrine, 1822, its origin and importance.

1825-1829.—*John Quincy Adams's Administration.*—Tariff of 1828—leads to the defeat of the Whigs and the election of Jackson.

1829-1837.—*Jackson's Administration.—Domestic* history;—United States Bank—nullification, 1832—Clay's Compromise. *Foreign* relations;—the French indemnity.

1837-1841.—*Van Buren's Administration.*—Panic of 1837—Sub-Treasury Bill, 1840—political revolution.

1841-1845.—*Harrison—Tyler's Administration.—Domestic* history;—the Bankrupt Law—Dorr's Rebellion.—*Foreign* relations;—the Maine boundary—annexation of Texas.

1845-1849.—*Polk's Administration.*— *Domestic* relations now give direction to *Foreign* policy—Oregon boundary—chain of causes leading to the Mexican war—boundary claimed by Texas—Mexican war, May, 1846, to Feb., 1848.

NOTE.—*Read* the details; give the leading military events in sequence, omitting all dates, excepting years. Teach with the following grouping. *Northern operations*—Taylor east of the Rio Grande—west of it—Wool—Kearney—Doniphan—Fremont. *Southern operations*—Scott's campaign.

Treaty of Guadalupe Hidalgo—its terms—discovery of California gold in 1848—its important subsequent influence upon the national development.

1850-1853.—*Taylor and Fillmore's Administration.*—The Slavery question the leading element in the subsequent history—the California question, 1850—its alleged relation to the Missouri Compromise—death of Taylor—Clay's Compromise Bill, 1850.

1853-1857.—*Pierce's Administration.*—Effects of the Fugitive Slave Bill—the Kansas-Nebraska Bill, 1854—it annuls the Missouri Compromise—rise of a new party, "Free-soil" or Republican—civil war in Kansas, its causes—flow of immigrants into that territory.

1857-1861.—*Buchanan's Administration.*—Continuation of the Kansas trouble—John Brown's affair—its effects—split of the great Democratic party—four Presidential candidates—election of Lincoln—extreme doctrine of State Rights—secession of South Carolina, Dec., 1860—Fort Sumter—more States secede—Confederate government formed, Feb., 1861.

1861-1865.—*Lincoln's Administration.*—Civil war—Fort Sumter, April 12, 1861—effects upon the North—the President's proclamation—more States secede, making eleven in all.

NOTE.—*Read* the details of the war ; show the importance of the question of foreign intervention, and the efforts on both sides in regard to it.

In the *Review* show that the operations of the Confederates were mainly defensive, except in the great sorties of Lee at Antietam and Gettysburg, of Hood at Nashville, and of Early at Chambersburg—all of which were repelled. That the main objects of the aggressive movements of the Union troops were, 1st, the destruction of Lee's army; 2d, The opening of the Mississippi—that after the opening of that river by the fall of Forts Henry and Donelson, and the subsequent capture of New Orleans and Vicksburg, the lines were contracted by a movement from the northwest to the southeast, ending in Sherman's march from Atlanta to Savannah and Goldsboro'. The leading incidents will then readily fall into place.—Show the importance of the blockade, the chief function of the fleet—also, but very briefly, the enormous expenditure of men and money on both sides, and the measures by which they were obtained.

1865-1869.—*Johnson's Administration.*—Death of Lincoln—the two subjects of leading importance—1st. Providing for the public debt — 2d. Reconstruction — the 13th Amendment — the President and Congress quarrel—impeachment—the French in Mexico, and the demand of the United States Government—purchase of Alaska—laying of the first Atlantic telegraph cable.

1869-1873.—*Grant's Administration.*—Pacific Railway—14th and 15th Amendments—the Alabama question—leading provisions of the treaty of Washington—the Geneva Arbitration—the settlement of the northwest boundary question.

Addenda—The rapid development of the country since 1815 —the leading elements in that development—emigration and immigration—the Erie Canal and the Lakes as the great waterway—steam and steamboats—railways—telegrapns.　In the biographical review include a notice of prominent men, such as Calhoun, Clay, Webster, Seward, Greeley, Morse, etc., etc.

ELEMENTARY SCIENCE.

Natural Philosophy.—The suggestion to use "a simple text-book" should not be interpreted as a recommendation to dispense with oral instruction in this branch.　On the contrary, the proper use of the text-book is as an auxiliary, as a general guide to the teacher in the selection of subjects, and as an important help to the pupil in preparing at home for the recitation of a lesson which has been previously explained and illustrated in the class-room.

Any system of procedure which omits this preliminary oral instruction is certainly not worthy of the name of *teaching*.　The text-book should be indeed brief and simple, and its illustrations must necessarily be few.　But the teacher should supply the further illustration and experiment which will certainly be found to be necessary; it is also of especial importance that the pupils should themselves be in every way encouraged and led to report such instances of the applications of the principles they have been taught, as *they* can themselves discover in the phenomena and incidents of their daily life and experience, both in and out of school, so that, as far as possible, they may form habits of observation and reflection.

The teacher will find a wide difference in the readiness with which individual pupils will conceive and apply scientific principles.　With a few, the bare statement of a principle will often enable them to point out its simpler applications. The results of a certain order of experiments, and the simpler deductions from them, will be promptly anticipated by such minds. But it will not be so with all; and with some, only by careful and repeated illustration will the principles which interpret the facts presented, be clearly apprehended. In all experiments the pupils themselves should be made as far as possible participants. In reviews they should be called upon to repeat the experiments or statements made by the teacher or given in the text, and to give the proper explanation. They should also be encouraged to try further experiments for themselves at home, and to furnish an account or a repetition of them in the class-room, if possible.

The teacher should also particularly remember that it is not necessary to follow slavishly the exact order or selection of topics given in the text-book. The teacher, and not the book, should be the master. An intelligent pupil will not be long in finding out whether or not the statements in the text are the limit of his teacher's acquisitions. The great majority of young minds are hungry for this sort of knowledge, and it will unquestionbly be the teacher's fault if that appetite be not at the same time both gratified and stimulated.

Care should be taken, when the scientific meaning of a common term differs greatly from the popular one, to point out clearly such difference, in order that the pupil be not misled by thinking that he knows that of which he is really ignorant. Among the many cases in which this will be found necessary, the terms *porosity, porous, solid,* and *impenetrability* may be taken as instances. It is by no means necessary that the pupil should be able to give an exact and comprehensive scientific *definition* of such terms; a few analytical ques-

10

tions by the teacher will readily show if the subject is understood.

When a lesson from the text-book is to be given for home study, it should first be carefully illustrated and explained. No teacher will be likely to do this as well as he should, if he give the subject no thought until about to assign the lesson. After receiving these explanations the pupil will be far less liable to misconceive or, as sometimes happens, to fail utterly to comprehend the statements of the text. As far as the subject will allow, he should be led through the medium of *experiment* to a knowledge of the *facts*. The facts once ascertained, the *principles* underlying them may be deduced. A limit will, sooner or later, be reached, where the more recondite parts of the subject, so far as they may be entered upon, *must be taught empirically*, in consequence of the pupil's limited knowledge of other departments of science.

For instance, suppose that the teacher has already experimentally established in his pupil's mind a general idea of the terms *force* and *gravity*, and that he now wishes to lead him to know that " the *weight* of a body is the *measure* of the *force* of *gravity*" acting upon it, and after that to establish the *law of its variation*. Let the teacher or one of the pupils borrow a common spring-scale—the smaller and simpler the better—let a pupil *pull*, and at the same time notice that he is exerting a *force*, that the position of the index will vary with the *degree* or *amount* of force, that the *motion* is in the *direction* of the force, however the instrument may be held ; now place a succession of heavy bodies in the scale, and let him notice that the *effects* are identical with those produced by his muscular force. He will no longer *vaguely* conceive that the effect produced

upon the scale is because the body is *heavy* (which was
to him a vague term), but because the earth actually
pulls it as he did, though no connecting bond is visible,
as when *he* pulled. A knitting-needle suspended and
balanced upon a thread and acted upon by a simple
magnet, will clearly convince him that a *force* may be
exerted by one body upon another without actual contact. You have clearly defined for him the idea that
"the weight of a body is the measure of the earth's attraction upon it." If now you wish to teach the law
of the *variation of the weight* of a body of invariable
mass, as should indeed be done, the next step must be
empirical. The pupil's deficiency in mathematics for-
bids any other course of procedure. The "Law of
Gravitation" must be *stated to* him, together with the
reason for so doing without proof. It will develop in
many a mind an earnest desire to supply that deficiency.
The law of the *variation* of weight may now be readily
deduced by first adding to the pupil's mathematical
knowledge the technical meaning of the term *square*,
and then giving a variety of simple arithmetical problems to illustrate it.

There is, perhaps, no graver or more common error
in relation to this subject, among earnest teachers who
are called upon to teach it, than the notion that this
requires expensive or complicated apparatus. The very
contrary is the case in the great majority of instances.
Expensive apparatus, with its show of brass and glass,
has a direct tendency to repress the most precious element and evidence of a teacher's success—experiment-
ing at home by the pupils themselves. The principles
of the *lever* may be just as well developed by means of
a pen-handle, a pointer, or a window-pole, as by a polished brass or steel bar; a large spool makes an excel-

lent *wheel and axle ;* a ribbon-block a good single pulley, fixed or movable; a slate, a book, or a shingle, an *inclined plane ;* a pocket-knife will soon furnish a good *wedge* from a little piece of board, while the use of the blade itself is an excellent illustration of the application of the principle; and a large screw or a discarded auger-bit, with a knitting-needle or a pen-holder for a lever, makes an efficient *single screw.* And so through every department of the subject. Nothing marks more fully the ability of a teacher than fertility in such resources. Strings, tops, balls, and marbles; pop-guns, potato-mills, bean-shooters, and putty-blowers, and the thousand and one nameless articles to be found in pupils' pockets, furnish an exhaustless mine of apparatus, and good apparatus too, for the skillful teacher. The immortal Dalton wrought out his atomic chemical theory with apparatus which may be excelled in many a junk or old bottle shop ; and the teacher determined to succeed will find that " where there is a will there is a way."

SYLLABUS OF TOPICS.

(*To be illustrated as far as possible objectively.*)

CONSTITUTION, FORMS, AND PROPERTIES OF MATTER.—Illustrate the following terms—body or mass, molecule, atom ; solid, fluid, liquid, gas; sensible or cellular pores, as in bread or sponge ; physical or intermolecular pores, as in iron, water, air, and every form of matter ; porosity.

Extension, impenetrability, rarity and density, compressibility and expansibility, inertia, mobility.

FORCE AND ITS FORMS.—*Attraction and repulsion :* refer briefly to the fact that atoms and atomic forces are treated of in chemistry. Indestructibility of matter to be briefly explained.

MOLECULAR FORCES.—*Cohesive force :* the properties of matter which are dependent upon cohesion ; tenacity, flexibility, brittleness, hardness, ductility, malleability; the properties dependent upon cohesion and molecular repulsion; elasticity. Illustrate the elasticity of flexure; of compression; of expansion; of torsion. Relations of solids, liquids, and gases to molecular attraction and repulsion.

Adhesive force: properties dependent upon adhesion; capillary attraction and its uses in organic and inorganic nature.

Divisibility of matter—into particles by mechanical force; into molecules by heat, solution, etc.—What forces are overcome in each case, and by what other force.

MECHANICAL FORCE.—*Gravity*—why called universal gravitation; its simplest phenomena; its law; weight, a measure of gravity.

MECHANICS OF SOLIDS.—Center of gravity; line of direction, plumb-line; stable, unstable, and indifferent equilibrium.

Simple Machines.—Lever, with simple problems in mental arithmetic; pulley, wheel-and-axle, inclined plane, wedge, screw.

MECHANICS OF LIQUIDS (*Hydrostatics*).—Mobility of liquids, and its cause; their small compressibility; pressure in every direction; gravity the primary cause; equality of pressure at a given point; variation of pressure with depth; meaning of the term *level;* why still water has a level surface; why the hydrant water flows from the open tap; at what height it ceases to flow, and why; other illustrations of the same principle; what that principle is; the hydrostatic paradox; the hydraulic press; specific gravity; the hydrometer; why iron ships float.

MECHANICS OF GASES (*Pneumatics*).—*Air*—its compressibility, expansibility, and elasticity; chief mechanical difference from liquids; its weight; its pressure in all directions; upward pressure and how shown; the mercurial barometer, its construction, principle, and uses; Torricelli's experiment; Pascal's experiment; the aneroid barometer; height of the atmosphere, and gradual diminution of its density.

Astronomy.—The teacher should, at first, endeavor to awaken an interest in the subject by referring to some of the most impressive and beautiful phenomena connected with the sun, the moon, the stars, planets,

comets, and meteors. He should endeavor to induce
the pupils to observe more attentively these phenomena,
and to excite their curiosity to know about them. Encourage them to ask questions in relation to what they
observe; as, Why does the moon change its appearance?
Why does the sun rise so far from the east point, or set
so far from the west point at certain times in the year?
What bright star was in the west on a certain night, at
a particular time? and other such questions, some of
which the pupils are, of course, to be told cannot be
answered until they have further studied the subject.
Thus they will learn to study the science from nature
as well as from the book.

Let the general phenomena of the heavens be first
explained; the movements of the sun, moon, stars, and
planets in relation to the horizon; the circles of daily
motion; the difference between planets and fixed stars;
how to distinguish some of the former, etc.

The following topics may then be taken up in their
order: The *Earth*, its form, magnitude, motions, etc.;
Circles, and angular *distances* on the Earth and in the
heavens; *Day* and *Night;* the *Seasons*, etc: these topics
should be illustrated by the use of a Tellurian, and
Problems for the Globe should be used for the purpose
of exercise and illustration.

Next, teach the general arrangement of the *Solar
System.* Inferior and superior planets—their magnitudes, revolutions, position of orbits, periodic times,
and apparent motions.

The *mathematical definitions* necessary for the proper understanding of this portion of the subject should
be taught incidentally thereto.

FIRST GRADE.

LANGUAGE.

Reading, Spelling, Definitions, and Word Analysis, continued as in the preceding grade.

English Grammar.—Analysis, Parsing, and Syntactical criticism and correction, continued; the anomalous and idiomatic forms to be taught and explained.

Composition.—Exercises on selected themes; Practice in Letter Writing, commercial and social.

MATHEMATICS.

Mental and Written Arithmetic.—Continued and reviewed, including the rules pertaining to the mensuration of regular plane surfaces and solid bodies; with exercises in analysis and calculation, continued.

Algebra.—Through equations of the first degree.

Geometry.—The geometry of plane figures, with practical applications.

GEOGRAPHY AND HISTORY.

Geography.—The Outlines of Physical Geography.

History.—The Outlines of Ancient and Modern.

ELEMENTARY SCIENCE.

BY ORAL INSTRUCTION, OR WITH A SIMPLE TEXT BOOK.

Natural Philosophy.—Simple outlines completed, to include Acoustics, Pyronomics, Optics, Magnetism, and Electricity.

Astronomy.—Elementary, continued and completed.

Chemistry.—Elementary principles and facts.

WRITING AND DRAWING.

Penmanship.—Instruction to be continued as in the preceding grade, with practice in the writing of paragraphs, verses, business forms, notes, superscriptions, etc.

Drawing.—Drawing objects of regular form in perspective, block combinations, etc., with shading; copying pictures of familiar objects, animals, etc., with easy landscapes, as far as the time may permit; also (for males) simple architectural and mechanical drawing.

MISCELLANEOUS BRANCHES.

Book-keeping.—Single and double entry; with careful instruction in the principles of the latter.

Constitution of the United States.—History of its adoption; its various provisions and amendments; the reasons for the same to be explained as far as may be necessary or appropriate.

How to Teach

LANGUAGE.

Reading, Spelling, and Definitions.—See the preceding grade.

English Grammar.—The exercises of this grade comprise those of analysis, parsing, and composition. Sentences of an irregular or idiomatic construction, should be presented to the pupil, with the view to show how far their analysis can be made to harmonize with the usual syntactical rules, and to teach the just limits of their use. Anything bordering on *slang* should be discountenanced and condemned. An improper construction—that is, one that contravenes well-established rules and principles—should not be sanctioned by any ingenious analytical contrivance or substitution.

The exercises in analysis should embrace the careful and critical study of select passages from some of the best English and American writers; as Shakespeare, Milton, Pope, Cowper, Young, Bryant, Longfellow, etc., etc. Prose writers, such as Addison, Johnson, Irving, etc., should also be drawn upon for exercises,—always, however, with a critical end in view,—to discover and correct errors, as well as to find excellencies and beauties.

Such exercises, to however limited an extent it is

10*

possible to carry them, will always exert an important influence upon the pupils' style of composition, if not of daily speech. They will serve, moreover, to cultivate the taste of the pupils, and to awaken an interest in their minds in the study of English and American literature. A good reading-book will be found an important auxiliary in carrying on the instruction here suggested.

Composition.—The exercises in composition in this grade, as in those preceding it, should be, to some extent, *impromptu,* so as to develop that fluency and readiness in the written expression of thought which is of so much service in almost every sphere of life. The writing of letters, etc., as suggested in the outline course, should receive a very careful attention at this stage of the pupils' progress.

MATHEMATICS.

Arithmetic.—In this grade, the teaching of arithmetic consists in large part of a review of what has gone before, with exercises sufficient in number and difficulty to familiarize the pupils with the principles, and render them expert and accurate in their application. For suggestions in regard to this part of the work, the teacher is referred to the preceding grades.

The advanced work should comprise the following: *Exchange, Equation of Payments, Proportion, Partnership, Square Root,* and *Cube Root,* with their simple applications, and *Mensuration.* The exercises employed to teach these departments of arithmetic, should be of as practical a character as possible; and all the processes should be specially analyzed, the rules given being in all cases deduced from the analysis. A careful explanation of the *business transactions* involved in any of the rules or their applications, should always be given before the pupils are required to solve the problems. Failure more frequently arises from a want of this knowledge than from a deficiency in arithmetical attainment.

The following *syllabus* contains a brief summary of what is suggested to be taught in this grade.

SYLLABUS OF TOPICS.

EXCHANGE. Its nature; bills of exchange; par of exchange; acceptance; domestic exchange—to include two cases:—1. To find the cost of a draft when its face and the rate are given; 2. To find the face, the cost and rate being given; foreign exchange —including the consideration of bills on England and France (cases as in domestic exchange); analysis as in percentage.

NOTE.—Remember that the old par value of the pound sterling is now prohibited by law, and that the new legal value is $4.866⅔.

EQUATION OF PAYMENTS. Cases:—1. To find the average time of payment, when the items have the *same date,* but different credits; 2. When the items have different dates; 3. To find the average time for paying balance of account, having both debits and credits. *Analysis,* on the principal of *interest,* reducing each principal concerned to $1.

PROPORTION. Ratio; proportion defined; relation of antecedents and consequents; ratio of 4 to 12, $4:12=\frac{4}{12}$; method of finding the missing term; simple and compound proportion distinguished; problems involving each: these problems should be only such as are required to illustrate the principle, since they are ordinarily to be solved by analysis previously given.

PARTNERSHIP. Terms defined. Cases:—1. To find each partner's share when the profit or loss is divided according to capital only; 2. To find it when time is considered. *Analysis,* fractional, or by means of proportion.

SQUARE ROOT. Involution and evolution defined: simple examples of each; powers of roots; illustration of what is meant by finding the square of a number; what is meant by square root. Illustrate by *simple powers*, integral and fractional— common fractions and decimals (the latter carefully). Problems in which the root contains denominations other than units. Illustrate by geometrical construction (square of the sum of two lines).

The following are specimens of "simple applications," which should be taught in this grade :—Given the *area*, to find the side of the square containing it.

Given the length and width of a rectangle, to find the side of a square equivalent to it.

NOTE.—In teaching the pupils how to find the area of a rectangle, avoid giving the erroneous impression that we absolutely multiply the length by the width, as expressed by *denominate numbers*. Show that the number of *superficial units* corresponding to the *linear* units of the length, is multiplied by the number (abstract) of linear units in the width. Thus, if the length be 10 feet, and the width 5 feet, the area must be, not 5 feet times 10 feet, but 5 times 10 square feet, equal to 50 square feet.

Given any two sides of a right-angled triangle, to find the other side. Teach and *illustrate* the geometrical theorem on which this problem depends. Give various questions requiring an application of this problem.

CUBE ROOT. How to extract it, with an illustration of the process. This is best given by means of the blocks constructed for that purpose. If the pupil has studied Algebra sufficiently, a demonstration by the Binomial Theorem may be given. The *formula* representing the cube of the sum of two quantities, will enable the pupil to remember clearly the details of the rule.

The *applications* of the Cube Root should include the computation of the contents of similar solids.

MENSURATION. This should at least include the following cases :—1. To find the area of a parallelogram when the base and altitude are given; 2. To find the area of other quadrilaterals, with sufficient data; 3. To find the area of triangles; 4. To find the area of a circle; 5. To find the diameter and circumference of a circle when the area is given; 6. To find the solid contents, from sufficient data, of a cube, parallelopiped, prism, pyramid, cylinder, cone, and sphere; 7. To find the contents of a cask, or other vessel, with the requisite data.

Every *topic* to be treated in the arithmetic of this grade should be introduced by corresponding *mental exercises*, the slate being used only when the numbers involved are too large to be readily retained in the mind. The pupils should be very frequently practiced in this mental work. The *text-book* in mental arithmetic should be sparingly used, and great care should be exercised in assigning lessons for home-study in this branch.

Algebra.—This subject should be taught as a peculiar *mathematical language*, by means of which the relations of quantities and the results of their combinations may be expressed, and thus the reasoning in regard to them facilitated. The symbols, both of quantities and relations, or operations, should at first be carefully taught and illustrated.

The simple operations of addition, subtraction, multiplication, and division, should not be exhaustively treated, as is usually done, before the pupil is made acquainted with the nature and use of equations. The equation is to algebra what the proposition is to ordinary language. It is the means of definitely expressing a mathematical truth, either particular or general. *Inequations* (technically so called) express truths, but not exactly; as, when we say, $x + y \gtrless 5$, we do not indicate *how much* the sum of x and y exceeds 5; but if we say, $x + y = 6$, we express a precise fact. It is suggested, therefore, that equations be presented very soon after the preliminary explanation of the symbols employed. The examples of equations first presented should be of the simplest character; and their use in the solution of problems should be *objectively* shown. This may be done by employing a few very easy questions, such as are given in some of the text-books, for mental solution; as, What number is that, to the half of which if 5 be added the sum will be 11 ? Even the dullest pupil can be easily made to perceive the use of expressing that condition so that it can be clearly kept in view; as (x representing the unknown number) $\frac{x}{2} + 5 = 11$.

In solving such a problem, the successive steps or *processes of reasoning* should be kept in view. Thus, subtracting 5 from each member, the result (expressed by a second equation) is, $\frac{x}{2} = 6$; and, multiplying by 2 the result (expressed by a third equation) is $x = 12$, which gives the solution. (Applied axiom to be referred to.)

Such an exercise, properly performed, will develop more intelligence than whole months of mechanically working out by blind rules long sums in addition, subtraction, multiplication, and division, such as Multiply $x^2 - 3x + 5$ by $x^3 - x^2 + 2$; Divide $x^3 - y^3$ by $x - y$, etc., etc. These exercises are proper in their place, but of themselves they have but little, if any, educational or practical value.

Syllabus of Topics.

1. Preliminary explanation of symbols, both *letters*, as representatives of quantity, and the signs of relation or operation, as, $+ - \times \div =$ etc.; exercises to familiarize the pupil with their significance and the mode of reading them.

Note.—It will be of great service to accustom the pupil to read algebraic expressions in such a way as at once to indicate their meaning; as, $a + b$, the the sum of a and b; $a - b$, the difference between a and b; $a \times b$, the product of a and b, etc. Exercises in finding the numerical value of expressions, when particular values are attributed to the representative letters, will greatly aid in accomplishing this result. Thus, find the value of $\frac{a^2b - b3}{c}$ when $a = 3$, $b = 2$, $c = 1$, etc.

2. Easy problems in arithmetic, the solutions of which may be facilitated by the use of equations, the latter to be of the simplest form, and involving only an application of the pupil's acquired knowledge of symbols. This will at once show the pupils the value of the algebraic notation, and interest them in the study of the subject, as being of practical value.

3. *Mental practice* in solving such problems, by means of equations. Most of the text-books in use will afford a sufficient variety.

4. Practice in solving equations of this character; each equation to be read previously in the form of a problem; as $\dfrac{x}{3} - \dfrac{x}{8} = 10$; which may be read:

What number is that one-third of which exceeds one-eighth of it by 10?

The method of *clearing equations of fractions* and *transposition* should be taught, not by applying mechanical rules, but as processes of analytical reasoning. Thus in the equation above given, the pupil will easily be made to perceive, that the multiplication of both members by 24 will produce an equation without fractions.

(The intermediate step $\dfrac{24x}{3} - \dfrac{24x}{8} = 240$ should be at first used.)

5. After the pupils have acquired a clear idea of the nature and use of equations, and some expertness in operating with those of a simple character, those of a more difficult or complex form should be presented, giving occasion for the use of the operations of addition, subtraction, multiplication, and division, which can then be more exhaustively treated, with sufficient practice on the part of the pupil.

6. The nature of literal equations or *general expressions* should be then taught, and examples given, some of which may be made to involve an application of all these processes.

Such as the following are suggested:

(1.) $\dfrac{x+a}{b} - \dfrac{x-a}{c} = d$

(2.) $\dfrac{x-a}{b} + \dfrac{x-b}{a} = 2$

(3.) $\dfrac{x-a^2}{b} - \dfrac{x-b^2}{a} = 0$

(4.) $\dfrac{x}{a-b} - \dfrac{x}{a+b} = 1$

(5.) $\dfrac{(a+b)x}{a-b} - \dfrac{(a-b)x}{a+b} = \dfrac{1}{4}$

Such equations as the above involve much useful practice, not only in adding, subtracting, multiplying, and dividing, but also in fractions and in factoring. The latter should receive careful attention.

6. The method of solving equations containing more than one unknown quantity—involving the various methods of *elimination* —should follow this, and sufficient practice in the *solution of problems* should also be afforded. The latter, with the preparation herein indicated, may be made a most important aid in training the mind to careful and exact analysis, and logical reasoning— perhaps the most important object, generally, of the study of this subject.

Note.—This syllabus is not designed to be entirely exhaustive, but to afford hints as to the order and method of presenting the most important topics.

Geometry.—This subject, from its extremely *abstract* character, is quite difficult for young students fully to comprehend. It is essential that the abstract ideas with which it is concerned should be developed in the minds of the pupils at the preliminary stage of the study. Unless this is done, they cannot be benefited by the instruction, nor, indeed, take any interest in it. They will, moreover, be wholly incapable of carrying on the processes of reasoning involved in the demonstrations, unless they clearly apprehend the nature of the truths to be proved, as well as of those assumed as premises, or arguments.

The first idea to be developed is that of a solid, as conceived in geometry, involving *three dimensions* of extension; next, that of a surface, abstracted from the solid, involving *two dimensions ;* next, that of a line, abstracted from the surface, involving *one dimension;* and, lastly, that of a point, as indicative of a position in the line, or at either of its extremities, and involving *no dimensions.* These terms, reversing the order, should then be defined; namely, *point, line, surface, solid.*

Unless these fundamental conceptions are clearly and thoroughly impressed upon the minds of the pupils, no true progress can be made.

The *classification* of lines and surfaces may then be taught, the fundamental idea used being that of *direction ;* as of a straight line, *never changing* its direction ; a curve line, changing it *at every point ;* of a broken line, changing it at certain points. The classification of surfaces into *plane, curved,* and *broken* may be made in an analogous manner.

With this, the idea of *parallel lines* may be made to harmonize by conceiving them as lying *side by side* (literal meaning of *parallel*), and all in the same direction, *i. e.,* tending to a point *at an infinite distance,* or tending to points, at a finite distance, which, wherever assumed, are at the same distance from each other (the latter may be the easier to develop at first).

The idea of a plane *angle* should be made to harmonize with these conceptions of a straight line and parallel lines, being conceived as expressing the *difference* in *direction* of two straight lines that meet at a point.

Note—This, it will be seen, harmonizes with the idea of parallel lines, which tend to a point at an infinite distance, and hence *never meet,* and cannot form an angle; while the straight lines that form an angle tend to a point at a *finite distance,* and meeting at that point, form the angle.

The definitions of Geometry form the groundwork of the subject, constituting the basis upon which all the subsequent reasoning rests; hence, it is very important that these definitions should be clearly understood and carefully committed to memory.

It is desirable, before the pupils are required to study demonstrations, that the different methods of *reasoning* should be carefully explained, and that they should, to some extent, be exercised in the same. This can easily be done by bearing in mind that geometrical truths

have reference to a comparison of magnitude, and hence involve the idea of *equality* as a definite fact, and *inequality* indefinitely. Thus, it is required to be proved that the sum of the three angles of a triangle is *equal* to two right angles; also, that, of any two sides of a triangle, that which lies opposite to the greater angle is greater (not how much greater). Hence, as a preliminary exercise, the following might be given:—
Question—If A is equal to B, and B is equal to C, how does A compare with C? *Answer*—They are equal. *Question*—Why is A equal to C? *Answer*—Because they are both equal to B. *Question*—How does that prove it? *Answer*—Because things that are equal to the same thing are equal to each other. *Question*—Can that be proved? *Answer*—It cannot; it is self-evident. *Question*—What are self-evident truths called? *Answer*—They are called *axioms*.

A variety of such exercises may be employed; and, in this way, the pupil, before beginning formal demonstrations, may be made clearly to apprehend the nature of geometrical reasoning—so different from that which he has generally employed during all his previous studies, or which he is accustomed to use in daily life. If the foundation, as here suggested, is well laid, the pupil will soon find it as easy a task to *read* his geometry, and to learn it by *reading* (not *rote study*), as to read any other book of science.

Of course, in hearing recitations in geometry, the teacher should vary the method, so as to preclude entirely the possibility of any rote study, or merely *verbal recitation*. For this purpose, the *figures* employed should be different from those in the text book, the *letters* used in connection with the figures should be changed, or numerals used in their stead. The demonstrations should sometimes be given without using either letters or numerals; and, in the case of such as are very easy, the figures themselves may be dispensed with. In most cases, the pupil should be required briefly to recapitulate the arguments employed.

The amount of ground to be covered in this grade is defined as the "Geometry of Plane Figures." The following Syllabus (intended to be only suggestive) embraces everything required.

Syllabus of Topics.

I. Elementary definitions—axioms—symbols.

II. Theorems relating to straight lines, angles, and polygons: 1. *The sum of any two adjacent angles is equal to two right angles.* 2. *Vertical angles are equal to each other.* 3. The various theorems pertaining to the angles formed by the intersection of two parallel lines and a third line. 4. Angles having their sides parallel are equal. 5. Triangles are equal, (*a*) when they have two sides and the included angle in each respectively equal; (*b*) when they have two angles and the interjacent side in each respectively equal; (*c*) when they have three sides in each respectively equal. 6. The sum of the three angles of a triangle is equal to two right angles. 7. The sum of the interior angles of a polygon is equal to twice as many right angles as the figure has sides, less four right angles. 8. The sum of the exterior angles of a polygon is equal to four right angles. 9. Theorems relating to a comparison of the perpendicular and oblique line drawn from the same point to the same straight line. 10. Only one perpendicular can be drawn from a given point to a given straight line. 11. The greater side of any triangle is opposite to the greater angle; and the converse. 12. The opposite sides and angles of a parallelogram are equal; and the converse. 13. Any problem, either after, or in connection with, these theorems, which can readily be performed; as, to construct an equilateral triangle, to bisect a given straight line, or a given angle, etc. In order to aid in the solution of these, it will be necessary to teach the definition of a circle, its construction, and parts.

Compass and ruler exercises may also be profitably interspersed.

III. Ratio and Proportion.

IV. The Circle:—1. *Relations of angles to chords.* 2. *Relations of angles to arcs.*

V. Area: 1. *Comparative areas of parallelograms and of triangles.* 2. *Measure of areas, of a parallelogram, of a triangle, of a trapezoid, etc.* 3. *Of squares described on the sides of triangles.*

VI. Similarity of figures: 1. *Of triangles.* 2. *Of polygons.*

VII. Problems, pertaining to the circle, the polygon, area, and similar figures.

VIII. Practical applications in mensuration. (See arithmetic.)

Outlines of Physical Geography.—Some departments of physical geography, though perhaps not known to the pupil by that name, have always been the necessary introductory element to the most rudimentary outline of political geography.—Describing the course of a river, the position of a peninsula or a cape, the direction of a mountain chain, or the boundaries of a continent, is as truly a part of physical geography, as is the explanation of the oscillation of the tropical rain-belt, of the formation and transport of icebergs, or of the theories of the trade-winds and ocean-currents.

The physical geography specially described in this grade is a *comparative* science. It considers the world as an organic whole, and includes the study of its planetary conditions, of the mutual relations of all its parts, internal and external—the land, the sea, and the atmosphere,—together with the geographical distribution and conditions of the various forms of vegetable and animal life, and of the various races of mankind.

In the brief time that can be allowed to so comprehensive a subject in a single grade, it is obvious that only the simplest outline can be presented. The work has been carefully prepared for in the geography of the preceding grades, to which attention is here specially invited.

A synopsis of the points included in the grade is here appended. If a text-book is used, *the teacher should first be thoroughly familiar with its contents,* so that it may be employed principally as a reading or reference-book from which appropriate *selections* may be read in the class. If any other course be pursued, most of the text-books treat the subject so extensively that the pupil will necessarily leave it, at the end of the term, with only an unfinished foundation and no superstructure.

SYLLABUS OF TOPICS.

The Earth as a Globe—its form and dimensions, and how ascertained.

The Earth as a Planet—the zones, and their causes.

The Interior of the Earth—its probable condition, and how inferred. (Treat briefly.)

The Surface of the Earth—its division into land, water, and atmospheric envelope; the land divided; the ocean not; comparative extent of land and water.

The Land Surface—(Omit Geology). Comparison of the continents in their direction, contour, elevations, and area; comparison of the great mountain systems of the continents; volcanoes; distribution of; theories of volcanic and earthquake phenomena (very brief); comparison of the plateau belts; of the great plains; the great islands and archipelagoes, their distribution and arrangement.

NOTE.—To illustrate the comparison of the continents by the several classes of elevations, give upon the blackboard rough chalk diagrams of sections of the continents.

The Ocean—its subdivisions and great areas compared; its level; its great currents, their function and some one theory of their origin (very brief); its tides and waves, and their effects. (Both very brief.)

The Atmosphere—its constituents; vital importance of its watery vapor and its carbonic acid to plants and animals; evaporation from the ocean surface, especially in the torrid zone; the atmosphere and the watery vapor as the Earth's blanket.

The Winds—the trades, and counter-trades; theory of (very brief); region of variable winds—(very brief); the winds as carriers of ocean vapor; solar heat the great cause of oceanic and atmospheric circulation.

The Great Rain-belt—its annual oscillations; tropical, rainy, and dry seasons; the mountains as condensers—illustrations.

Drainage—the river systems of the several continents compared; their existence and direction in relation to the winds and mountain ranges; causes and location of deserts—illustration; lakes; snow in the frigid zone, and on lofty mountains in the torrid zone; glaciers, their origin and motion (very brief); icebergs, their origin.

Vegetation (very brief)—warmth and moisture necessary to; general characteristics of tropical vegetation; examples of tropical plants; examples of plants of subtropical and temperate regions; of arctic regions; the great forest belts, their location and causes; prairie belts; desert belts; effects of certain plants on human industries and development (very brief).

Animals (very brief)—comparison of the characteristics of the several zones and continents as to animal life; examples.

Man—the various races, their numerical proportion, leading peculiarities, and distribution.

The pictures and illustrative diagrams and maps of any good text-book will, if properly used, very greatly simplify and expedite the study of nearly every department of the subject, and will render definite ideas that might be otherwise vague.

History (*Outlines of Ancient and Modern*).—The *general suggestions* given in relation to the history of the United States (see Third Grade) are, to a very great extent, applicable to this grade. The much greater extent of time to be covered in teaching ancient and modern history, together with the vast number and diversity of nations which it embraces, necessitates, in a much greater degree, the fixing of a good outline in the mind of the pupil, as preliminary to a more minute study of the subject.

This outline should be brief, but should show clearly the chronological and geographical relations of the nations, the history of which is to be studied, and, to some extent, their ethnological relations. When this has been done, it will be perfectly easy to take up the history of any nation comprehended in the outline, and to treat it intelligibly.

The use of maps, charts, and synchronous tables, will aid very much in impressing firmly upon the pupil's mind such an outline as is here suggested. The maps used should show clearly and accurately the territorial extent and relations of the various nations generally treated of in ancient, mediæval, and modern history. All names of places referred to should be carefully pointed out on the map, so that their exact location may be constantly kept in view. This will aid the memory very much, as it brings into play the faculty of conception.

In the arrangement of topics the *order of time* should be carefully followed at first, and the date (year) of each important event kept before the mind of the pupil. A few leading dates should be carefully memorized. After the history of different nations has been studied, the leading events of each should be arranged in synchronous tables. The reigns of contemporaneous sovereigns, for example, should be compared, and the connection of events in each carefully studied.

Reviews, such as are suggested in connection with the United States history, by a chronological, geographical, and biographical arrangement of topics, should be given with sufficient frequency.

The following syllabus presents the topics which should be embraced in the outline above suggested :

Syllabus of Topics.

1. The nations and countries of the most remote antiquity— *Egypt* and *Ethiopia, Babylonia* and *Assyria, Lydia, Media, Syria* and *Palestine, Persia.* Of these only a brief sketch need be learned.

2. GREECE—the mythologic period (very brief); the period from the beginning of the Persian war to the Roman conquest of Greece. This will include the rise and fall of the Macedonian Empire, with its divisions under Alexander's successors.

3. ROME—the legendary period; the foundation of the Republic in its various stages, including the contests between the orders of Patricians and Plebeians; the successive wars with the Samnites, Carthaginians, etc.; the civil wars, including the triumvirates; the fall of the Republic, and the foundation of the Empire under Augustus. The territorial conquests should be shown in connection with this.

4. THE ROMAN EMPIRE—its territorial acquisitions and changes from Augustus to the division of the Empire at the death of Theodosius, including a brief sketch of the principal reigning emperors, and the invasions by the Goths, Huns, and Vandals.

5. THE WESTERN EMPIRE, from Honorius to its fall under Augustulus (brief), including the barbaric invasions.

6. THE EASTERN EMPIRE—from Arcadius to the taking of Constantinople by the Ottomans; a brief sketch, including the wars with the Goths, Saracens, Seljuks, Mongols, and Ottomans.

7. THE SARACENIC EMPIRE—a brief sketch of its foundation, its territorial conquests and extent, its divisions, and its fall.

8. FRANCE—the invasion of Gaul by the Franks, and foundation of the *Merovingian Dynasty;* a brief sketch of it; the *Carlovingian Dynasty,* including Charlemagne's conquests. and the revival of the Western Empire; the *Capetian Dynasty* to the end of the Reign of Louis XI. This will include the *Crusades.*

9. ENGLAND—a brief sketch of British History before the time of Egbert; from Egbert to the Tudors. (England may be studied first, if it is preferred.)

10. Other nations contemporaneous with England and France. (Very briefly.)

11. MODERN HISTORY—in a similar manner; *England* and *France,* as the leading nations; other nations, including *Germany, Prussia, Russia, etc.*

12. AMERICAN HISTORY—not immediately connected with U. S. History.

Other parts of the world as *China, India, etc.*, may be omitted in this preliminary outline—which is all that can generally be pursued in the Common Schools.

This history should be so studied as to induce the pupils to read standard writers upon the most important topics. The instruction should embrace advice and direction as to the best writers in each period and nation. *Historical selections* will be found valuable for this purpose.

ELEMENTARY SCIENCE

(BY ORAL INSTRUCTION OR A SIMPLE TEXT-BOOK.)

Natural Philosophy.—For general suggestions, see preceding grade.

SYLLABUS OF TOPICS.

Acoustics.—Preliminary—a general idea of the transmission of vibrations illustrated—the nature of sound—sounding bodies—a medium necessary—the air as a medium—other media—limits of audibility of vibrations—velocity in air and other media—loudness does not alter the velocity—reflection of sound—echo, its causes and limits—physical distinction of noise from music—pitch in music—effects of tension upon vibrating wires—influence of sound boards—tuning-forks—speaking-trumpets, speaking-tubes — resonance — murmur of shell — the ear, its construction and action—the wonderful physical condition of the tympanum when listening to a full orchestra.

Pyronomics.—Heat—known only by its effects—effect on the nerves—effect upon the constitution of bodies—transmission of heat—the three methods of transmission illustrated—air a bad conductor and worse radiator—important relation of this fact to clothing, to vegetation, etc.—heat as a sensation—rela-

11

tion of terms hot and cold—sources of heat—quantity and effects of solar heat—its relations to physical geography — source of the heat developed by friction—motion of mass converted into molecular motion—heat only a mode of vibratory motion —force as indestructible as matter—source of heat in combustion—the thermometer—principles employed in its construction—nature and determination of the zero—evaporation—its causes—effects on temperature of bodies—phenomena of boiling—temperature of boiling water—why invariable at a given elevation—economic applications—why the boiling point varies with elevation—boiling in a closed vessel—the steam-engine—its essential elements and general principles—high-pressure and low-pressure engines.

Optics.—Light—moves in straight lines — shadows — sources of light—vibratory nature of light (only refer to it)—velocity of light—how known—law of intensity illustrated—photometry by shadows—non-luminous bodies—how seen—reflection—its law—mirrors, and their uses (treat more fully of the plane mirror than of the others)—refraction—its simplest phenomena —its law—lenses—uses of, especially the convex lens—color —the prism and the solar spectrum—the order of the colors (refer very briefly to thermic and actinic rays)—Frauenhofer's lines (brief)—phenomena of the rainbow—the colors of objects —primary colors—the eye and vision.

Magnetism.—Magnets, natural and artificial—forms of artificial magnets—polarity—attraction and repulsion—magnetic induction—temporary and permanent magnets—the Earth a magnet—magnetic needle, and why it points to the north.

Electricity.—Frictional electricity—conductors and non-conductors—electricity not a fluid but a polarizing force, related to magnetism—attraction and repulsion—electric induction—insulators—effects of points—atmospheric electricity—its origin— lightning-rods—the flash—the white hot air—the thunder—popular fallacies as to electric fluids, thunder-bolts, heat-lightning, and the cause of thunder — current electricity from chemical action—a battery, its wires and poles—polarized condition of the parts—how to develop heat and light—uses made of these—simple helix—simple galvanometer—magnetism developed by electric current—temporary magnet and magnetic telegraph.

Astronomy.—The topics embraced in the preceding grade should be carefully reviewed in this grade, as far as may be necessary to secure thorough preparation for the advanced portions of the subject, which constitute the special work of the grade. The use of the globes should be continued, in order more fully to familiarize the pupils with the Doctrine of the Sphere—so important to a clear understanding of astronomical facts.

The interest of the pupils in the observation of astronomical phenomena should be sustained by calling their attention as frequently as possible to facts which they can verify in this way. By degrees, the pupils should be induced to familiarize themselves with the locations, at different seasons of the year, at a given time by the clock, of the most conspicuous constellations and stars. The use of the Celestial Globe, or a planisphere, will furnish valuable aid in the accomplishment of this. The positions of the planets Jupiter, Saturn, Mars, Venus, and Mercury, among the stars, should be kept constantly in view, together with their apparent motions, and general progress eastward. The use of a good almanac will afford assistance in accomplishing what is here suggested; also in calling attention to the more unusual phenomena connected with eclipses.

The following topics should be specially treated in this grade:

SYLLABUS OF TOPICS.

1. THE SUN—its magnitude, real and apparent; distance from the earth (give a *general* idea of the manner of finding this, although a minute knowledge of *parallax* may be reserved for the more advanced part of the subject); solar spots—theory with regard to their cause, their apparent motions, what is deduced from this. The *Zodiacal light* may be briefly referred to in connection with the Sun.

2. THE PRIMARY PLANETS—in succession, commencing with

Mercury, the pupil to learn the most important facts in relation to their orbits, magnitudes, telescopic appearance, synodic and sidereal periods, axial rotations, apparent motions, seasons, satellites, etc. The *Asteroids*, their orbits, etc. Any interesting facts in relation to the history of astronomical discovery should be communicated incidentally, as this will serve to make the subject more attractive.

3. The Moon—in a similar manner, teaching about its *phases* and their cause, its revolutions, periods, *Harvest Moon*, *Librations*, and a brief general description of the lunar surface (*Selenography*).

4. Eclipses—solar and lunar; total and partial, how caused; comparative frequency—ecliptic limits. *Transits*, their cause—why important.

5. Tides—flood and ebb, spring and neap, how caused; principal facts connected with them; the tidal wave; height of tide at different places—primitive and derivative tides.

6. Comets—their peculiar appearance, the different parts of which they are composed; different kinds of comets; periodic times of the comets of short period—interesting facts in relation to the *orbits, size, mass, density*, and apparent magnitude of conspicuous comets.

7. A brief account of *Meteors*, their supposed nature and origin—cause of the periodic displays of meteors.

8. Stars—classification—the constellations—names, classification of, brightest stars in each—apparent change in position due to *precession;* cause of precession; exercises in finding the constellations visible at any time; the *galaxy;* proper motion of the stars; multiple stars; variable and temporary stars; distances of stars, how found; *parallax*, diurnal and annual.

9. Nebulæ—classification of; their nature and appearance; general location and appearance; the location and appearance of the most noted.

10. Time—how measured; solar, sidereal, and civil day; why the solar exceeds the sidereal day; why the solar days are unequal; equation of time; tropical, sidereal, and civil years, how and why they differ in length.

11. Astronomical Refraction—its effect upon the apparent positions of the heavenly bodies; variation at different altitudes.

12. General Review.

In giving instruction in this subject, its special office as a means of training the *conceptive faculty*. should be kept steadily in view. Facts of observation and facts of *inference* should be carefully distinguished. Apparatus and diagrams will afford some aid in enabling the mind to grasp the more difficult facts of inference; but the actual *observation* of the phenomena to be illustrated should precede, as far as possible, the use of these. Thus, a good *tellurian* will illustrate clearly the causes of the change of the seasons, and a diagram may be made to show the reason of their unequal duration; but the facts of these changes and inequalities must first be clearly apprehended by the mind. If this is done, the natural curiosity to know the cause will make the pupils more attentive to the instruction given. Cumbrous and complicated machinery, without the attentive observation of the natural phenomena, and the conceptions based upon them, rather serve to give false notions than to impart clear ideas of the actual facts. A good planisphere will prove a valuable aid in the study of uranography.

Nor should the teacher fail, in connection with the instruction, incidentally to impress upon the pupil's mind that, in studying the laws of the universe, he is contemplating the works of a beneficent Creator, infinite in wisdom and power. No subject is so well qualified as astronomy to give just ideas in this respect, and, while performing a peculiar and most important office in the training and development of the intellectual powers, to exalt the understanding and give elevation and tone to the whole character.

Chemistry.—The instruction given in chemistry in the common schools, like that given in physics and in the natural sciences, must necessarily be at the most only rudimental. Whole sections of each subject must be omitted. In every department of oral instruction in science, the principal object should be to form the mind to proper habits of observation. This, together with the knowledge of the facts and principles of science incidentally thus imparted, is a *preparation* for the systematic study of these sciences, rather than a formal attempt to impart a knowledge of their complete outlines. Yet this knowledge of the facts and principles thus obtained, is in itself of so great practical importance as to render it an indispensable part of any proper scheme of common school education.

The process employed should, as far as practicable, be the same as that suggested for the instruction in natural philosophy. The lesson, when not a review, should usually begin with an experiment. The facts to which the attention of the pupils is particularly directed, should, as far as possible, relate to the chemistry of common things or of every-day life. They should be so taught as to leave in the mind of the pupil a determination and a conscious ability to know more of a science so highly practical, so intensely interesting, and so obviously within his own power to acquire.

As in Natural Philosophy, the greater part, or even the whole, of the necessary apparatus may, with a little ingenuity, be extemporized. As a stimulus to the inventive powers of the pupils, this is in itself an important matter in practical training, and will, perhaps more than anything else, insure the further prosecution of the subject by the pupils themselves. There are so many excellent text-books in the rudiments of this science, all abounding with practical hints and illustrations, in relation to the construction of such apparatus, that it is not necessary here to do more than refer to them.

The following syllabus of topics, together with a few experimental illustrations therein introduced, is chiefly intended to show how the objective process of instruction may be applied to the study of facts in chemistry, the subject being quite as profitably and easily approached from any one of a dozen starting-points, other than the one here selected. No other department of science can be made to show the value of this process more clearly, or to furnish more important mental discipline. Experiment must be made to raise questions in the mind of the pupil, only to be answered by deductions from further experiment.

A small portion only of the subject can here be sufficiently expanded to illustrate the process, the further details being necessarily left to the ingenuity of the teacher.

SYLLABUS OF TOPICS.

FORCES.—(Begin with a very brief review of the following points in Natural Philosophy.) All changes in matter are effected by forces; examples of *physical* changes wrought by *physical* forces, in pulverizing, solution, fusion, polarization, etc., in which the substance remains unchanged in composition and general properties.

Chemical changes; those in which the substance has changed its properties; experimental illustrations: (use no chemical names or terms at this stage of the work; use well-known common names as far as possible at first, such as sulphur, copper, blue vitriol, alcohol, etc.)

Exp. 1st. Show copper filings and pulverized sulphur; let the properties of each be objectively noted; melt them together slowly; notice the *heat* given out in the process; examine the substance produced by the combination; it is neither copper nor sulphur; compare with a similar mixture of melted sugar and sand; solution will show these last unchanged.

Exp. 2d. Burn sulphur in air; the sulphur disappears, and an invisible sour gas is formed, perceived by the lungs and the smell; has been made from the sulphur and the air.

Exp. 3d. Burn alcohol or kerosene in air: show water as a product; heat given out in all these changes of substance.

Chemical attraction: such changes are produced by a *force* known as chemical attraction or chemical affinity: the *atoms* of sulphur and copper attracted each other and formed a new substance; (omit its name); this force frequently breaks old combinations to form new and stronger ones.

Exp. 4th. Make a solution of blue vitriol (copper sulphate), in a small vial, dip a clean knife-blade into it; copper is deposited on the blade; ask what substance must have been contained in the transparent blue vitriol; *tell* that this copper was combined with another substance which has taken up some of the iron, at the same time rejecting or throwing down a part of the copper.

Elements (nearly all to be *told*); iron and sulphur called elements; why; there are many elements (65); some, like iron and copper are metals; therefore called *metallic elements;* all the rest, like sulphur, are called *non-metallic elements;* about a dozen elements compose the greater part of the material of all known substances; nearly every substance, water, rocks, plants, and animals consists of chemical compounds.

Carbonic acid (carbonic dioxide; carbonic anhydride; use none of the names at first). What is it that bubbles in soda-water? How do you know that it is not air? Its taste; its smell; why called acid (reserve the scientific definition of an acid).

Exp. 5th. Show marble fragments, or chalk (not the *plaster* cylinders used upon the blackboard). Show muriatic acid; dilute a little with water; taste it; an acid; pour the dilute acid upon the marble or chalk. (A small bottle, bent tube, and receiving-bottle for the gas are necessary.) Smell the gas; compare changes which have taken place with those of copper and the iron in Exp. 4; one acid has taken the place of the other; the acid gas must have been solid; the *force* which held it so compressed.

Exp. 6th. Burn a piece of marble or chalk in a charcoal fire; lime kilns; marble *changed* to lime; properties different; *tell* that the great heat has driven off the gas.

Exp. 7th. Make and filter lime-water; agitate some of the gas of Exp. 5 with lime-water in a bottle; water becomes milky; the gas has united with the lime as before burning; chalky sediment settles; lime water a *test* for this gas; meaning of the term *test.*

Exp. 8th. Agitate the gas from soda-water with lime-water: result identical with the last; therefore the gas in soda-water is the same as that from the marble.

Exp. 9th. Burn a candle in an open wide-mouthed jar; close the jar tightly; candle soon goes out; a part of the candle has disappeared; test, as before, the air that is left in the jar; therefore the same gas.

Exp. 10th. Let the burning candle smoke or smut white paper; tell and show that the smut or lamp-black is charcoal; its better name, carbon.

Exp. 11th. Burn ordinary charcoal; it seems to have dissolved in the air; gather the air from it; test it; now use the popular name, *carbonic acid gas* (other and better names to be learned hereafter); therefore carbon in the candle; in kerosene; in all fats, coal, bread, wood, etc. Show by over-baked bread, meat, by wood, etc.

Exp. 12th. Blow breath through a straw or a pipe stem into lime-water; test shows abundant carbonic acid; from bread, vegetables, and other food.

Exp. 13th. Collect from marble a quantity of the gas; show that it will not support combustion; fatal to life; the gas in mines, wells, vats, etc.; suicide with charcoal; necessity of thorough ventilation.

In the same manner *oxygen* may now be considered, its properties and functions shown, and its principal compounds, including the carbonic acid of the preceding experiments. Hydrogen, chlorine, and nitrogen may be next in order.

Review. At this stage it is desirable to review, rearrange, and explain the knowledge already acquired, under the following heads:

Chemistry of water: hydrogen, oxygen; solution of solids and gases in water; hard and soft waters; mineral waters.

Chemistry of the atmosphere: combustion; nitrogen; carbonic acid; its relations to plants and to animals; illuminating gas.

Chemistry of rocks and soils: limestone and lime; quartz,

11*

sandstones, and silica; clay, slate, and alumina; granite, feld-spar, potash, soda, etc.; common salt.

Chemistry of plants and animals: starch, gum, sugar, lignin, vegetable and animal oils, albumen, gluten, etc.

Special topics: bread-making, soap-making, glass-making, fermentation, distillation, photography, etc., etc.

MISCELLANEOUS BRANCHES.

Book - keeping.—After the forms required in single-entry book-keeping have been taught, which should be quite brief, the nature of double-entry book-keeping should be explained, by showing the relation of *debit* and *credit*, and how the former in one account may be exactly balanced in another, so that one set of entries may be made to verify the accuracy of another, and thus prevent the admission of any errors which may not be readily discovered and rectified.

2. The *classification* of accounts should be followed by an explanation of the three books—Day-book, Journal, and Ledger. Journalizing simple entries in the Day-book should then be taught; and sufficient exercises given to impart readiness and accuracy in the process. The keeping of a simple and brief set of accounts will then render the whole process and theory intelligible to the pupils' minds, and will also render them sufficiently expert in their application.

3. All the common *business forms* should be taught; as the form of bills, receipts, bank checks. promissory notes, bills of exchange, invoices, etc., etc. *Business correspondence* should also receive some attention. It is of great importance to render the pupils expert in writing a good business letter. In every exercise fluency, legibility, and grace in penmanship should be

carefully attended to. *Quantity* and *quality* should both
be insisted on in this respect.

Constitution of the United States.—The
recommendation to teach the *Constitution of the United
States* applies to pupils of both sexes in this grade. It
would appear to be essential that those who pass
through a full course for common schools should have
some knowledge of the simple principles and requirements of the organic law of the nation—the distribution of the powers of the general government, and
the rights, duties, and obligations of an American
citizen.

The Constitution itself should be the text studied,
the pupils being made familiar, as far as possible, with
the language of the instrument, and also instructed in
the meaning and intention of the several provisions.
Several matters, purely technical, will need to be carefully elucidated, such as *ex-post-facto laws, bills of at-
tainder, habeas corpus*, etc., etc. The history, English
and American, particularly the former, with which
these are connected, will prove a most instructive and
interesting subject for comment by the teacher.

Questions as to the construction of certain points in
the Constitution, which have been in agitation at various times, during the past history of the country, would
prove, in boys' classes especially, as far as time and opportunity may admit, very beneficial for discussion, as
tending to impart readiness in speech, as well as self-
reliance and freedom in thought and opinion.

GENERAL SUGGESTIONS

RELATIVE TO THE CLASSIFICATION AND INSTRUCTION OF PUPILS IN SCHOOLS.

Reviews.—Such a review of previous lessons, in connection with each new lesson on the same subject, should be given as will cause the pupils properly to associate together the facts learned in all of them, and thus lead them to acquire a comprehensive as well as a familiar knowledge of each subject contained in the grade or the course.

General reviews of subjects should be had at least as often as once during each month; and in these the leading facts learned in previous grades should be included.

Progress of Classes.—Whenever it is found that a class has advanced further in one or more subjects of its grade than it has in others, less time should be devoted to these subjects, and more to others, so that the grade of the class may be equalized in all its studies. No study of a succeeding grade should be introduced into a class of a lower grade until the class has completed the requirements of the grade in all the branches of study included therein.

Progress of Pupils.—It often happens that a few of the pupils of a class will so far outstrip their fellows in a single month, as to render it necessary to transfer these rapid learners to a class of the next higher grade. While great care should be exercised not to stimulate the excessive mental activity or precocity of young pupils, yet the disparity of progress in pupils of the same class may sometimes be used as an incentive to urge forward those who are extremely sluggish or inert. This may be done by promoting in a public manner, at the end of each month, two or three of the pupils who are found to have made the greatest improvement, into a higher class of the same grade. In doing this, however, care must be taken not to disturb the gradation by permitting pupils to omit important branches of study. As a general thing every pupil should be required to spend the whole time which may be prescribed for the grade.

Recitations.—No class in the primary grades should be required to spend more than half an hour, at one time, in the same exercise. The mind, as well as the body, needs rest. A change of subject, and a change in the manner of conducting class exercises, are both necessary in order to furnish opportunities for rest during school hours.

The recitations should be spirited exercises. The questions should be as definite as possible. The teacher should carefully avoid implying in the question any of the facts or principles that should be stated directly by the pupil. The habit of repeating the pupil's answer should also be avoided. Pupils should be invariably required to use natural and proper tones in recitation, to enunciate distinctly, and to avoid grammatical errors. If this be not done, the lessons in reading and grammar will be of little avail to break up pernicious habits of speech, which the teacher, by his neglect, will have assisted to fix.

Unless thoroughly familiar with the details of the text-book, the teacher needs special and renewed preparation quite as much as the pupils. Without this, he will not succeed. In hearing the recitations, he should carefully discriminate between the statements found in the text-book and additional ones which he may have found necessary to make in the preparatory explanation of the lesson, and which the pupil may have had no opportunity to con over.

Lessons for Home Study.—In every class, however well graded, the pupils will differ much in age, health, mental capacity, and home advantages. A correct and judicious classification will reduce this inequality to a minimum; but there will still remain a wide field for the exercise of discrimination, care, and caution on the part of the class teacher. The lessons should, in all respects, be adapted to the average ability of the pupils of the class; but, even beyond this, some allowance will often have to be made in the case of pupils of quite inferior mental capacity or opportunities for home study. Teachers must bear in mind that the one great object of home study is to train the pupils to self-exertion,— to give them the ability to depend upon their own efforts as students, and by degrees, to dispense with the aid of a teacher. It is, therefore, of supreme importance to avoid everything that would discourage, or deprive of self-reliance; and nothing has a stronger tendency in this direction than the imposition of excessive tasks.

Teachers are especially admonished to be considerate toward pupils of a delicate constitution, an over-excitable brain and nervous system, or in temporary ill-health. Many children of this class are precocious in mental activity and exceedingly ambitious to excel; and the greatest care is required to prevent them from injuring themselves by an inordinate devotion to books and study.

The *length* of the tasks imposed should, therefore, be

most carefully scrutinized and adjusted. The practice of assigning a *fixed number* of words, lines, paragraphs, pages, or examples, without a minute inspection of their nature or contents, is often accompanied with disastrous results. The pupils are wearied and discouraged; and the parents, finding the work of the school-room transferred to the home circle, lose all confidence in the judgment and ability of the teacher.

The teacher should ascertain the methods which pupils employ in home-study. Verbatim study, excepting in case of important definitions, is to be discouraged. While making the necessary preliminary explanations, a brief abstract of the leading points should be written upon the blackboard, and made the basis of the recitation. This will do much to induce a rational method in study, and prevent a slavish adherence to the text.

The teacher should advise with his pupils as to their time and opportunities for home study. Household duties, cramped and noisy homes, and deficient light, no doubt greatly obstruct, in many cases, the pupils' efforts. These should be, as far as possible, ascertained and allowed for. Very small print should be entirely excluded from home lessons on account of its tendency to produce myopy, when studied by artificial light. Many hours of confinement in a crowded class-room, with the long-continued and close attention required there, renders rest and relaxation, with some kind of physical exercise, indispensable to growing boys and girls. The teacher should, at least, advise that these come before home-study.

Physical Training.—The pupils should be exercised, as much as may be practicable. in such a way as to expand the lungs, develop the muscular system, and impart an easy and graceful carriage to the body. In schools for boys, the marching drill should be employed in the ordinary evolutions of the schools, with such instruction as may be requisite to make it effective. Light gymnastic and calisthenic exercises should be employed as far as may be necessary or suitable for the general objects of physical training, or as a pleasant and beneficial relaxation after the severer mental exercises.

Where formal exercises in calisthenics, etc., are not employed, the pupils should have sufficient intermission for recreation in the play-ground. Time thus given to physical exercise will always prove a gain in the exercise of the mental powers. When pupils are under efficient discipline, their performances, at their lessons, are always better after exercise in the play-ground,— for the excitement, as it subsides, leaves the intellect more active and hence readier for class-room work.

In the case of young pupils, even while in the class-room, it is desirable that they rise at intervals for a few minutes, to exercise, by varied movements, both the upper and lower limbs.

Manners and Morals.—Such instruction should be given daily to the pupils of all the grades as will foster a spirit of kindness and courtesy towards each other, a feeling of respect toward parent and teacher, and a love for cleanliness, order, law, and truth. The reading lessons and the ordinary incidents of the school-room may be made the means of inculcating the great moral truths common to all well-ordered minds.

Children learn to love and practice kindness, neatness, truthfulness, and politeness by observing these traits in those around them. It is, therefore, exceedingly important that the teacher should present living illustrations of these qualities, by her own conduct before the pupils, during all her intercourse with the class.

Social relations, the dependence of each individual upon his neighbor—the necessity of labor—the benefits of society and government, should be illustrated and taught by means of easy and familiar lessons suited to the age and capacity of the children. As the development of the moral nature is of greater importance to the welfare of the individual and the community than any other part of education, no opportunity should be omitted for training children in such habits as will cause them to grow up truthful, honest, self-governing, and law-abiding citizens.

GOVERNMENT AND DISCIPLINE.

In all the rules and methods of discipline employed, the true object of discipline should steadily be kept in view ; namely, to train the pupils so that they may form *right habits.*

Firmness, vigilance, and uniformity, in dealing with children, are of the first importance. The teacher should never resort to violent means, as pushing, pulling, or shaking the children, in order to obtain their attention. All such practices constitute a kind of corporal punishment which, whether that species of coercion be permitted or not, should be most carefully avoided.

Modes of punishment especially painful to the corporeal system, such as the sustaining of wearisome burdens, unnatural and long-continued attitudes of restraint, standing, kneeling, etc., are exceedingly wrongful and injurious. Equally so is the confining of delinquents, by tying them or shutting them in closets. These are all a resort to mere physical force, instead of moral incentives, and involve no appeal to a sense of honor or duty in the child. They do not properly assert the *authority* of the teacher, nor do they really produce *obedience* on the part of the pupil.

When corporal punishment is resorted to, it should be of a proper character—never partaking of that continuous infliction of pain which we denominate torture, and never administered except in a spirit of mildness, and deep regret at its necessity. When all those persuasive incentives and agencies which constitute *moral suasion* have been appealed to without avail, and there is no other recourse, corporal punishment may be resorted to in order *to save the pupil*, but for no other reason. The necessities of discipline may seem to require it, and they certainly do, if in order to meet them the teacher must choose between chastising his pupil in this way and depriving him of the benefits of the school instruction and training, and thus insuring his moral destruction.

In directing the various movements required of the pupils, care should be taken never *to touch them.* The teacher should take such a position before the class as will command the eye of every pupil, and thence direct by the voice, or by a signal. Pupils must be habituated to the impression that the teacher will give his commands but *once*, and that they must be obeyed *at once*.

Harsh tones of the voice are unnecessary and improper. Words of disapprobation may be uttered by the teacher in a tone of *decision*, without the use of any severity that would imply resentment, anger, or antipathy on the part of the teacher. On the contrary, the language used, and the tones of the voice, should always express a feeling of *sympathy* with the child. This is the way to win the youthful mind, and to bend the will, through the affections ; a different course will antagonize it, and prevent all real submission, securing only a temporary semblance of obedience.

"As is the teacher, so will be the school." It is, therefore, requisite that teachers should rigidly discipline themselves by carefully cultivating habits of neatness, cleanliness, and order, gentleness of manner, a watchful self-control, and a cheerful spirit. In speaking, let the rising inflection of the voice prevail ; then, the falling inflection of reproof will be more impressive and effectual.

Teachers should seek to obtain the sympathetic regard of the children by giving a due attention to their wants and requests, which should be fulfilled as far as may be proper and reasonable. Children are quick to perceive and to resent injury or injustice. The child who asks for the privilege of a drink of water, for instance, may be suffering acutely ; and, if not accorded relief, when this seems to be perfectly practicable on the part of the teacher, feels a sense of outrage which, for a time, if not permanently, impairs its respect and regard for the teacher. The cultivation of a due feeling of *sympathy* for the children will wholly prevent this. The possession of this feeling in its fullness is the best foundation for success in both discipline and instruction.

Encouragement inspires confidence ; and children, more than others, need it. Let it be given in all cases where this can be honestly done. To a want of this in the discipline of classes, are to be ascribed the timidity and reserve so often manifested among pupils by a hesitating manner, a low voice, and a tone of inquiry in response, especially to strangers. A proper degree of encouragement renders them confident and spirited, eager to tell what they know, and in an audible tone of voice. Encouragement has a peculiar influence in promoting both mental and moral improvement.

Public exposures and badges of disgrace belong to a class of punishments which, if ever resorted to, should be employed under careful limitations, and with great circumspection and prudence, for it requires a skillful, discreet, and conscientious teacher to use them safely and with advantage. In the discipline of girls, they should be avoided altogether, as destructive of that nice sense of shame and that delicate sensibility to reputation which are to be most carefully fostered in the female character.

Cleanliness, method, and regularity are among the first and most necessary elements of popular education. Every rule requisite to maintain or impart these should be diligently and punctiliously enforced.

Education is unfinished until the physical powers are brought into subjection to the understanding and the dictates of morality and social refinement. Children should be taught how to sit, to stand, to move, to walk. Rules are required for this; but they need to be only few and simple, and the nice and watchful observation of children renders it quite easy to enforce them, provided they are not capriciously applied. Children must first be taught them, and then *never* permitted to violate them without admonition or correction.

Teachers should never forget that their pupils are constantly and closely watching their conduct, and that they are prone to imitate whatever they observe. They should, therefore, see nothing that they may not safely imitate. There is an "unconscious tuition," the silent influence of which produces the most permanent effects.

The character of children is greatly affected by their

surroundings. These should, therefore, be neat and orderly. The rooms in which they assemble should be clean, the desks and other furniture, as far as possible, without injury or defacement, and everything giving evidence of constant and punctilious attention. Children, from the contemplation of these things, unconsciously acquire habits of order, neatness, and regularity, which have an important bearing upon their usefulness and happiness in after life.

The basis of *good order* is attention. It does not require that the pupils should occupy, for any certain time, a fixed position; that they should be compelled to strain their glances upon a given point; that they should be as motionless as statues. All this is unnatural; and whatever is unnatural is really *disorderly.* The postures should be graceful, easy, and uniform, but should be frequently changed; the movements, while as simultaneous as perfect attention would necessarily produce, should also be easy and natural.

Good order involves impression rather than repression; it does not consist in a coercion from which result merely silence, and a vacant gaze of painful restraint, but it results from the steady action of awakened and interested intellect,—the kindling of an earnest purpose and an ambition to excel. Hence by making punishment the first, instead of the last, resort, the true object of educational discipline is defeated. The prevailing atmosphere of the class-room should be always that of kindness and love, equal to that of a parent, in whose place indeed the teacher is for the time; and it will be almost invariably found that everything essential to effective discipline will spring from an interchange of confidence and regard between teachers and the pupils committed to their instruction.

Those who have the management and instruction of our Common Schools should exercise the greatest care that their teachings and influence be not exclusively intellectual,—that they tend not merely to inform the mind, but to form the character,—not only filling the head, but impressing likewise the heart. Even where the operations of these schools are confined to *teaching*, let the kind of knowledge and the mode of imparting it be dictated by considerations having in view moral and religious, as well as intellectual, improvement. Let the knowledge imparted be always such as will refine, ennoble, elevate. When scientific truth is presented, let the pupil be led to look not simply *at* nature, but "through nature up to nature's God;" let him learn the laws and phenomena of the physical universe with the spirit of the Psalmist, when he exclaimed, "When I consider the heavens, the work of thy fingers, the moon and the stars which thou hast ordained, what is man, that thou art mindful of him, and the son of man that thou regardest him?" Thus may instruction in every class and grade be made effectual, without the dogmatic teaching of sectarian tenets, in subserving and promoting the best interests of its pupils, both temporal and eternal. Any scope or intention short of this would certainly be inconsistent with the intelligence, as well as the moral and religious character of our age and country, and must render our Common School education, as a means of fostering and supporting the free institutions of our Republic, unworthy of support or vindication.

A SCHOOL LIBRARY.

Its Necessity.—Of all the means necessary to a teacher's true and lasting success in the mental and moral training of his pupils, few, if any, are equal in importance to a proper school library,—not necessarily a large library, or an expensive one, but a library consisting of interesting and instructive books, such as boys and girls may readily be led to love to read.

The pernicious character of the greater part of the cheap literature found in many so-called newspapers and in other cheap forms of publication, needs but little comment. Its enormous quantity shows that it is extensively read, and it is well known that it finds its chief market among the young. An enfeebled mind and a vitiated taste, as shown in a craving for exciting and unnatural stories, and in a positive dislike for instructive and truly interesting reading, as being too tame and insipid to hold the attention, are among the common and least injurious results of an unchecked indulgence in the mental dissipation which this trash induces. Its darker shades and more injurious and debasing consequences need not here be dwelt upon. The proper antidote and substitute for this wide-spread poison is good reading.

Such a library is also the indispensable supplement to the systematic mental instruction given in the class-room. If, for instance, care be taken and opportunities sought during the lessons in geography, history, or in any of the departments of science, to introduce some little book from the library, and to read a few interesting paragraphs illustrating the lesson, a brief notice and commendation of the book at the close of the exercise, with a few hints as to how best to read it, will utilize many a valuable work that might otherwise remain untouched upon the shelves.

Once introduced into the world of good books, and fairly interested in even one of its many departments,—once tasting and enjoying the wholesome sweets of a sound and ennobling literature, a young man or a young woman, it may be safely trusted, will not abandon it for that to which allusion has been made. A teacher has failed in one of the most important of all of his functions, if, being in possession of a good school library, he has not fixed, in at least some of his pupils, the habits and love of self-culture, by leading them to become habitual readers.

Its Character.—Great care and discretion are necessary in the selection of books for a school library. As far as possible they should be *small books*. The greater part of the suitable works in history, biography, travels, etc., are readily selected, and should include such works as Abbott's Histories, Scribner's Library of Wonders and Library of Travel, Chaillu's works, the Rollo books, etc., together with a fair proportion of good standard works, such as those of Prescott, Bancroft, Lossing, Hume, and Macaulay, the Student's Series of Histories, Translations of Josephus, Herodotus, Thucydides, etc. In selecting from the great number of works of imaginary travel and adventure, written with the professed purpose of giving to youth instruction in the physical geography, natural history, and social condition of various countries, all those in which the narrative is overdrawn, and therefore teaches error, should be rejected. Natural history and the other subjects treated of in the oral instruction in science, should be abundantly represented. If works of fiction are admitted they should be selected with reference to their moral purity and their permanent value as additions to literature, rather than because they are new and are advertised as popular. Many a school library has been filled with ephemeral trash and made the instrument of mental degradation rather than of elevation, by want of care ·in this respect. Such old classics as Robinson Crusoe, Paul and Virginia, and the Vicar of Wakefield, should not be wanting. A few of the leading popular poets should also be represented by small volumes. In their selection of books, pupils should be advised by their teacher, so that they may not attempt works beyond their present ability to read with profit.

Uses.—Among the many ways which may be suggested for making a systematic use of the library as a means of culture, the following is given as an illustration:

Let us suppose that some new books have been purchased, and that one of them is Abbott's Life of Madame Roland, and that the teacher has himself first read it, or at least looked over it, and marked a few short but interesting passages. Before the class or before several of the higher grades assembled for the purpose, the teacher hangs the map of Europe. In a brief conversational lecture he states to the class or school a few of the leading points in relation to France and Europe at the period referred to, then reads a brief but interesting selection or two from the first portion of the book, and commends the book to their notice. With such an introduction many pupils will read the work, while without it they would not have thought of so doing. It will generally be found that history and biography are usually not read by the pupils because they have none of the preliminary conceptions relating to the subject which the method above indicated supplies.

12

Books of travel present peculiar advantages for this method, and are among the most instructive portions of current literature.

An excellent plan with individual and advanced pupils is for the teacher to select some interesting book, sufficiently brief and simple, and in place of the usual exercise in composition, to require of the pupil an abstract of limited length, with the selection of a page or two of peculiar interest or importance, to be read aloud, with such explanation or remarks as the subject may suggest.

SYNOPTICAL TABLE OF THE PRIMARY SCHOOL GRADES.

	TENTH GRADE.	NINTH GRADE.	EIGHTH GRADE.	SEVENTH GRADE.	SIXTH GRADE.
Language.	Reading words which are familiar by use. Sounds. Letters. Spelling.	Reading in a First Reader. Meaning of Words. Sounds of Letters. Spelling.	Reading through a First Reader. Meaning of Words. Sounds of Words. Spelling—oral and by copying.	Reading in a Second Reader. Meaning of Words. Sounds of Words. Spelling—oral and written.	Reading through a Second Reader. Definitions. Words analyzed by sounds. Spelling—oral and written.
Arithmetic.	Counting and adding objects. Figures to 100.	Adding with figures. Reading and writing figures to 999. Roman Numbers to I. V. X. L.	Adding simple columns. Numeration and Notation through millions. Multiplication Table to 6x12. Roman Numbers to CC.	Addition and Subtraction with practical examples. Multiplication commenced. Multiplication Tables to 12x12. Tables of Measures commenced.	Addition and Subtraction reviewed. Multiplication continued. Division—long and short. Tables of Weights and Measures.
Object Lessons.	Form—common shapes—ball, square, etc. Color—common colors. Objects—names and uses. Human Body—principal parts.	Form—rhomb, circle, crescent, cone, etc. Color—shades of common colors. Objects—parts and uses. Human Body—names and uses of parts of limbs.	Form—pyramids, parallel lines, surface, angles, etc. Color—primary and secondary. Human Body—bones and uses. Animals—familiar ones. Plants—names of trees, plants, etc. Objects—parts and qualities.	Form—polygons, and other forms. Color—harmony. Human Body—organs of senses. Animals—comparison, groups, families, etc. Plants—roots, leaves, etc. Objects—qualities. Occupations—tools, etc.	Form—shapes compared and described. Human Body—continued. Animals—compared and classed. Plants—leaves and flowers. Objects—mineral, vegetable, animal. Occupations—productions, etc.
Drawing.	Drawing.	Drawing lines, etc.	Drawing plane figures.	Drawing continued.	Drawing continued.
Writing.	Printing on slates.	Writing small letters.	Writing simple words.	Writing on slates and paper.—Capitals.	Writing with pen and ink.
Geography.				Place and Direction.	Geography—direction — location, countries, etc.

SYNOPTICAL TABLE OF THE GRAMMAR-SCHOOL GRADES.

	FIFTH GRADE.	FOURTH GRADE.	THIRD GRADE.	SECOND GRADE.	FIRST GRADE.
Reading.	Third Reader—first half. Exercises on subject-matter. Review of Punctuation, Roman Numbers, and Elementary Sounds.	Third Reader—latter half. Exercises as in preceding grade.	Fourth Reader, with special elocutionary exercises to teach expression. Special exercises in vocal culture.	Fifth Reader—special vocal and elocutionary exercises as in preceding grade.	As in preceding grade.
Spelling.	Oral and Written.—From reading lessons; also miscellaneous words and words derived therefrom. Words and short sentences from dictation.—Capitals.	As in preceding grade.	As in preceding grade, with special attention to syllabication.	As in preceding grade.	As in preceding grade.
Definitions.	From reading lessons; also exercises in forming these words into sentences.	As in preceding grade, with easy exercises in the applications of prefixes and suffixes.	As in preceding grade. Review of prefixes and suffixes and their combinations with easy roots.	As in preceding grade, with word-analysis, or *Etymology.*	As in preceding grade.
Grammar.	Empirical correction of common errors in speech.	Analysis, Parsing, and Construction of simple sentences, with such definitions only as are necessary.	Analysis, Parsing, and Construction of easy compound and complex sentences. Short compositions in the class-room.	Analysis, Parsing, and Construction, continued. Exercises in False Syntax. Composition, continued.	Analysis, Parsing, and Syntactical Criticism and Correction, continued. Anomalies and idiomatic forms. Composition on selected themes. Letter-writing.

Arithmetic.	Through Simple Rules and Federal Money. Tables completed and reviewed.	Fractions, Common and Decimal. Practice in preceding grade for rapidity and accuracy.	Denominate Numbers, with practical applications. Review of preceding grades.	Commercial Arithmetic, including the percentage rules.	Arithmetic continued and reviewed. Mensuration of planes and solids. *Algebra* through simple equations. *Geometry* of plane figures, with practical applications.
Geography and History.	Simple Outlines of the World, with Definitions. Outlines of N. America and West Indies.	United States in detail.	South America and Europe with outline review of preceding grades. *History of U. S.,* 1492 to 1763.	Asia, Africa, and Oceanica, and general outline review. *History of U. S.,* 1763 to present time.	Outlines of *Physical Geography.* Outlines of *History, Ancient and Modern. Constitution* of the U. S.
Elementary Science.	Food, clothing, and building materials. Zoology.	Botany in spring and summer. Mineralogy in fall and winter.	Review of preceding grades. Physiology and Hygiene.	*Natural Philosophy* (simple outlines of), Mechanics, Pneumatics, and Hydrostatics. *Astronomy,*—ordinary phenomena, and Solar System.	*Natural Philosophy* simple outlines completed. *Astronomy*— Elementary—completed. *Chemistry* — elementary facts and principles.
Writing	On slates—continued. On paper—as in preceding grade.	On slates, with practice for experiness. On paper, review of elementary forms. Words without capitals. Words with capitals.	On slates—as in preceding grades. On paper — difficult elementary forms, phrases, and short sentences.	As in preceding grades, but more advanced.	Continued, with short paragraphs, business forms, notes, and superscriptions. *Book-Keeping.*
Drawing.	Review:—Straight lines in various positions and combinations; rectilinear figures, as squares, triangles, etc.	Review of preceding grade, with curves, circles, ellipse, etc.	Review, and add scrolls, simple geometrical solids, and drawing from simple copies.	As in preceding grades, with sphere, spheroids, hemisphere, and shading begun.	Regular forms in perspective — Block Combinations—Copying Pictures. *Architectural and Mechanical Drawing.*

NUMERAL FRAMES,

OF VERY SUPERIOR STYLE.

The Abacus, or Numeral Frame, has come down to us from ancient times. Although long disused, it is now not only a **very popular,** but an almost **indispensable aid** in teaching Children

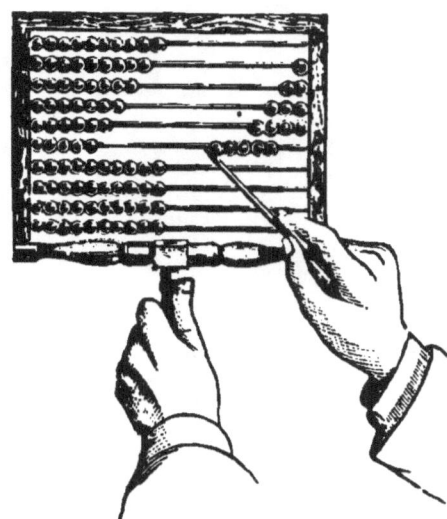

to count, and in giving them correct ideas of numbers and of their first lessons in addition, subtraction, multiplication, etc.

The balls, nicely and smoothly turned from wood, are painted four different durable colors and varnished. The handles enter the frame with a screw, and are taken out for safe shipment.

In strength and style of finish, our Numeral Frames are not equaled by any others made.

WE MAKE THREE SIZES:

No. 1—size, 9 in. by 11 in., with 100 balls ....Price, $1.25
No. 2—size, 10 in. by 12 in., with 144 balls .... " 1.50
No. 3—size, 20 in. by 27 in., with 144 balls .... " 5.00

The balls of Nos. 1 and 2 are about a half-inch in diameter, and those of No. 3 are 1¼ inch. No. 3 has a different handle, a place being cut out of the frame for grasping, or for hanging it up in view of the school.

NEW FORMS AND SOLIDS.

Containing sixty-four pieces—there being forty-eight Plane Forms,
fifteen Solids, and a six-inch Rule, among which are
several NEW Forms and Solids, not
included in any other set.

Each Form is stamped with its Number in the List.

1. Equilateral Triangle.	16. Hexagon.	31. Hemi-Sphere.
2. Right Angled "	17. Heptagon.	32. Prolate-Spheroid.
3. " " "	18. Octagon.	33. Oblate.
4. Obtuse " "	19. Nonagon.	34. Ovoid.
5. Curved "	20. Decagon.	35. Cylinder.
6. Triangle—1 curved side	21. Circle.	36. Cone.
7. Isosceles Triangle.	22. Semi-Circle.	37. Conoid.
8. Scalene "	23. Quadrant.	38. Cube.
9. Square.	24. Segment.	39. Square Prism.
10. Oblong.	25. Sector.	40. Triangular Prism.
11. Rhomb.	26. Ring.	41. Hexagonal "
12. Rhomboid.	27. Crescent.	42. Square Pyramid.
13. Trapezium.	28. Ellipse.	43. Triangular "
14. Trapezoid.	29. Oval.	44. Six-inch Rule.
15. Pentagon.	30. Sphere.	

This is the only set which is accurately and scientifically made. It
is the only set which is approved for use in the schools of New York
City.

PRICE, (neatly put up in substantial wood box), $2.75.

Also, **Geometrical Forms** and **Arithmetical Solids.**

26 Pieces, in box, . . . $2.50.

SCHOOL GLOBES.

Our New School Globe. Probably the reason why so few of our schools are supplied with a globe is that there has been no **good globe** to be obtained at **a moderate price.**

Our New Five-Inch Terrestrial Globe will precisely supply this want. The map is **new**—clearly and finely engraved—prepared expressly for taking the place of the large and expensive globes. The "Grand Divisions" are boldly colored. The water is white, distinctly showing the principal Islands, Peninsulas, Capes, Gulfs, Bays, etc., etc.

It is mounted in a light and durable manner, with strong brass mountings, inclined axis, on a neat black walnut stand.

Securely packed in box with sliding cover.

PRICE, - - - - - **$2.25.**

A Hemisphere Globe, (made by cutting a solid five-inch globe through the Poles,) **showing also the two Hemispheres on a flat surface,** will be found a great convenience to the teacher. The two parts are united by a brass hinge. **Price,** - - **$2.00.**

Our Complete List of Globes comprises all the Globes, large and small, which are known. It will be mailed on receipt of stamp.

J. W. Schermerhorn & Co., *Manufacturers*

14 Bond Street, New York.

OUR GYMNASTIC APPARATUS.

" Mens Sana in Corpore Sano."

It is made of well-seasoned wood, varnished and polished. Dumb-bells and Indian Clubs are made of maple ; Wands of white ash or black walnut ; Hand-rings are very strongly made of three sections—black walnut, cherry, and maple. Besides great strength, they have the merit of beautiful appearance.

PRICE LIST.

Dumb-bells—four sizes :

Nos. 1 and 2, for children.....................per pair, $0 60

Nos. 3 and 4, for youths and adults............ "   75

Rings—two sizes :

No. 1, for children........................ "   75

No. 2, for youths and adults.... .... "   75

Wands—in required lengths, nicely turned.......... each,   30

same, with metallic balls.................. "   75

Indian Clubs—five sizes of short clubs :

No. 1,	weight per pair about	2	pounds	..........per pair,	1 25
No. 2,	" " "	3	"	.... "	1 50
No. 3,	" " "	4	"	.... "	1 75
No. 4,	" " "	5	"	.... "	2 00
No. 5,	" " "	6	"	.... "	2 50

Six sizes of long clubs :

No. 1,	weight per pair,	7 to 8	pounds..........	"	3 00
No. 2,	" "	10	"	....	"	4 00
No. 3,	" "	12	"	....	"	4 50
No. 4,	" "	14	"	....	"	5 00
No. 5,	" "	16	"	....	"	5 50
No. 6,	" "	20	"	....	"	6 00

Any size or style to order. Liberal discount **on quantities.**

Kehoe's Book on use of Clubs, illustrated.....:.........1 00

Manual of Calisthenics, illustrated, Watson.............1 25

Hand-Book of Gymnastics, highly illustrated, Watson.....2 00

J. W. Schermerhorn & Co.,

Manufacturers and Publishers,

14 Bond Street, New York.

www.ingramcontent.com/pod-product-compliance
Lightning Source LLC
Chambersburg PA
CBHW060611030726
47498CB00005B/1637